SILK TOWN
INDUSTRY AND CULTURE IN MACCLESFIELD
1750-1835

Hull University Press

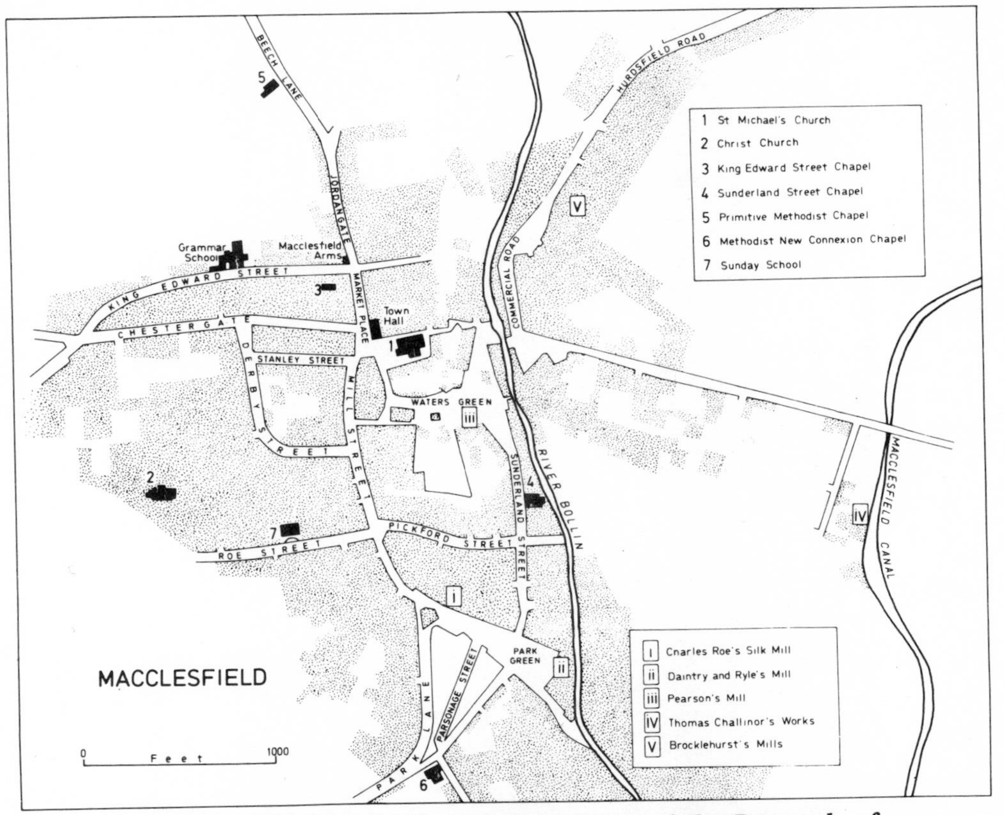

This map has been adapted from *Plan of the Borough of Macclesfield, 1838* (publisher, J. Cawley).

SILK TOWN
INDUSTRY AND CULTURE IN MACCLESFIELD 1750-1835

GAIL MALMGREEN

University of Massachusetts

HULL UNIVERSITY PRESS
1985

ISBN 0 85958 447 X

Reprinted 1987

Phototypeset in 11 on 12pt Times and printed by
The University of Hull.

Contents

List of Tables

Abbreviations

CCRO	Chester City Record Office, Earwaker Coll.
Coll.	Collection
CRO	Cheshire County Record Office
d	old pence
EHR	*Economic History Review*
HJC	*House of Commons Journals*
HO	Home Office
MC	*Macclesfield Courier*
MCH	*Macclesfield Courier and Herald*
MPL	Macclesfield Public Library, Local History Coll.
n.p.	no place of publication
PMM	*Primitive Methodist Magazine*
P.P.	British Parliamentary Papers
PRO	Public Record Office
s	old shillings
THSLC	*Transactions of the Historical Society of Lancashire and Cheshire*
TLCAS	*Transactions of the Lancashire and Cheshire Antiquarian Society*

Acknowledgements

This study of Macclesfield grew out of a Ph.D. thesis at Indiana University. My first debt of gratitude is to three scholars who guided me through that project and then encouraged me to develop and expand it. M. Jeanne Peterson, who directed my thesis work, has been an inspiring teacher, a mentor in every sense. The final version has benefited from her constant support, her rigorous criticism, and her editorial skill. I was fortunate, as well, to be able to work with Martha Vicinus, whose love and respect for the culture of the industrial North is conveyed unforgettably to her students and friends. She led me to the subject and kept me at it. My original research in England was supported by a two-year scholarship from the Department of Economic and Social History at Hull University. As head of that department, John Saville generously assisted me in every possible way; his own work has been a model and his advice invaluable.

My thanks to Peter Bailey, Spencer Gelband, Ann Higginbotham, Victor Kiernan, Abigail Malmgreen, Stuart Piggin, Iorwerth Prothero, MaryJo Wagner, and the members of William Hutchinson's Colloquium at Harvard Divinity School, all of whom read the manuscript, or parts of it, at various stages. Their perceptive, sometimes sobering, comments and queries drove me to many additions and revisions. Thanks, also, to those who patiently listened, argued, answered questions, and offered assistance and moral support along the way, among them, Robert J. Bezucha, Janet Blackman, Bruce Calder, Hilary Chambers, Geoffrey Crossick, Jennifer Kermode, Bea Marchino, S. Ian Mitchell, Keith Neild, James Obelkevich, Eileen Simpson, and David Whalley. From all of them I have learned more than can be briefly expressed.

David and Naomi Reid have been the best of colleagues. I am the beneficiary, not only of their boundless hospitality, but also of their expertise in Lancashire and Cheshire labour history. David Reid first introduced me to the riches of the Local History Collection at Stockport Central Library ten years ago, and he has been the mainstay of my trans-Atlantic research efforts ever since.

The staff of the Cheshire County Record Office have been both gracious and efficient in helping me to make their extensive collections of Macclesfield material the backbone of this study. Thanks are also due to the staffs of the Chester City Record Office, Chester City Library, Manchester Central Library, John

Rylands University Library of Manchester, Chetham's Library, Birkenhead Central Library, Goldsmith's Library, Guildhall Library, Indiana University Library, and the Harvard-Andover Theological Library, and to Ruth and Edmund Frow of the Working Class Movement Library, Old Trafford, Manchester.

The staff of Macclesfield Public Library offered every facility at their disposal. Mrs J.R.C. Callander and Mrs Marie Moss welcomed me to their homes and made available their private collections of manuscripts. Mr E.A. Rose generously shared his unrivalled knowledge of Cheshire Methodism, and Drs Clive Field and Frank Baker directed me to essential Methodist manuscripts.

Finally, I am grateful to Joyce Bellamy of Hull University, who has been a copy-editor *par excellence*. She has shepherded the manuscript through production with meticulous skill and has improved it immeasurably in the process.

No one can hope to know a town without exploring it on foot, to get a feel for its unique personality. Any visitor to Macclesfield today will notice that a small renaissance in local history is taking place there. Thanks largely to the work of local historian Jill Norris and the staffs and supporters of the Macclesfield Silk Heritage Trust and the Paradise Mill Museum, the town is recapturing much of the beauty and dignity of its earlier days. In preserving the physical traces of past life and labour, and by reviving memories that had become faint and faded, they remind us that Macclesfield's history was made, not by silk or the silk trade, but by ordinary people, hoping and struggling, first for subsistence, then for security, and finally for a better future. This book is a contribution to that story, and an attempt to indicate how the distribution of economic and political power affected its course.

G.M.

I

A Town built on Silk

A great many English towns can be located in the more or less uncharted territory which lies between the purview of urban history proper and the study of rural life. In many market towns, border towns, satellites and suburbs, ecclesiastical centres, and the smaller ports and industrial towns change was a two-way process: newcomers and new practices were received and accommodated, but with due regard to community tradition and the sensibilities of old residents. It was in such places, and not in the 'shock cities', that most Britons experienced town life during the industrial revolution and well into the nineteenth century.[1] Yet historians have usually followed the early social investigators in concentrating on the most startling examples of growth and upheaval, or on crisis conditions. Alan Armstrong has made this point in the introduction to his study of early Victorian York: 'Not appearing to present obvious pathological characteristics, country towns, both large and small, tended to be ignored. Yet in fact, they were still the norm, so far as urbanization in the mid-nineteenth century was concerned.'[2]

Macclesfield is just the sort of town social historians of industrialisation have been inclined to overlook. Though it industrialised rapidly and thoroughly during the second half of the eighteenth century, it never attained the proportions of a city. This transformation from a small but thriving market centre into a middle-sized textile manufacturing town by no means obliterated, and indeed was predicated on, intimate economic and cultural ties with an agricultural hinterland.

The town is situated on a steep rise of land overlooking the

Bollin River at the margin of the flat fertile pasturelands of East Cheshire. The foothills of the Pennines loom just to the east. Even after the pressures of industrialisation began to push Macclesfield's boundaries outward in several directions, engulfing neighbouring hamlets, the town centre retained its medieval form. At the crown of the hill was the market square, dominated by the tall, graceful tower of St Michael's Church, a handsome Gothic edifice originally built in 1278 by King Edward I. Behind the church a wide flight of stone steps, still one of the striking landmarks of the town, descends sharply, past fragments of a medieval castle wall, to the river valley below. In the eighteenth century the town's common lands, already given over to extensive industrial encroachments, lay on both sides of the river. These were formally enclosed, divided, and sold off in 1804. Two broad water meadows on the town side of the river, Waters Green and Park Green, were favourite sites for fairs, communal festivities, and open-air meetings of all kinds, and became the first concentrated areas of factory-building. Several new streets were laid out by the end of the eighteenth century, to connect the 'greens' with each other, and with the old town centre.

Bordering the market square were several large inns, a variety of tradesmen's premises, and the town hall. On market days the square was packed with wagons, barrows, stalls, and tables, and crowded with farmers, factors, labourers, artisans, vendors, and prospective purchasers of every degree of respectability. Narrow streets with medieval names — Dog Lane, Back Lane, Barn Street, Backwallgate — ran outward from the market-place, escaping quickly into the open fields. In the nineteenth century many of these old streets took on new and grander titles with national and county associations — Stanley Street, Derby Street, King Edward Street, Brunswick Street — in keeping with the dignity of the newly-extended rows of shops and dwellings that lined them.[3] In 1824 the old town hall building, along with some decrepit shops around it, was cleared away to make room for an imposing new structure, a grey, grim, classical-style building, rather like a Greek temple greatly enlarged.

Most of the life and work of the town was carried on within a few steps, or a short walk, of its central square. All ranks of residents — the wealthy merchants with town houses in Jordangate or Chestergate, shopkeepers and handloom weavers in their tidy row-houses, and the poorest labourers in crowded tenements near the river — lived in close proximity to one another. Clustered around the town centre were the offices, workshops, warehouses, churches and chapels, and inns and public houses suitable to each grade on the social scale. Neither a rampaging mob intent on smashing the windows of the high and mighty, nor the local magistrates who turned out to read the riot act to them, would have had very far to go on their respective errands. A kind of rough community solidarity, nurtured in part by sheer physical compactness, persisted in the town, even in the face of rapid growth and unsettling economic change.

As an ancient borough, first chartered by the crown in 1261, Macclesfield conscientiously guarded its municipal independence and corporate privileges. It was fortunate to be at a safe enough distance from the bishop's palace, and sufficiently removed from the orbits of the great county families, to escape direct interference in its affairs. Though the town welcomed the nobility and gentry of the county as visitors, as patrons, and especially as customers, deference in Macclesfield tended to be a voluntary or habitual response rather than an enforced one. The mayor and Corporation[4] were entrusted with the regulation of trade and the collection of market tolls and fines, the preservation of the good order of the town, and the right of appointment to a number of local offices — among them town clerk, coroner, constables, governor of the poor-house, and the two curacies of St Michael's. In the eighteenth century the town could boast neither a parish church nor a representative in Parliament. The parochial honour belonged to nearby Prestbury, a village which eventually dwindled into insignificance beside its more prosperous neighbour. And the town had to be content with only county representation in Parliament until the 1832 Reform Bill. Still, in addition to its traditional functions, Macclesfield had a long-established and flourishing economy based on the manufacture of silk, first as a cottage industry and later in factory production. The town was the social, financial, and professional centre for a considerable region, and in general a magnet to the countryside around. It retained the air of a bustling country town, clinging, as a historian of Lincolnshire has aptly put it, to 'a precarious urbanity'.[5]

Macclesfield's setting in an agricultural county specialising in dairy products, meat, and vegetables for the urban food market, was advantageous to its industrial development in several respects. Traditionally, East Cheshire had been able to produce an abundance of food with a minimum of labour. Because small and medium-sized family farms employing relatively few farm labourers per acre were the norm, a burst of population growth, as in the second half of the eighteenth century, meant a surplus of labour available for employment in workshops and mills.[6] The population boom and attendant urban growth in their turn stimulated the demand for food so dramatically that Cheshire farmers soon found themselves competing with industry for labour. Contemporary observers of Cheshire agriculture agree that wages rose during the latter part of the century and that rural prosperity was widespread, except for the smallest farmers and casual day labourers.[7] Henry Holland reported in 1808 that the highest farm wages were offered in the neighbourhood of Stockport and Macclesfield, where agricultural labour was most scarce.[8] The prosperity of East Cheshire farmers brought trade to the town's retail merchants, commissions to solicitors, auctioneers, and factors, and a flow of capital towards the town — as farmers' sons moved in to try their luck at business, and farmers' daughters brought dowries to urban husbands. The children of farm labourers, eager to better themselves, made their way in a continuous stream towards the spinning mills and weaving shops.

Macclesfield's geographical situation also helped to foster its economic growth. The streams of the southern Pennines, with their fast and regular flow of clean, soft water, were well suited to the needs of silk mills and dye-houses.[9] The Bollin River and several subsidiary streams, which could also be used for power, flowed through the town's common lands. Macclesfield was on the main coach and carriage routes from London to Manchester, Chester, and Liverpool, and by 1780 all the major roads converging on the town were turnpiked.[10] In the late eighteenth century the London road, via Leek, was modified to take traffic through Derby and Leicester rather than Coventry, thereby opening up the Midlands hosiery trade to Macclesfield's silk producers. In the silk manufacture both raw material and finished products were light and compact enough to make land transport economically feasible, so the lack of a local canal until 1831 (and of railways until 1845) did not pose an insuperable barrier to development.

Yet the town was also in a sense isolated. The Derbyshire Peaks, rising sharply just a few miles east of the town, provided an obstacle to easy intercourse with Derbyshire and the woollen centres of the West Riding of Yorkshire. Merchants, chapman (i.e., wholesale dealers, middlemen), and peddlers regularly made the hazardous trek across the Peaks, but in winter snow often blocked the passes (as it still does today). The nearest urban concentrations — Coventry and Stoke-upon-Trent in Staffordshire, Manchester to the north, and Chester and Liverpool to the north-west — were too far away to overshadow the town, but close enough for regular contact. Substantial neighbouring towns, Stockport, Knutsford, Buxton (Derbyshire), and Leek (Staffordshire), all about ten to twelve miles distant, were not so near as to challenge Macclesfield's pre-eminence as a minor regional centre. And no nearby village could rival the town as a provider of market, retail, and professional facilities for a large area of south-east Cheshire.

Macclesfield grew quickly after 1750, more quickly than its natural rate of increase would have decreed. Without census returns, and until a comprehensive statistical analysis of the parish registers is undertaken, only a very rough estimate of the rate of growth of the town's population in the eighteenth century can be made. The earliest reliable account is found in the survey of the condition of his diocese drawn up by Francis Gastrell, Bishop of Chester, in about 1720. Gastrell reports 925 families.[11] The bishop's information, provided mainly by local incumbents, appears to have been carefully collected, collated, and amplified by available documentary evidence. Gastrell's figure, if use is made of Peter Laslett's suggested multiplier of 4.75 for 'mean household size',[12] gives a total population of about 4400.[13] The next estimate of the town's population, from a churchwardens' report of 1754, gives a total of 'near 6000', a plausible enough figure.[14] Local historian John Corry mentions a count taken 'by two intelligent residents in 1786', which resulted in a total of seven thousand residents, a suspiciously round number, but again a plausible one.[15] From such fragmentary data it can only be concluded, generally, that the town grew slowly during the first half of the century, and gained momentum thereafter; growth reached a maximum rate between 1800 and 1830.

Table I : 1

Macclesfield, Population Growth, 1801-61[1]

Year	Total Population	Males	Females	Percentage Change	National[2] Percentage Change
1801	8,743	3,979	4,764	—	—
1811	12,299	5,629	6,670	+40.7	+14.0
1821	17,746	8,421	9,325	+44.3	+18.1
1831	23,129	11,005	12,124	+30.3	+15.8
1841	24,137	11,454	12,683	+ 4.4	+14.3
1851[3]	29,648	14,183	15,456	+22.8	+12.7
1861	36,101	16,690	19,411	- 7.5	+11.9

1. *Sources:* J.N. Jackson, 'The Population and Industrial Growth of Macclesfield' [*c.* 1851-1951] (Manchester University Ph.D., 1960) Appendix, Table 2.2; and Chester City Record Office, Earwaker Collection, CR63/2/34, 'A Table of the Population . . . of the Prestbury Division of the Hundred of Macclesfield', a summary table of data from the Censuses of 1801, 1811, and 1821.
2. For England and Wales.
3. All figures up to 1861 are for the old township of Macclesfield. New borough boundaries, incorporating into the town parts of the industrialised villages of Sutton and Hurdsfield on the east bank of the Bollin River, were drawn up in 1835. Growth for the new borough as a whole from 1841 to 1851 was + 19.7%, indicating the heavier concentration of new residents in the old core of the town. 1861 figures are for the new borough.

The first official census, in 1801, gave a total of 8743;[16] this figure was doubled by 1821 and nearly doubled again by 1851. [See Table I:1.] The rates of growth for the first three decades of the nineteenth century, far exceeding national rates for the same period, are striking. Between 1831 and 1841 there was a slump in population growth, which Stella Davies attributes to depression in the silk trade, discouraging in-migration and encouraging out-migration.[17] If Davies is correct, this was a delayed reaction, however, since the trade depression began as early as 1826 and probably reached a high point in the period 1828 to 1831. Another spurt of growth occurred from the early 1840s until about 1860, and thereafter the severe decline of the silk trade brought about mass emigration, a great deal of it to America, where emigrants from Macclesfield were largely responsible for making Paterson, New Jersey, the silk manufacturing centre of the United States.[18] The town's population contracted steadily until the Second World War, and did not reach its 1861 level again until the 1960s.

By 1801, the first year for which there was a breakdown of male and female inhabitants, there was already evidence of the preponderance of females (54.5 per cent) which later earned Macclesfield its nickname of 'the women's town' and which reflected the exceptional opportunities for women's employment in the silk industry.[19] In 1811 about 90 per cent of the town's families described themselves as being chiefly engaged in 'trade, manufacturing, and handicraft', as against 8.9 per cent employed in agriculture. By 1821 those occupied in agriculture numbered 2.7 per cent.[20].

It is clear that a substantial proportion of the population increase during the industrialising years was due to migration, and especially to migration from nearby rural areas and from just over the county borders in Staffordshire and Derbyshire.[21] Later, drawn by news of 'the establishment of the silk manufacture to an extent and perfection formerly unknown in England',[22] silk-workers came from Dublin and London, Coventry and Leek, and silk towns like Middleton and Failsworth in Lancashire. The heavy influx of Irish seems to have started in the 1790s and continued unabated through the period.[23] In 1841, when census returns first gave some indication of place of birth, 79 per cent of the town's population was Cheshire-born. By 1851, 58 per cent were native to Macclesfield itself, 15 per cent came from elsewhere in the county, 10.35 per cent were Irish-born, and 1.56 per cent London-born.[24].

The migrants included both unskilled country people, seeking to learn a trade, and experienced workers in search of better pay and more regular employment. A representative story is that of Ann Jones, a native of Newry, Ireland, who was arrested in Macclesfield in 1809 as a 'rogue and vagabond'. She said she and her husband came from Ireland about seven months before 'to get work, and that they have worked in Manchester and were going towards London, having heard that better work was to be had there.'[25] Such casual and seasonal labourers led a strenuous, wandering life, and even skilled artisans were often forced to keep moving in search of employment. Weavers and spinners tramped up and down between Manchester, Stockport, and Macclesfield, following the work, or rumours of work, and sometimes switching back and forth between the cotton and silk trades, picking up new skills as needed. A great many migrants were deserted, widowed, or single unprotected women, seeking a living for themselves and their children, if any. Typical of many such cases is that of Martha Hill, a 21-year-old cotton-spinner from Manchester, found wandering at Macclesfield, pregnant and 'not able to give a good account of herself' in 1812.[26] Another young female pauper told the magistrates she had been born in London, moved to Chester at the age of fourteen, was later apprenticed to a cotton-weaver, and was presently (1825) a silk-weaver.[27]

Young women like these were attracted to the town by the hope of finding work in the silk industry. Yet, as their stories show, not all could be assimilated comfortably. Some checks on the town's growth were endemic to the silk trade itself. A glance at any collection of eighteenth-century portraits or furnishings will reveal the widespread demand for silks, in the form of gowns, suits, handkerchiefs, scarves, ribbons, laces, stockings, gloves, upholsteries, and draperies, in the middle and upper ranks of society. But in the context of the rapid expansion of the domestic market for all sorts of consumer goods in this period, silk remained essentially a luxury article. It was subject to the vagaries of changing fashion and the market for it was cyclical and concentrated in the haunts of the privileged and wealthy — that is, primarily in London. The raw material, including the cost of transport from abroad and duties, was expensive, as was the skilled labour necessary to work the delicate fibre; so a high level of risk was built into the trade.

Most important, the domestic silk manufacturer continually faced potentially ruinous competition from the superior and more cheaply produced output of the French and Italian industries. Both of these countries had the advantage of being able to produce their own raw silk, as well as a lower cost of living. Lyons, with its 52,000 silk workers by the end of the eighteenth century, had the largest concentration of industrial workers in one trade in Europe.[28] Without the high protective tariffs imposed on imported wrought silks the English industry could not have taken hold as it did in the eighteenth century, and there was always pressure on Parliament to tighten regulation.[29]

For all their pride in local achievement and prosperity, provincial silk manufacturers continued to look to London when gauging the 'state of the trade' or preparing a protest to the Government. The workmen likewise often followed London's lead when organising themselves into trade associations or in voicing their collective grievances. Any indication of a government move towards free trade in silk goods was greeted by a concerted wail of protest from both London and the provincial trade, and from both employers and operatives. Finally, the 1860 free trade treaty with France dealt a crippling blow to all but a few specialised branches of the trade.

I

Why did silk-spinning (and later weaving) move outside the capital in the eighteenth century? The answer lies in technological advances in the industry. The mechanisation of spinning, combined with availability of abundant supplies of relatively cheap labour, encouraged both the factory and domestic production of silk thread in towns and villages near the main turnpike roads out of London. But the training and skill necessary for handling silk meant that the spinning industry tended to move first to communities which already had colonies of French or Flemish immigrant silk-workers — for example, Norwich, Coventry, and Canterbury. The first entrepreneurs of the new provincial industry were Londoners, seeking to avoid the higher costs of the metropolis by 'putting out' their work. Technological advances and economies of scale eventually drew the cheaper branches of the trade farther and farther from London, and local investors and factory-masters soon took over the provincial trade.

For Macclesfield and other provincial silk centres there continued to be an element of competition with the Spitalfields trade. London was not only the prime market for the finished product, it was also, from the time of William III, the only port in

England through which raw silk could legally be imported. The chief sources of supply in the eighteenth century were Italy, Turkey, China, and India. From London much of the raw silk was sent out to the provinces to be twisted or 'thrown' into thread, which was then returned to Spitalfields to be woven. The metropolis had long enjoyed what amounted to a monopoly on the fanciest goods — velvets, brocades, cloth of gold and silver, and elaborate figured silks — designed and executed by ingenious craftsmen mainly of Huguenot descent.

The revolutionary technical development in the industry during the eighteenth century was the introduction of water-powered, factory-based silk-spinning. Machine-spinning of silk was introduced into England by the brothers John and Thomas Lombe.[30] John Lombe had gone to Italy in about 1715 and there managed to learn the carefully-guarded arts of power-spinning. On his return to England in 1717 he and his brother built their famous silk factory — soon to be the model for similar mills elsewhere — on an island in the River Derwent near Derby.[31] The Lombes enjoyed an impressive success, and from this time the old system of hand-spinning of silk declined rapidly, though the older techniques held on for some time in London, where both space and water-power for the new-style mills were lacking.

Macclesfield was one of the first English towns to imitate the Lombes' achievement, and there were several reasons why this should have been so. In the local area the manufacture of silk- and mohair-covered buttons, 'wrought with the needle, and making a great figure in full trimmed suits', had flourished since the sixteenth century.[32] The work was carried out mostly by women and children under the putting-out system, though button-making also provided some work for skilled male workers, in the production of the moulds and the metal 'backs' which were then covered with thread or cloth. Small workshops and warehouses dotted the streets adjoining the market-place, and local entrepreneurs developed useful contacts with London traders, who would supply raw silk or twist (i.e., silk thread) on credit and contract for the finished product. Silk cloth and small wares were also distributed through several counties by chapmen and peddlers, some of whom were nicknamed 'flashmen' since they frequented the wild, hilly country between Macclesfield, Buxton, and Leek, a district known locally as 'Flash'. Their vagabond life

Table I : 2

Macclesfield, Silk and Cotton Enterprises: 1794-1834

TYPE	1794	1814	1817	1825	1834
Spinning firms (throwsters and twisters)	10	—	41	76	55
Manufacturers	19	38[1]	22	65	54
Dyers	7	4	5	8	10
Smallware mfrs (incl. buttons, trimmings, ribbons, hatbands)	18	3	9	—	7
Hat manufacturers	—	6	15	9	9
Cotton mills	2[2]	14	9	3	3
Total	56	65	101	161	138

1. This figure includes both spinning firms and manufacturers.
2. Both of these firms are listed as 'cotton and silk' manufacturers.

Sources: [Peter Barfoot and John Wilkes], *The Universal British Directory of Trade and Commerce* . . . vol. III (London: Barfoot and Wilkes, [1794?]).

[William Holden], *Holden's Annual Directory. Class the Fifth, Combining the Calico, Cotton, Silk, Woollen and . . . Other Connected Manufacturers* . . . (London: W. Holden, 1814) p. 217.

John Corry, *The History of Macclesfield* (London: author, 1817) Appendix.

[J. Plant and T. Gregory], *The History and Directory of Macclesfield and Its Vicinity* (Manchester: W.D. Varey, 1825) pp. 97-180.

[J. Pigot], *Directory of Cheshire* (Manchester: J. Pigot and Co., 1834) pp. 39-43.

Table I:2 *continued*

Variations in method of compilation and standard of accuracy make comparisons between early directories hazardous. Generally there is a trend towards greater inclusiveness, from the earliest brief listings of 'principal tradesmen' to lists of individual residents with their occupations, like Pigot's 1834 guide. As a result the leap in the figures between Holden's old-style listing of 1814 and Corry's detailed study of 1817 is exaggerated. Only very general trends are indicated here.

'Manufacturers' is usually used to designate firms which engaged primarily in weaving, either on their own premises or by putting-out. I have also included in this column broader categories such as 'silkmen' and 'merchants'.

For a full account of early directories and the vagaries of their composition, see Jane E. Norton, *Guide to the National and Provincial Directories of England and Wales, . . .* (London: Royal Historical Society, 1950).

combined with an unsavoury reputation as sharp dealers, passers of false coin, and denizens of low inns and alehouses, earned them the suspicion of the more settled population.

The scale of this trade was impressive. One Macclesfield button merchant might lay out as much as £12 to £18 per week in wages in the small village of Wilmslow alone — with the average weekly wage for women estimated at 3*s* 6*d* in the mid-eighteenth century.[33] The accounts of button-dealers Brocklehurst, Acton, and Street show an annual profit at the same period of nearly £1500.[34]

Changes in fashion caused a slump in the silk button trade as early as 1710, and even an act of Parliament in 1718, requiring that all buttons be made from material different from that of the garment itself did not reverse the trend. The appearance of cheap metal buttons, mass-produced in Birmingham, added to the competition and left many Cheshire button-workers unemployed by mid-century.[35] Nevertheless, there were still ten good-sized button-making firms in Macclesfield as late as 1787, and traveller John Aiken reported that the button trade was still 'considerable' in 1795.[36] Pigot's *Directory* for 1817 lists four dealers, two in the town and two in the countryside; all of these, however, are listed as 'button and twist manufacturers', thus indicating the course followed by many button manufacturers to salvage their prosperity.[37]

The falling off of the button trade left Macclesfield with a pool of available labour, substantial capital for redeployment, a distribution network, and valuable contacts with silk merchants in London and elsewhere. Reversing its long-standing protectionist and xenophobic stance, the Corporation now sought new industry actively, revoking in 1729 severe restrictions against 'ingenious strangers' who might seek to start a business in the town.[38]

Local tradition traces the beginnings of large-scale silk-spinning in Macclesfield to the enterprise of one Peter Orme, a Huguenot, who is said to have opened a spinning workshop in the market-place, near the old town hall. Hand-throwing,[39] or spinning, to serve the button trade, was certainly carried on at least from the seventeenth century; only the scale increased later, with masters gathering their workpeople together in large sheds, sometimes referred to as 'mills'.[40] The extant land tax lists for the town, beginning in the 1740s, are full of references to mills, shops, 'shades' (i.e., sheds), crofts or twisting crofts, and workhouses.[41] The term 'mill' was used variously in the early days, to refer to large handicraft workshops, to factories proper (i.e., those with power-driven machinery), and to the spinning machinery itself, as in the case of the 'Dutch mill', an improved spinning apparatus which multiplied the output of each hand-worker. The use of Dutch mills, and the greater investment they required, seems to have encouraged the organisation of large enterprises, where many hand-spinners worked under one roof, on machinery owned by the master. It is known that a spinning mill owned by Michael Daintry in Park Green was in operation by 1735, when the young James Brindley, then apprenticed to a wheelwright and millwright in Sutton, was called in to repair some machinery damaged in a fire. It is not known whether the machines he worked on were power operated. Brindley, born a few miles away, near Buxton, performed the Daintry repair as his first solo job, and it became part of the legend of his phenomenal skill. He worked on textile mills in East Cheshire and Leek for the next few years, before embarking on larger projects, culminating in his historic commission as surveyor and engineer of the Duke of Bridgewater's famous canal.[42]

The father of modern industry in Macclesfield, and the first entrepreneur of whom there is any detailed knowledge, was Charles Roe.[43] The son of Thomas Roe (1670-1723), vicar of Castleton in Derbyshire, Roe was born in 1715 and first came to Macclesfield in 1740. Nothing is known of his early life, or of how he first became involved in the button and silk trade. There were, however, family connections with the town. An older brother, William, was prime curate of St Michael's Church from 1724 until his death in 1730; another brother, James, held the same living from 1756 to 1765, and was a highly respected figure. In 1744 Charles Roe leased some land at the western end of Park Green, having previously demolished an old dye-house on the site which had been converted into a twisting-shed by the former lessee, Joseph Pickford. Roe was familiar with the Lombes' silk mill at Derby and followed its style closely in planning his own new mill; he is said to have secured an exact model of the Lombes' machinery (their patent had run out in 1732), which he had copied for his mill. The remains of Roe's original mill were recently demolished, but it is possible to recapture its appearance from a representation of it on Roe's monument in Christ Church, Macclesfield, the church Roe himself built in 1775 for his friend the popular evangelical preacher David Simpson. The memorial plaque shows the main mill to have been a four-storey building, L-shaped in plan, surmounted by a bell tower, and powered by a large water-wheel.[44] This mill was to become a prototype for the local textile industry, its basic features reproduced again and again; perhaps the most famous surviving (and fully restored) example of a mill in this style is Samuel Greg's 1784 cotton mill at Styal, Cheshire.

By 1750 Roe had entered into partnership with Samuel Lankford, silk merchant, and in the following years the two leased more land, converted more buildings, and improved the mill's water supply. By the early 1760s Roe had acquired two additional partners and was beginning to sell out his interest in the mill, in order to free his time and capital for even more ambitious industrial projects. In 1762 the firm's total worth was £16,611 18*s* 2*d*, of which £2800 was the value of the buildings, machinery, and utensils. By 1764, when Roe finally liquidated his interest, the total value was over £19,000.[45] Roe got out at the right moment, since trade slumped badly in the years 1764 to 1766. In 1773 the firm, now Lankford, Robinson, and Stafford, went bankrupt.

Charles Roe continued to play a leading role in the town's affairs; having served as mayor in 1747/8, he was chosen alderman on many occasions thereafter. The most important industrial venture of his later years was the Macclesfield Copper Company, founded in 1758 in partnership with Rowland Atkinson, a brother-in-law of Roe's and headmaster of Macclesfield Grammar School. A copper-smelting works was constructed on part of the town's common land, leased from the Corporation at a rent of 5*s* per year.[46] The smelting project had the advantages, at first, of local ore, from Alderley Edge, local coal, abundant water, local clay for pots and bricks, and calamine ore, from which zinc is smelted, brought in from Flintshire and Shropshire. The company prospered and extended its operations widely. By the mid-1760s local supplies of coal were nearly exhausted, and this crisis, along with the general need in East Cheshire for cheaper transport for heavy commodities (including cheese, salt, timber, and stone, as well as coal and metal ores), led Roe to project a detailed scheme for a canal to link Macclesfield with the Weaver Navigation at Northwich. A lively publicity campaign won Roe and his fellow 'navigators' the support of leading merchants and land-owners, and Roe testified before a House of Commons committee in 1765 that, with the canal, carriage costs for some products could be cut by as much as two-thirds, and the quantity of goods transported could be doubled. But the scheme failed, largely as a result of the hostility of the great canal proprietor, the Duke of Bridgewater. The Duke's surveyor, Brindley, testified to the technical difficulties involved in the new canal scheme and 'the great injury the Duke's navigation is likely to receive.'[47] W.H. Chaloner concludes that 'the industrial development of Macclesfield was sacrificed to the Duke of Bridgewater's megalomaniac desire to be "the largest dealer as a carrier in Europe".'[48]

As the copper-smelting business expanded Roe and his partners sought new supplies of ore. In 1764 they leased Parys Mountain in Anglesey and began mining copper ore there in 1765. John Walker, a Liverpool merchant who later became a partner in the company, advertised 'an assortment of rowl'd copper from Charles Rowe, Esq. and Co.' for sale in June 1765, and in 1767 the company opened an additional smelting works near Liverpool. By 1782, the year after Roe's death, the company showed a net annual profit of £15,000.

Following Charles Roe's death the activity of the firm shifted more and more away from Macclesfield. William Roe (1746-1827), the only one of Roe's seven sons to devote himself to the family business, was concerned mainly with the Liverpool works.[49] Thus, the Roe enterprises, so outstanding for their scope and daring, made a less enduring contribution to the town's economic history than their grand beginnings portended.

The success of Charles Roe's silk mill did, however, inspire the building of many others. By 1758, according to John Corry, at least twelve large mills had been established, either by new construction or through the conversion of older button-making workshops.[50] Development was mainly along the stream banks, with elaborate systems of reservoirs, weirs, sluices, and culverts devised to channel the water more efficiently for power. As new mills and their attendant outbuildings and workers' cottages were built along the Bollin River and Dams Brook the town expanded to the south and east. These early mills were constructed of local materials, brick, stone, hewn timber, hand-forged nails and brads, with heavy oak beams, stone-flagged roofs, and brick walls, diminishing in thickness with each storey. The power provided by water-wheels was 'conveyed to the spinning machinery by vertical and horizontal line shafting which, from an engineering point of view, favoured a multi-storey structure. Excessive lengths of shafting all on the ground floor would have produced much friction, thus slowing down the machinery.'[51] Winding stone staircases in projecting towers connected the storeys, creating something of a fire hazard, and baskets of bobbins and raw silk had to be laboriously hand-carried from floor to floor. Ceilings tended to be low; ventilation and heat (provided by open coal fireplaces) were sometimes inadequate, although the necessity for cleanliness and the maintenance of a moist atmosphere in working with silk encouraged employers to see that inner walls were whitewashed and ceilings lathed and plastered to minimise dust seepage from above. Large mill buildings were sometimes built on speculation, with individual floors, or parts of floors, rented out to a number of small masters. Smaller sheds, garrets, warehouses, and workshops were also sub-divided in this way — resulting in a complex pattern of financially interrelated enterprises.

Usually unadorned except for a triangular pediment in the centre of the front facade, framing a clock-face and capped by a small cupola to hold the bell which summoned spinners to their work before engines brought steam-whistles with them, the early mills had a quiet, unobtrusive attractiveness. Their simple brick walls, broken by even rows of small-paned windows, gave them almost a domestic style and scale. One observer finds them 'reticent and retiring', adding a note of calm and order to the cramped and chaotic town streets.[52] And so they do, now that their water-wheels are motionless, their candles and oil lamps extinguished, and their thousands of spindles stilled and gone.

Not all new industry in Macclesfield was power-based; apparently many button manufacturers simply transferred their capital and premises to silk-throwing by hand methods. A prime example is the Brocklehurst mill, which became the largest and most diversified firm surviving to the present time. John Brocklehurst joined the old button-making firm of Acton and Street in about 1748, and the business was taken over, in stages, by the Brocklehurst family. The three original partners seem to have started with about £4000 in capital; this amount they trebled within eleven years. Fragmentary records from the 1750s show that the partners took out total profits ranging from £490 to £668 per year while ploughing back amounts ranging from £636 to £973.[53] The Brocklehurst mills expanded dramatically in the second half of the eighteenth century, and by 1789 the firm was trading all over the British Isles and as far afield as New York and Moscow.

The mills at Hurdsfield are a sprawling complex of buildings representing nearly every stage and type of industrial architecture to be found in Macclesfield. A small Georgian-style block of mill and office wings around a central courtyard, probably the original premises of Acton and Street, is still used as the company's general offices. This block is flanked by newer and larger mill wings, which probably housed handloom weavers, and perhaps hand-throwing machinery as well, in the eighteenth century. The absence of any trace of a water-wheel suggests that power-spinning was not introduced until the 1820s, when a new wing was constructed to house steam-driven machinery. Because of the delicacy of the fibre, power-weaving developed very slowly in the silk industry; handlooms continued to be used for fine work into the twentieth century. Thus, the early weavers' struggles were, for the most part, directed not against mechanisation but against manufacturers who tried to impose the norms and discipline of mass production and the factory system on domestic workers. Power looms did excite hostility when they appeared; the first few to be seen in Macclesfield, installed by the Brocklehursts in the late 1820s, were greeted by a window-smashing crowd of demonstrators.

The Brocklehursts took a leading part in civic and philanthropic activities; they supplied the town with a number of mayors and aldermen and were staunch members of the small Unitarian chapel off King Edward Street. William Brocklehurst, who moved to Hurdsfield in 1729 and is referred to as a chapman, came from a land-owning family from Kettleshulme, Cheshire. It was his son John (1718-91) who laid the foundations of the family's textile empire. This pattern is often repeated in the family histories of the town's early industrialists: the profits of land-holding were combined with those of wholesale (or even retail) trading, the family built up a large putting-out business, and finally the transition to factory-owning was made. Holdings of farmland, dwelling-houses, and other rentable property were carefully preserved and expanded as a supplementary source of income.

The second John Brocklehurst (1755-1839) was affectionately remembered as a portly figure 'with powdered hair, and the fashionable queue of the time of George III'. Although he considered himself a Whig and was 'a warm admirer of Charles James Fox',[54] he occupied himself primarily with business affairs. Political ambition emerged only in the next generation, when John Brocklehurst III (1788-1870) became one of Macclesfield's first M.P.'s in 1832. He was educated at Macclesfield Grammar School and resided in the town all his life. Described as a charitable man, 'simple and unostentatious in his personal life', he refused a baronetcy three times.[55] He held his parliamentary seat for thirty-six years, from the First Reform Act to the Second, and passed the seat on to his son in 1868. As an M.P. he became a leading spokesman for what might be called the Whig outlook in the silk trade: 'although a Free Trader so far as the necessaries of life are concerned, he believed that as silk might be regarded in the light of a luxury . . . so Protection was absolutely necessary for its prosperity.'[56]

The Brocklehursts' chief rivals for the town's economic, social, and political leadership, after Charles Roe's sun had set, were the Ryle family. The senior John Ryle, an austere figure, became, in

1773, the town's first mayor with Methodist sympathies. In partnership with Michael Daintry[57] he ran the Park Green Mill, so successfully, it is said, that he left his young son John Ryle II a fortune of some quarter of a million pounds. The younger Ryle's story is amusingly (and indulgently) told by a historian whose informants knew Ryle well:

> Mr. Ryle was well educated, open-hearted, utterly unselfish, generous to a fault. Nature intended him for a country gentleman, and if her design had been fulfilled, as a country gentleman he would have shone. For business, however, he was totally unprepared. It so happened that his sister married a Mr. Wood, a cotton-spinner. The spinning did not pay. Mr. Ryle, a kind and liberal man, advanced large sums of money. Poor man . . . he was destitute of experience, he thought it would all return; of course it never did . . . . To recuperate himself, at Mr. Wood's suggestion, he embarked in banking, honourably, consistently, trustfully, as in everything else.[58]

Ryle, with Michael Daintry, took over the town's first bank, that of Hawkins, Mills and Co., founded in 1787. They did well at first, then opened a Manchester branch in 1821, apparently over-extended themselves, and finally failed in 1841. An orthodox Tory and protectionist, John Ryle II became M.P. for Macclesfield in 1831, soon retired from active business, and withdrew to a country estate, Henbury Hall, in about 1834.

The Brocklehursts followed the Ryles into banking, but were more cautious. Taking over another local bank, that of Critchley and Turner, they opened their doors for business in a building directly in front of the Unitarian Chapel in 1816. This venture was successful, and was eventually absorbed by the District Bank Ltd. Like the famous Macclesfield pennies — trade tokens which the Macclesfield Copper Company had used to pay its workmen in the 1780s — the banknotes of the Brocklehursts and of Daintry and Ryle became familiar currency in the district.

II

Soon after 1800 a major technological advance in the silk spinning industry occurred, when steam power began to be used to drive twisting mills. Boulton and Watt of Birmingham sold a twenty horsepower, double action '(Beam) Crank Type Engine' to J. and G. Pearson's silk mill in Waters Green in 1804.[59] Their ledger also notes sales of engines to 'cotton mills' in Macclesfield in 1800 and 1802, but the customers are recorded as 'Daintry and Royle [i.e., Ryle]', the well-known silk manufacturers. The mill where these engines were installed stands at the eastern end of Park Green; it was built in 1785 as the successor to Daintry's small mill where Brindley had worked in 1735. In 1810 the first mill to be built expressly for steam-powered spinning was constructed as an extension of Charles Roe's mill, at the opposite end of Park Green. This mill, a 'skyscraper' of its day, ushered in a new age. Six storeys high and rectangular in plan (34′ x 74′, with a 10′ floor-to-ceiling height — loftier than in the older mills) it had an engine and boiler accommodated in lean-to sheds attached to the main block.

Between 1810 and 1820 several new steam-driven mills were built and a number of older factories converted to steam power. Steam technology meant an increase in the amount of capital needed to set up in the trade. For example, John Brocklehurst spoke of a large spinning mill costing £7000 to construct, independent of machinery, in the early 1820s. The equipment for this mill cost an additional £4000.[60] Added to the fixed capital investment was the necessarily large inventory of raw material and finished goods likely to be on hand at any time. One middle-sized firm of silk manufacturers lost more than £4500 worth of goods in a fire at their King Edward Street premises in 1824.[61]

The advent of steam production left its mark on the geography of the town. Silk mills now tended to be located adjacent to main roads, to assure a ready supply of coal. The imposing Chester Road Mill, for example, stimulated the development of a new district of shops and cottages to the west of the town centre. An advertisement for a bankruptcy sale in 1826 gives a vivid description of this mill, and suggests the high level of risk involved in early factory ventures:

> All those two valuable and compact silk factories with the engine house, and the buildings belonging thereto situate in Chester Road in Macclesfield and late in the occupation of Messrs. Hapgood and Parker together with the steam engine and fixed and main gearing therein. Also 10 cottages, stables and joiners' shops. The steam engine, which is of 12 horses

> power, is nearly new and in good repair. The buildings are wholly new and they are justly considered the most complete and desirable works in the town of Macclesfield.[62]

At first local coal, from small mines on the town Common and from the surrounding villages of Hurdsfield, Rainow, Bollington, Adlington, and Pott Shrigley, was sufficient to run the Macclesfield mills. Horse-drawn 'rail-roads' brought coal from the pit-head to the turnpike road, where coal wharves were constructed for local distribution.[63] But local mines soon began to give out, and industrialists were forced to look farther afield. Demands for a Macclesfield Canal were pressed with renewed urgency. The delay in canal building, and the shortage of capital for new mill construction, resulted in old premises, using a combination of steam-driven and water-powered machinery, remaining in use into the 1830s and 1840s.

After the spinning of silk was well established locally the weaving branch of the industry also took root in Macclesfield. The spread of silk-weaving from London to the provinces may have been stimulated in part by the agitation of the London weavers to maintain their customary prices in the face of renewed competition from French silks after the Seven Years War. The culmination of the London weavers' struggle was the passage in 1773 of the Spitalfields Acts, which set standard prices for various types of woven goods, and may have induced some weaving masters to look elsewhere for cheaper labour.[64] In any case by the 1790s plain weaving, 'the manufacture of silk handkerchiefs, shawls, and other kinds of broad silk' became a feature of the trade of Macclesfield.[65] According to one master weaver, Macclesfield wares consisted of 'bandannas and black figured handkerchiefs till about the year 1809, when the figured and fancy trade was introduced.'[66]

Local tradition has it that the mysteries of the weaving trade were imported into the town from London and Dublin. The first weaving-masters may have been Messrs Leigh and Voce; they began in a small shop near the market-place, employing immigrant weavers, who soon began to instruct local workers in the art. By 1794 Barfoot and Wilkes' *Universal Directory* lists nineteen 'manufacturers', a term which probably includes both weavers working in their own homes and the contractors who employed them. [See Table I:2.]

Weaving developed on a dual basis, as both a domestic and a factory industry. Weavers' houses, with two floors of living-space below topped by a garret, with characteristic long windows and skylights to provide maximum light for the delicate work, were built in great numbers, especially between 1815 and 1825.[67] Outside wooden stairs led up from the back yard to the third-floor shops, so that workmen could enter and leave without disturbing the family below. The work was let out both by 'manufacturers' and by the spinning mills themselves. The scale of the trade may be judged from the testimony of a committee of weavers in 1818 that there were 402 figured looms and 604 plain looms in private houses and upwards of 234 looms in factories. There were said to be 313 married and 129 unmarried 'out-door' weavers, and 867 children of weavers working.[68] In 1824/5, when the directory lists sixty-five manufacturing firms [See Table I:2.], there were 550 master weavers (with looms in their own houses) and 4775 others employed in weaving (journeymen, apprentices, factory-workers, etc.).[69] To serve the weavers (and the London market for thrown silk) the Macclesfield spinning industry at this time employed 276,000 spindles, manned by 10,229 workers, according to the testimony of John Brocklehurst, M.P., in 1832.[70]

When the Brocklehursts introduced power looms to their Hurdsfield mills in the late 1820s they ushered in yet another phase in mill development. Single-storey weaving sheds now became a feature of the larger mill complexes, since the intense vibration of the power-driven shuttles made installation of power looms on upper floors impracticable. 'Shuttles oscillating between the shuttle boxes, and the beating up of the weft would have caused the upper floors to sway with catastrophic results, ... Silk "throwing" machinery, however, is much lighter in weight and runs with an even movement . . . . Thus "throwing" machines could be installed to a height of four to five floors.'[71] Only in the 1840s, when iron-girder construction made mills more sturdy could power looms be accommodated on upper storeys.

Customary practices, originating in the domestic weaving shops, came to influence the relationship between employer and worker in the factory as well. For example, the artisan weaver had always been responsible for the cost of his house-rent, lighting, heat, quill-winding (i.e., bobbin-winding, usually performed by children), setting up the warp, and the upkeep of his loom. The total of all these expenses, in the 1810s, probably averaged about 2*s* 6*d* to 3*s* a week.[72] When mill-owners like the Brocklehursts began to employ weavers in the factory, a fixed sum was kept back from their earnings to cover these overhead costs.[73] By the 1820s most looms in private houses seem to have belonged to the weavers themselves, rather than to the factory-masters, so there would not have been loom-rent to pay.[74] Journeymen, on the other hand, did pay weekly rent (2*s* 6*d* in the 1810s) to the master weaver whose loom and work-space they used; they often paid extra for candles and quill-winding as well.[75] Apprentices paid no expenses, but they received only board and lodging, if they lived in, or half the value of the work they produced, if they lived out.

III

The consequences of the eighteenth-century 'revolution' in silk-spinning for Macclesfield were revealed by a parliamentary investigation in 1765. The trade had experienced a temporary, post-war slump in 1763/4, and there were complaints about smuggling and unfair competition from foreign silks. Evidence was solicited from Macclesfield employers, and these figures, attested by the Reverend James Roe, two churchwardens, and the overseer of the poor, indicate that during good times seven large firms alone had employed 2470 workers and another twelve smaller firms employed 1000 between them.[76] Even allowing for some exaggeration of the case, this is a tremendous work-force, at a time when the town's total population was only about 6000. The outcome of the parliamentary inquiry was an act reducing the import duties on raw silk, and the throwsters duly testified to an improvement in their business the following year, while continuing to press for prohibition of the import of wrought silks.[77]

The boom in spinning and weaving extended to other communities in East Cheshire. In nearby Congleton, for instance, a large mill was constructed by John Clayton of Stockport, who leased the garden of the town workhouse for the purpose. His mill, built in 1755 at a cost of £2000, with a water-wheel designed by Brindley, employed 400 to 500 people and made silk twist for the Coventry ribbon market.[78] Good-sized mills were constructed in remote hamlets like Wildboarclough and Gradbach, in the

Pennine uplands. The silk industry also took hold in Stockport itself and prospered there — though it was always eclipsed by the town's thriving cotton industry.

The impressive expansion of the provincial silk trade was based on close links with London, still the prime market for finished goods and a necessary source of raw material, capital, credit, and distribution facilities. Macclesfield throwsters travelled regularly to London to arrange for contract work, and John Stafford, solicitor and Town Clerk, was dispatched several times in the 1760s to confer with the London trade or to deliver evidence to investigative bodies.

John Sherrard, silk throwster of Spitalfields, told the House of Commons in 1765 that he employed as many as a thousand workers outside London, ninety per cent of them women and children.[79] Of these, 400 were in Cheshire. It is not clear whether Sherrard referred to people directly employed by him (and supervised by overseers in his employ) or to subcontracting through provincial masters. The two systems existed side by side, but subcontracting seems to have been the more general practice in Macclesfield. There is one case of a London silkman listed as co-owner of a Macclesfield warehouse in the 1780s, and John Corry mentions a London silk-throwster who owned premises in Mill St in 1814.[80] But most industrial property in Macclesfield was probably locally-owned, with some investment from Lancashire.

London firms apparently preferred to have Macclesfield throwsters ship most of their product back to the capital, where some of it would then be redistributed throughout England. The Brocklehurst mills, for instance, held outstanding accounts of £3121 owed by only nine large London firms, as against eighty small accounts owed by customers in Scotland, in 1789. Clearly the Brocklehursts were covering the Scottish market directly, through their own travellers, and leaving England to the London merchants.[81] The traditional habit of dealing through London seems to have persisted, though there was always some direct distribution from Cheshire. Chapmen carried silk wares to markets, fairs, and private customers throughout the North. Some master spinners and handloom weavers actually hawked their own product, or part of it, from town to town on a seasonal basis. One old weaver who ended his days in the workhouse recalled how, for sixty years, he had tramped to Scotland every summer, selling his silk goods at farmhouses along the way.[82]

Macclesfield merchants, from the very largest to the smallest, acted as 'undertakers' to London dealers, that is, they received raw silk from London and contracted to twist, dye, and/or weave it, either on their own premises or by letting it out to domestic workers. This arrangement greatly reduced the amount of ready capital needed for carrying on the business, and resulted in a multi-tiered system of contractors and a hierarchy of workshops of all sizes and types. Dyeing became an important branch of the local industry,[83] and large numbers of artisans and labourers were employed in subsidiary trades — as mechanics, reed-makers, millwrights, carpenters, carters, etc.

Cotton manufacturing briefly gained a foothold in Macclesfield in the 1780s.[84] But, as can be seen from Table I:2, the cotton trade quickly declined relative to silk. Local historian John Wootton, speculating on the triumph of silk over cotton from 1815 or so, concluded that the workpeople preferred 'the general cleanliness and healthiness' of the silk manufacture, and that the earlier mechanisation of all phases of cotton production (drawing labour and capital to the large, modern mills of Manchester and its vicinity), left many hand-workers in country districts little choice but to turn to silk: 'So it may be remarked that the country silk weaver, in his relative position as regards his fellow-workman in the town, was not a creation so far as the silk-weaving business [is] . . . concerned; he . . . may be looked upon as the last remnant of the cotton manufacture in its domestic state.'[85] The outworkers employed by Macclesfield manufacturers in country villages became a sort of sweated branch of the trade, doing the cheapest kind of work at the lowest rates.

By the 1820s Macclesfield could truthfully advertise itself as the leading centre of silk manufacture in the kingdom. But other sources of employment, many of them generated by the textile boom, coexisted with silk.[86] Small retailers of all kinds flourished in the town, as did a number of artisan groups.[87] Hat-making, a skilled trade long established in Cheshire, naturally gravitated to the supply of silk.[88] Some shoe-making was also carried out on a mass-production, though not a mechanised, basis.

Local historians assert that Macclesfield in 1756 had only eight streets — the other thoroughfares being mere lanes and alleyways. By 1834 the town had acquired not only a great many more streets but six booksellers, twenty-four schools and academies, seven confectioners, eleven milliners and dressmakers, fifteen medical men, and five clock-makers. Undoubtedly a solid industrial base was beginning to generate a superstructure of urban sophistication. Macclesfield became 'a town with a dual personality. . . . On the one hand there was the weekly market, the five annual fairs, the shops of the merchants, the church, the grammar school, and the legal functions of the old foundation; on the other the more juvenile enterprises of silk-throwing, silk-weaving, cotton-spinning, copper-smelting, and the manufacture of buttons, hats and hat-bands.'[89] A survey of the Corporation Minutes for the eighteenth century, dominated as they are by entries about repairing the roads, collecting market tolls, the appointment of beadles and pig-catchers, and the payment of bell-ringers or the reimbursement of 'persons who were sufferers in the late Riot in this Borough, by having their Meal and Flour taken from them.'[90] gives the distinct impression that the industrial revolution took place there almost silently, without much discussion, debate, or public intervention. However quiet, the 'revolution' was certainly thorough; when the town Common was finally enclosed in 1804 the work consisted mainly of parcelling out the land between numerous proprietors who had already leased land for industrial purposes. Many of these encroachments, legal and illegal, were of forty to sixty years' standing; the Corporation had made 180 leasing arrangements between 1760 and 1800.[91] The very absence of controversy about industrial development reflects how deeply involved the leading burgesses were in the process.

Yet the Macclesfield merchant was in many respects a traditionalist, who went out to meet progress in a deliberate and formal style — in the powdered wig of the era of George III. Even the Macclesfield Whig was apt to be the sort who thought free trade a very fine thing — for the next man. Economic dynamism was tempered by local tradition and borough custom, and the pace and nature of economic and social change in Macclesfield had as much to do with Casterbridge as with Coketown. The result, as will be shown in later chapters, was a subtle and complex range of social responses and cultural attitudes. Cultural provincialism was challenged and leavened by a ready receptivity to religious innovation; almost simultaneously the town gave itself over to industrial expansion and a considerable part of the population embraced a passionate Methodist commitment. One of the purposes of this study will be to investigate what each of these developments may have had to do with the other.

II

Masters and Servants

In Macclesfield, as in the larger urban centres, industrial growth brought social readjustments in its wake. The pace was less revolutionary and the conscious response more hesitant than in Manchester, Bradford, or Nottingham, but undeniably innovation was keenly felt in such a small, settled community, and resistance to change could be especially stubborn where the population was still small enough to be mobilised in protest easily and quickly. An evolution in social relations can be traced between about 1750 and 1835 — complex, uneven, and loosely parallel to, though not strictly determined by, the economic transformation of the town. Just as the large factory came to dominate the town's economy without sweeping away the small workshop, a new consciousness of class identity, and sometimes class antagonism, emerged without obliterating older notions of status and social responsibility.

In 1766 the Reverend James Roe of St Michael's Church published one of his annual sermons addressed to the town's 'societies of artificers'. The sermon was designed to be preached to an audience of small masters and journeymen on one of those trade holidays when the assembled societies marched through the town, each member grandly dressed and bearing a long staff bedecked with coloured ribbons. Acknowledging the societies' functions as social and benefit clubs, Roe praised the virtues of brotherhood, mutual assistance, and harmony, which would guarantee 'Peace and Prosperity, Ease and Tranquillity, public and private'. The ideal of a close-knit community, bound together by common religious and moral values, and a common impulse towards modest prosperity and worldly distinction, was a vision the good clergyman could recommend equally to the humblest workmen and to 'men of superior Rank and Abilities'.[1]

Roe's artisan audience may well have enjoyed this moment of self-congratulation. They had, after all, only recently emerged into local prominence in an economy no longer dominated by agriculture. But the small masters' Utopia was an anachronism almost at birth. Roe's hearers occupied a middling social stratum, sandwiched between a new class of big capitalists on the one hand and a growing body of unskilled, unapprenticed labourers on the other. Ironically the great spinning factories which spawned and sustained the most numerous local artisan group, the handloom weavers, were bastions of the new system of industrial organisation which would undermine and ultimately destroy the artisans' independence.

The Webbs characterised the artisan trade club of the eighteenth century as 'an isolated "ring" of highly skilled journeymen, who were even more decisively marked off from the mass of manual workers than from the small class of capitalist employers.' Enforcement of apprenticeship regulations made some trades a virtual caste monopoly, and 'disputes with their employers resembled rather family differences than conflicts between distinct social classes.'[2]

Master artisans, with their journeymen and apprentices, held themselves aloof from the much larger, less articulate body of domestic, unskilled, and casual workers. Among the latter, factory workers were beginning to emerge as a new and separate subgroup, a minority until the early nineteenth century. In both skilled and unskilled trades women and children made up what might almost be called a 'silent proletariat'. They found no place in the trade societies. Except as objects of complaint from workmen who feared their competition, or of attention from overseers of the poor, they hardly figured in the annals of labour until the Factory Act campaigns brought them into the limelight. Yet the existence of this large pool of relatively defenceless, unorganised workers is an important key to the resilience of factory masters in the face of trade fluctuations and resistance from the worker élite.

As James Roe's sermon suggested, eighteenth-century Macclesfield was a society of ranks, in the words of Asa Briggs, 'a network of social obligations but with gentle slopes of social gradation'.[3] Not that social conflict was absent, or that the lower orders lacked awareness of the barriers separating them from their rulers and overseers, and those on whom they depended for the very means of life. As E.P. Thompson has shown, the eighteenth-century 'plebs' shared a distinctive, self-shaped, and self-perpetuated culture. Tensions between the various levels of society, he concludes, while hardly revolutionary, produced a 'more active and reciprocal relationship than the one normally brought to mind under the formula "paternalism and deference".'[4] Bargaining between ranks was carried out sporadically, by gesture or direct action — 'theatre and counter-theatre' in Thompson's vocabulary of class relations. A structural equilibrium generally prevailed, in the nation as in the community, and riot rather than rebellion was the mode of lower-class protest.[5] Thompson takes most of his examples from the urban world of George Rudé's 'crowd', or from the rural domains of the squirearchy, but his schema applies as well to a town like Macclesfield.

Among the obstacles to the development of a militant, adversary relationship between social ranks in Macclesfield was the unusual situation of the silk industry, dependent on government protection and vulnerable to forces patently outside the control of local employers. So masters and workmen usually found it in their interest to present a united front, to speak for the whole trade in the national arena. More generally, communal bonds and loyalties produced, if not a cosy paternalism, at least a persistent expectation of reciprocal duty and mutual forbearance in time of trouble.

I

In labour history, especially before elaborate or continuous records were kept of industrial life, it is always easier to study disputes and upheavals in the normal routine of work than to learn about what went on in mills, workshops, and cottages during the long intervals of quiet. As D.C. Coleman has said, 'The noise of complaint makes itself felt in the records; the silence of contentment does not.'[6] Whether or not silence can safely be equated with contentment, the available sources can easily distort the sense of worker and employer 'mentalities'. One can hardly avoid overemphasising the moments of crowd activity. In an attempt to redress the balance, it is worth drawing together what evidence there is of the nature of the work-force and the conditions of labour in eighteenth-century Macclesfield, before moving chronologically through the crisis-punctuated history of master-servant relations.

Without census data, sketching the social profile of a town becomes an exercise in speculation, but most probably the pre-industrial social structure of Macclesfield resembled a blunted pyramid. At the bottom were those doing casual and heavy labour as well as the helpless poor: the old, the sick, and many unprotected women and children. At a slightly higher level were the domestic and factory textile workers, then came artisans and small tradesmen, and finally a mixed group of merchants, large employers, professional men, and property-owners jostling each other for precedence. The landed aristocracy was absent, and there had not yet emerged a clearly demarcated élite of big capitalists to take their place at the top of the social tree.

This is, necessarily, a roughly-drawn picture. Fortunately rather more detail may be gleaned from the pages of the early records of Christ Church, Macclesfield. For a few years in the 1770s the incumbent of this newly-opened church departed from the laconic style usual in eighteenth-century registers and recorded some biographical data on individuals mentioned, perhaps as an *aide mémoire* in getting to know his flock. The occupational information recorded there is summarised in Tables II:1 and II:2. Women's occupations are not listed but their fathers' are, hence both of these tables compare two generations of workers. Most of the detailed entries are for baptisms, with a few for burials; there are no marriage entries, as marriages could be solemnised only at the parish church (Prestbury). So, the lower end of the social scale may be under-represented through non-observance, but nevertheless, the general outlines are striking: we can see a solid concentration of population in the artisan and silk-worker groups, and a strong tendency toward intermarriage within and between these groups (Table II:1). Textile work is clearly a new occupation for men in the 1770s, and one that is (in the absence, as yet, of handloom weaving) very much over-shadowed by the older artisan crafts.[7]

Tables II : 1 and II : 2

Occupational Data from Christ Church, Macclesfield, Register, 1775-79[1]

II:1 Married Couples: Occupations of Husbands and of Wives' Fathers

Labourer (incl. Miners & Quarrymen)	Button- or Silk-workers (incl. Dyers)	Artisan	Retailer, Wholesaler, Clerk	Farmer, Husbandman
		H F		
F		H		
				H F
		H	F	
	H F			
	H F			
	H (mill piecer)	F (sugar boiler)		
F	H			
	H	F		
H				F
F		H		
			H	F
	H	F		
		H F		
		F		H
		H		F
	F	H		
H		F		
	H			F
F		H		
		H F		
	H			F
		H F		
		H F		
F	H			
		H	F (parish clerk)	
	H			F
F		H		
				H F
	F	H		
	H	F		

H = Husband. F = Wife's father. Total: 30 couples.

These groupings are rough; a wide range in both wealth and social status could be included in such categories as 'farmer' or 'silk-worker'. In most cases the appropriate category was clear; three instances where the proper attribution was debatable are indicated.

1. *Source:* CRO P/84/1

II:2 Occupations of Male Workers and their Fathers

Labourer (incl. Miners & Quarrymen)	Button- or Silk-workers (incl. Dyers)	Artisan	Retailer, Wholesaler, Clerk	Farmer, Husbandman
		F S		
		F S		
		(F S)		
				(F S)
		S		F
		F S		
	S	F		
	S			F
F		S		
	(F S)			
	S			F
S				F
			S	F
		S		F
		S		F
		F S		
S	F			
	S		F	
		F S		
	S	F		
		S		F
	S	F		
F		S		
			S	F
		F S		
				(F S)
S	F			
		S	F	
	S		F	
	F	S		

F = Father. S = Son. Total: 52 individuals.

Circled entries are those in which the father's and son's occupation is the same.

Table II:1 shows a striking number of farmers' and labourers' daughters marrying artisans, and only two instances of artisans' daughters marrying farmers or labourers. Table II:2 also reflects a marked movement in the younger generation away from agriculture and into the artisan trades. The very small number of sons following their fathers' calling is rather surprising, since wills, lists of freemen, and directories suggest that it was common for at least one son (and often other relatives as well) to carry on the family trade. Indeed, the regulations governing apprenticeship and entry into the freedom of the borough tended to encourage such a practice.

The economic backbone of the town, as the register makes clear, was the skilled artisan group, a varied lot. Jealous of his status and privileges, the mid-eighteenth-century artisan still dealt from a position of relative strength, either directly with his customers or with the merchant-manufacturers. Trade clubs offered not only sickness and funeral benefits but an atmosphere of congeniality and trust, in which trade business could be discussed and mutual assistance organised. The better-off artisan was often a householder and a ratepayer; he owned his tools and could expect to exercise some choice as to the hours of his labour and considerable control over his rate of pay. The workshop was a little community, hierarchically organised, with mysteries and prerogatives that commanded respect. Each trade had its customary rituals, penalties, and rewards, like the 'usual supper and drink' at a Macclesfield tavern, which marked the completion of young James Brindley's first important engineering job.[8] Masters, journeymen, and apprentices were bound together by shared expertise, and by the hope that any trained man might rise to fill a master's shoes.

Women and children could be found in many workshops; often but not always family members of the master, they functioned as a sort of auxiliary work-force, not quite fully integrated into the formal structure of the trade. While children did not usually start mill work before the age of seven, they could start much earlier at home. From the 1790s, when handloom weaving was established in the town, toddlers of three or four might be found helping with quill-winding, and by the age of ten or eleven boys and girls could begin weaving.[9] The discipline imposed in small workshops, while perhaps not as rigid as that of the factory, was often as harsh.

The handloom weavers were late-comers among Macclesfield's craftsmen, but they brought to the town a strong tradition of trade solidarity. Some had migrated directly from London or Dublin, where the weavers enjoyed legal protection of their wage rates and working conditions.[10] In their new home they sought to identify themselves with the older élite of artisans, but in the reorganisation of the trade by large capitalist employers their independent status was steadily undermined. Other handcraftsmen in manufacturing trades, notably the hatters and the shoemakers, suffered a similar social decline for the same reasons. The skilled trades sought to defend their status, first, by insisting on customary wage and price levels. A skilled man would expect to maintain a comfortable margin between his own wage and that of a common labourer, but the differential was not expressed only in terms of money; there were also non-economic factors to be added in, for example, control of leisure time, freedom from officious supervision, and dignified treatment in general.[11]

The apprenticeship system was the other main bulwark of the skilled trades. By controlling the supply of labour it was hoped that enough work could be assured, at a decent wage, for all. Young people were indentured by legal agreement between their parents, overseers of the poor, or other guardians and the prospective master.[12] After a trial period the usual term of service was seven years, but it might be less; apprentices were not usually bound beyond the age of twenty-one.[13] In most trades each master was limited to two apprentices.[14] Promising situations were much sought after, and parents sometimes paid a cash premium on binding their children.[15] Whether or not an apprentice lived with his master seems to have been determined, in Macclesfield, mostly by family circumstances and by distance from his or her native place. When an apprentice did live in, the master provided room and board and instruction in exchange for twelve hours a day (or more) of unpaid labour.[16]

Another common form of apprenticeship was the 'half-pay' system, under which the apprentice did not live in and the master allowed him or her a stipend of half his earnings.[17] This newer, more impersonal system could be a boon to small masters whose premises were too small to accommodate live-in apprentices, and to parents who wished to keep their children at home. But it became a source of bitter complaints by weavers and others who claimed that it was used as a cloak by masters who simply wanted a supply of cheap labour. Factory owners, it was charged, would hire youths at a few shillings a week, without bothering to draw up indentures, and turn them off when trade got slack. 'During the time they are hired, the masters I believe can send them to prison [for absconding] . . . but a master has the privilege of sending them off at the week's end; I imagine the bargain is more in the master's favour', one weaver testified in 1818.[18]

Both local oral tradition and the numbers of runaway apprentices brought before local magistrates suggest that life in the shop could be hard.[19] In 1810 Bridget Earnshaw, aged ten, was bound to an exceptionally cruel weaver: 'My master had a terrible instrument called a twig-whip. . . . If I looked away from my work he would beat me with this whip. . . . [Once] he seized me by the hair and threw me against the loom, bruising my head and blacking my eyes.'[20] Such horrific anecdotes, even if atypical, remind us of the master's power and of the vulnerability of friendless apprentices. Yet there were clear benefits for the apprentice even beyond the value of his or her training; for instance, indentured male apprentices were exempt from military service, and by serving an apprenticeship one could secure a 'settlement' which assured eligibility for poor relief.

Though girls were sometimes apprenticed, they seem to have been customarily restricted to the less skilled grades of work. For a woman, even with a kindly master, apprenticeship represented a form of dowry rather than a guarantee of future skilled employment. She might be fortunate enough to find a husband proud of her natural abilities and willing to instruct her further, but there were few who would say, with John Foster, master silk-weaver, 'My wife is as competent a weaver as I am myself, I think, and as competent to gate, or put in any figure, as I am myself.'[21] A widow might venture to run her own shop, but in general women were likely to be at a disadvantage to male workers at every turn.

The repeal of the apprenticeship clauses (and the wage-regulation provisions) of the Elizabethan Statute of Artificers in 1813/14 had signalled the beginning of a national assault on state regulations of employer/employee relations that culminated in the repeal of both the Spitalfields Acts and the Combination Acts in 1824. Rejecting the new *laissez-faire* philosophy, Macclesfield silk-weavers steadfastly continued to argue that strict control of apprenticeship would be in the interest of the whole trade: 'Besides affording protection to, and a mutuality of interest between master and servant, it secured a uniform standard of ability among the journeymen. . .'[22] But in Macclesfield it is already clear by the 1810s that the system had deteriorated and was widely evaded. Niceties of indenture were cast aside when small masters had to protect themselves from trade slumps by dismissing unwanted apprentices before their time was out, and the factory-owners took advantage of this floating population of half-trained labour by hiring them up for short periods at low wages.[23]

The flow of migrants into the town further confused matters, as it became more and more complicated to check the credentials of those who claimed to have served an apprenticeship in another town. In spite of repeated charges by established master craftsmen that the newcomers engaged in shoddy workmanship and sweating, the increasingly obvious fact was that a long training period was not as essential to some trades as it had been. In silk-weaving, technological advances, factory supervision, and the growth of the plain-weaving branches of the trade meant that boys, women, and unskilled newcomers could become tolerably proficient in a matter of months. Only in the weaving of luxury goods could the master weaver still command the respect and consideration his dignity required.

Innumerable gradations of status, both between trades and within each trade, provided a natural barrier against the development of class-wide solidarity.[24] In any dispute with an employer or master a workman would first turn to the men in his own shop or branch of the trade, although in an extended strike skilled workers could usually expect sympathy and support from other groups at roughly their own social level. Somewhat paradoxically, it was the threat of proletarianisation — of being reduced to the factory-worker's level — that eventually drew the skilled workers together, forcing them to take a more class-conscious stance. Their common history of resistance finally brought some of the skilled trades together, during the 1820s and 1830s, in tentative gestures towards a united defence of their status.

In general, the rise of the factory must be analysed in the context of the eighteenth-century population explosion, and as a response to industrial bottlenecks in the handcraft system occasioned by the remarkable expansion of both the domestic market and overseas trade in the last quarter of the century. The attraction of the early factories, for the labourer, was that they offered an alternative for those who might be redundant in agriculture or who could not find a place in the family economy of the cottage workshop. Most people came to the mills to find a means of subsistence and not to improve their standard of living.[25] In 1770, for instance, Arthur Young reported that a silk-spinning mill in Knutsford was paying women 4*s* to 5*s* a week and children 8*d* to 2*s* — wages no higher than in cottage industry (especially considering the longer hours and more rigid discipline of the mills). A 'threadmaker' in the same town paid his male factory hands 6*s* to 8*s* a week, about equal to what a farm labourer could earn.[26] In about 1776, according to John Corry, Macclesfield silk mills paid millmen and stewards (i.e., mechanics and overseers, the élite of factory workers) only 7*s* a week, women 3*s* 6*d*, and children (hired on a three-year contract) 6*d* a week the first year, 9*d* the second, and 1*s* the third. Corry goes on to say that there was soon a sharp rise in silk factory wages, attributed to competition for labour from the cotton mills, so that (presumably by the 1790s) millmen were paid 16*s*, women 8*s* 6*d* to 10*s*, and children from 2*s* 6*d* to 5*s*.[27] By the turn of the century industrial wages, especially for men, had clearly outstripped those in agriculture.

One of the components of the traditional 'moral economy' of the pre-industrial community, along with the 'fair price' and the 'fair day's work', was the notion that the large employer of unskilled labour was a benefactor to the poor, and therefore to the community as a whole. In 1698, for example, the Corporation of Macclesfield had proposed that some experienced button-makers should be appointed 'to have the care and charge of such poore children and other poore that are fit to be employed in twisting . . . and making buttons.'[28] The image of the entrepreneur as philanthropist lived on, and was regularly recalled by the manufacturers when they petitioned the Government for favours or protection.[29] When Daintry and Wood, Macclesfield cotton-spinners, took child workers from the Sutton workhouse in the 1790s they could claim to be keeping the poor rates down, as well as providing useful training and instilling the virtues of an orderly and industrious way of life.[30] A traveller's account of conditions at the Lombes' Derby silk mill in the 1770s captures the cheerful enthusiasm for the new system felt by many who were not themselves burdened by the necessity of labouring for a living:

> These mills employ about 200 persons of both sexes, and of all ages, to the great relief and advantage of the poor. The money given by strangers is put into a box, which is opened the day after Michaelmas Day, and a feast is made; an ox is killed, liquor prepared, the windows are illuminated, and the men, women and children employed in the work, dressed in their best array, enjoy in dancing and decent mirth, a holiday, the expectation of which lightens the labour of the rest of the year.[31]

But as more and bigger factories appeared optimism was tempered by doubts about the social effects of the new system. Millworkers came to be seen as something of an alien group, even vaguely threatening to the town's well-being. Thus, during a grain shortage in 1796, when townspeople were urged to use rye and other wheat substitutes, Mayor Michael Daintry could single out millworkers as the group that failed to make sacrifices for the sake of the community. Fine wheaten bread, he said, 'is chiefly (I believe) consumed by people who work in the Manufactories — and who in general pay little regard to Economy, or to the interest of the community.'[32] By 1817 Whig local historian John Corry, though he could look back nostalgically at the old-fashioned twisters' 'sheds' as having instilled 'decent and regular' habits productive of 'general contentment', thought the unchecked spread of large factories detrimental to health and morals. He felt they encouraged 'profligacy arising from ignorance and the promiscuous assemblage of multitudes of young persons; while the constant confinement of children in many instances occasioned deformity of limb, and debility of constitution.'[33]

From the employer's point of view, on the other hand, there was much to recommend the factory system. It allowed close surveillance and direct supervision; as Henry Critchley, who employed weavers under his own factory roof and also dealt with outworkers, testified in 1818, 'The factory is a place which I am constantly visiting; the houses of the out-door weavers we but seldom visit.' And as to the quality of the goods produced, 'I think those manufactured within the factory have a superiority over the others; . . . and I attribute it in some degree to the superintendence of the masters over them.'[34] This the independent artisans hotly denied; of course, those who specialised in the 'fancy' or luxury branches of any trade were best able to resist the competition of mass production methods, but in most trades there was a steady decline of the luxury sector as a proportion of total production.

Child labour remained a mainstay of the factory silk industry. There was no need to import 'pauper apprentices' as had been done in remote rural mills or in districts where parents objected to mill work for their children. Macclesfield children worked for wages, under contract, and their families or guardians provided their food and lodging. The conditions of hiring should not be confused with formal apprenticeship — though the term was often misleadingly used.[35] Though the initial agreement was usually for three years, the employer was free to dismiss any child when trade was slow.

By hiring so many young children, youths, and recent migrants the employers hoped both to benefit from cheap labour and to create a trustworthy body of experienced workpeople, used to the routine of the mill and isolated from the artisan traditions of self-government by trade committees. Yet discipline remained a problem. To augment their private authority employers had frequent recourse to the local magistrates' court (presided over in Macclesfield by the mayor) for even minor infractions of work rules. Many of the magistrates were themselves large employers in the textile trades. For example, Mayor Thomas Allen, a retired dyer, heard 141 work-related complaints from employers (excluding charges of theft) in just over two years on the bench (*c.* 1823-25).[36] The defendants were apprentices, millworkers, and domestic workers charged with such offences as leaving their service, faulty workmanship, and refusing to finish work undertaken. Interestingly, only twenty-four of these defendants were women, indicating that women were either less rebellious or more easily intimidated and disciplined within the workshop or factory.[37]

The weight of the law was by no means always on the side of the owner against the operative, or the master against the journeyman. Workpeople also saw the law court as a remedy, and Allen, who had a reputation for fairness, heard seventy complaints from employees (only seven of them women) in the same period. Matters of payment due were assessed on the merits of each case, usually with reference to customary practice, and judgment was often in the worker's favour. In one case a millowner who had summarily turned four children out of his employ was ordered to take them back.[38] The most serious cases were passed on to Quarter Sessions, where workpeople generally fared less well.

The most common complaint by employers against silk-workers was that of pilfering — a problem endemic in an industry whose raw material was so valuable and so easily concealed. By the nineteenth century the theft of raw and thrown silk had become a lucrative underworld business, called 'the Turkey trade' in local slang; Fagin-like master-minds operated their own warehouses and twisting mills, supplied with silk by rings of youthful accomplices.[39] Periodic campaigns against thieving, like that set off by the new anti-pilfering law of 1777, resulting in a flurry of prosecutions in 1778, seem to have done little good. Of 168 complaints for theft (24 against women) heard in the mayor's court in the years 1823 to 1825, most involved silk. Penalties were stiffened over the years — from a 5*s* fine for thread pilfering (first offence) in the 1770s to whipping, fourteen days hard labour, transportation, and even death (for more serious, repeated offences) in the early nineteenth century.[40] Much use was made of informers and of summary searches by constables, especially of inns and taverns known to be frequented by suspects.[41] But the losses continued and flared up dramatically in times of economic crisis.[42]

What the eighteenth-century operative's feelings were about life in the mill can only be guessed. Workers' voices begin to be heard later, usually when they are protesting, about wages, or hours, or the tyranny of employers and overlookers. The process of adjustment to the factory was difficult, but particularly so for those who had vivid memories of a pleasanter way of life. Adam Rushton, for example, who became a well-known local lecturer and Methodist preacher, was sent to work at Green's twisting mill in Macclesfield in 1829, when he was eight. As a sensitive, nature-loving child from a farming family he found the experience traumatic: 'The close impure air seemed to be stifling me. The clangour of machinery deafened me. I could hardly speak. . . . On being remonstrated with, I burst into tears.'[43] Under the friendly tuition of a young woman worker he soon got the knack of the work and had twenty or more swifts spinning quickly before him. In this 'new and arduous course of life' he worked a fourteen-hour day, with one hour and forty minutes for meals, for

1*s* 6*d* a week, raised to 2*s* 6*d* at age nine, and 6*s* at thirteen. Rushton always loathed his 'crushing slavery' and attributed to it his 'chronic weakness'. Even worse, for him, was the damage to his spirit, and in the Methodist Sunday school he found solace and, eventually, a means of escape.[44]

Apart from the rigours of long hours and monotonous work, mill life held real physical dangers for workpeople. Crowded, damp, insanitary, and often deafeningly noisy, the silk mills were nurseries of disease and deformity. In the days of unfenced machinery and no safety regulations accidents were a constant hazard, especially for children. Nearly all the fatal accidents recorded in Macclesfield textile mills involved young children, but injuries to adults also occurred. The wife of one cotton-manufacturer reportedly kept handy 'a bottle of stuff which . . . is particularly recommended for the cure of Green Wounds . . . in case of any accident happening to them or their work people by being caught in the machinery which frequently happens.'[45]

Sidney Pollard has noted that 'early entrepreneurs, looking for docile labour of a new kind, turned easily to unfree labour', to the workhouses and even to the prisons. For the worker entering the factory, 'there was a whole new culture to be absorbed and an old one to be traduced and spurned, there were new surroundings, . . . new relations with employers and neighbours, new marriage patterns and behaviour patterns of children.'[46] Even when dealing with 'free' labour, employers usually hired on a yearly contract, after a trial period. Thus the factory worker came to be likened to a 'servant', comparable to domestic or farm servants or miners, all of whom were bound to a master for a year at a time. As late as 1818 it was still 'the common rule' to hire for a year or longer, 'so that [the employers] may be certain of their services for a certain time.' A 'printed form of hiring' was used, and the workman or woman was often asked to produce a 'character' or reference from his or her previous employer.[47] Especially for those who had personal or family experience of the life of an independent craftsman or small master, the factory system was tainted by its many restrictions and evil associations.

Artisans could be so anxious to maintain their social distance they would deny, at least publicly, any knowledge of factory life, even in their own trade. When John Foster, spokesman for the self-employed handloom weavers, was asked by a parliamentary committee in 1818 how many weavers were employed in the mills, he replied, 'I cannot speak to that; I am not in the habit of going into the factories to learn that.' He could not say how many hours were worked there, or what wages were paid: 'I am not acquainted with their line of business at all.'[48]

Of course, the subjective response of any individual worker to the spread of the factory system would depend in part on perspective, on whether he or she came to the factory from 'above' or 'below'. For the artisan or the unwilling refugee from the countryside factory work might represent a great surrender of liberty and dignity. For others it meant a steady wage and some freedom from the constraints of village and family life. Work that might have seemed little better than slavery to a master craftsman could be a godsend to the casual labourer, or to large families, where a few extra shillings meant everything. Andrew Whittaker gratefully remembered how work at Greg's Styal cotton mill helped his family through the 'very bad' years of 1812/13: 'A man with a family could earn at that time 10*s* a week at the factory. . . . Samuel Greg were a very nice-looking man, and a very good man, too. My mother worked at the factory. He onst put five new sixpenses on five of the studs on the machine hoo [she] were working.'[49] 'A man with a family', like an abandoned wife, or a widow trying to apprentice her needy child might be in no position to argue.

In spite of the long hours and harsh discipline of the factory, there were always those who could see it as an improvement to get into one, or to get their children in. Casual labour, both outdoor and indoor, was in plentiful supply in Macclesfield throughout the period, except for a few wartime years. Both men and women worked as indoor help: some as house servants, but many more as cooks, laundresses, and seamstresses, or cleaning and serving in pubs and shops, running errands, and doing the heavy, dirty jobs in workshops, stables, and warehouses. Such labourers were often partly paid in room and board and lived under the constant prying eyes of master and mistress. For them, the factory might mean a money wage and a small degree of privacy and independence. Outdoor work, too, was likely to be dirtier, physically harder, and more irregular than mill work. The Corporation regularly hired men by the day for such jobs as road-making, walling, and clearing away refuse. Wages for heavy outdoor work stayed level at about 1*s* 2*d* to 1*s* 4*d* a day from the 1760s to the 1790s, and rose to 1*s* 6*d* to 2*s* during the war. (From the post-war slump straight through the 1830s unemployed men were frequently set to work breaking stones or sweeping the roads for as little as 1*s* or even 8*d*, a day.)[50] For many who had never known the life of an independent artisan, the factory could offer a roof over one's head, and a small step up in status.

Having looked at some of the major occupational groups in Macclesfield, what can be said of the overall impact of industrialisation on the town's work-force? Again, sources are scarce. Not until the mid-nineteenth century, when the national census was well under way, was detailed occupational data collected; and at first the categories used were so crude as to pose considerable problems of interpretation. Nevertheless, it is worth analysing the 1841 returns, which are the first to give a picture of the structure of the Macclesfield work-force (Table II:3). The table shows some continuity with eighteenth-century patterns, notably in the high percentage of tradespeople and artisans and in the absence of a leisured 'gentlemanly' or aristocratic group. But even more emphatically than forty or fifty years before, this is a textile town; all other occupational groups have shrunk before the silk-workers — and most of these textile workers were now in large factories. We can also see the near disappearance of some occupations which had once flourished, even among town-dwellers, especially agriculture, mining, and quarrying. As would be expected, the number of domestic servants is low in comparison with less highly industrialised towns. Perhaps the most unexpected finding is the relatively low percentage of women reported in the textile workforce. It is known from other sources that women continued to make up the majority of all factory-workers in the silk industry, and that of such workers about 60 per cent were under eighteen. Very likely the 1841 figures under-represent women and children employed in industry.[51]

II

The decades from 1790 to 1830 saw a protracted contest, expressed sometimes in subtle manoeuvring and sometimes in open warfare, as the larger employers sought to impose the imperatives (as they

Table II : 3

Abstract of Occupations in Macclesfield from the 1841 Census[1]

	Male	Female	Total Number	% of Work-force
Professions, incl. government and military	151	36	187	1.4
Commerce	120	3	123	1.0
Tradespeople and artisans	1059	297	1356	10.1
(Dress)	(541)	(239)	(780)	(6.1)
(Food, drink)	(266)	(27)	(293)	(2.3)
Textiles	4432	3924	8356	65.7
Building trades	376	2	378	3.0
Metals, chemicals, engineering	318	5	323	2.5
Mines, quarries, bricks, glass	86	1	87	.6
Agriculture	309	4	313	2.5
Domestic and other service	206	652	858	6.7
Other	544	90	634	5.0
(Labourer)	(353)	(29)	(382)	(3.0)
Total	7704	5017	12,720	

1. *Source:* 'Occupation Abstract, England and Wales', P.P. 1844, XXVII, 587.

Table II : 4

Occupational Data, 1801, 1811, 1821[1]

	1801	1811	1821
Families employed in agriculture	220	244	99
Families employed in trade, manufacturing and handicraft	1509[2]	2458	3240
All other families	14	26	323

1. *Source:* Chester City Record Office, Earwaker Collection, CR63/2/34, 'A Table of the Population . . . of the Prestbury Division of the Hundred of Macclesfield'. Compare with population figures for these years, in Table I:1, page 6 above.

2. The source gives '8509', an obvious misprint.

understood them) of mass production and a national/international market on resistant artisans. There were periods of mutual prosperity and temporary co-operation — of full employment, high wages, and compliance on both sides with customary trade practices — but the long-term trend was towards the extension of the factory system and its associated discipline. Although the expansion of factory-spinning had brought the silk-weavers to Macclesfield in the first place and greatly swelled the numbers of millwrights, dyers, hatters, and other craft-workers, by the nineteenth century skilled hand-workers were a shrinking minority of the total manufacturing population. In 1824/5, for example, it was claimed that the spinning mills provided employment for 10,229 individuals, while the handlooms supported 5214 weavers and two or three times as many quill-winders and other unskilled weavers' assistants (mostly women and children).[52] To make matters worse for the artisans, employers were increasingly able to bring the outdoor labour force either into the mill or under the same terms of employment that applied to mill-workers. The craft-workers' response was to refashion their older ideology and tactics of self-defence into weapons better suited to the new conditions of struggle.

The trade clubs and societies which flourished in the eighteenth century did so under the shadow of repressive legislation. Combinations, if defined as 'conspiracies' in restraint of trade, were liable to prosecution under the Statute of Artificers of 1563, the law of master and servant dating from the same period, or a long list of more recent and more limited acts directed at various individual trades. The proliferation of new legislation testified to the frequency with which the old was ignored or evaded. Many employers would negotiate peaceably with their workmen rather than incur the expense and delay of prosecution. Informal 'turn-outs', in which the men would leave their work and gather at a favourite pub for a few hours while an *ad hoc* committee of representatives argued with the master, were common. If a dispute did find its way into court, magistrates and juries sometimes lent a sympathetic ear to the men's grievances; in Macclesfield justices customarily consulted a respected workman on technical points and were 'guided in some degree by the opinion of that man.'[53] The new Combination Acts of 1799 and 1800, passed in a wartime anti-Jacobin climate, applied to all trades, apparently broadened the category of punishable associations, and substituted summary proceedings before magistrates for jury trials. In practice, again, this sweeping legislation seems to have been infrequently and irregularly used. Convictions were often delayed or avoided through technical arguments or appeals, and lenient justices sometimes displayed a prior loyalty to traditional notions of 'fair play'.[54] None the less, the employer had the advantage in money and power, and the punitive legislation was an embodiment of that advantage; it stood as a threat, and as a last resort.

The laws against combination may not have been often applied, and they certainly did not curb trade disputes, but they did spread fear and resentment. They were seen as unfairly denying to the workmen a weapon that could be used with impunity by employers. By their very existence these laws challenged the moral and political authority of the trade clubs. But combinations in defence of any trade as a whole were, of course, viewed in a very different light. As it happens, the first detailed account we have of trade agitation in Macclesfield concerns just such an instance of co-operation between men and masters.

In April 1803 Henry Addington, then Chancellor of the Exchequer, introduced into Parliament a bill to permit the importation of silk handkerchiefs and other East India silk goods. In response an angry meeting of the whole trade was held in Macclesfield and a committee appointed 'to collect subscriptions and conduct ye opposition of ye said Bill'.[55] The seven-man committee seems to have been composed of small master weavers, and the two paid agents, Richard Fowler and John Byrne, were allowed a comparatively generous 5*s* per day each in compensation for the earnings they would lose by devoting themselves to the project. Macclesfield served as regional centre for the protest, and committee members travelled to Congleton (where about £28 was donated), Manchester (about £47 donated), and Leek (£2 5*s* donated) to solicit support.

Substantial contributions from large manufacturers and smaller amounts collected in the shops and mills were applied towards agents' expenses, delegates' travel, paper, the printing of handbills and writing of petitions, and for 'ringers' to tell the town of meetings and other items of news.[56] But the largest expenditures went for entertainment of the customary kind; the agents' accounts indicate that most of the funds found their way to a Mr Frost, grocer and liquor dealer: £6 for miscellaneous drinking, another £2 17*s* for 'Weavers Eating, Ringers, etc.', £3 1*s* 'Expenses for friends', and £3 18*s* 4*d* '. . . at Robt. Good's for ye Throwsters', ending in a flourish on 16 June 1803 with a staggering £7 12*s* 6*d* for 'expenses of Mondays Eating Drinking Ringing Laughing Smoaking and at last quarrelling and almost fighting' and an exhausted final entry, 'To Frost's Bill up to ye close of this tedious and perplexing business.' When Addison's importation bill failed and the committee applied to its agents for the return of the unspent funds, it was not at all amused by the whimsicalities of Fowler and Byrne; they were charged with embezzling and misappropriation. In spite of the eccentricities, this record reveals the techniques by which all levels of the trade — with the masters as financial mainstay and the workmen providing the 'mass' protest — could be mobilised to a political end.

Unanimity and co-operation against an external threat did not, however, assure industrial peace locally. Soon after 1803 some of the masters could complain that 'combinations have of late been very general — In every branch of Manufacture carried out [here] the workmen have at different times turned out for an advance of wages and whilst the Men are out of Employment, they are supported by Subscriptions raised amongst the other Manufacturers.'[57] One of these strikes, in 1805, involved a group of male employees in the silk-throwing mill of Henry Critchley and Daniel Brinsley. It was apparently touched off by Brinsley's accusation that the men were idling and gossiping while fetching drinking water, and his threat to make a deduction from their wages. Tempers flared and the ringleaders were finally charged with conspiring 'with divers other persons to quit [their] service and raise the wages of themselves and other servants.'[58] There were secret meetings at night on Macclesfield Common, and outside support was forthcoming. One of the firm's female spinners, Sarah Taylor, told of meeting James Turnocks, a millman for Daintry and Ryle and Co., who said:

> 'Your men are out.' She answered 'Yes, I believe they are' he then asked what they intended to do. She said, 'I don't know I have not been at my work' he then said they talked of gathering for them, to which she replied, 'Do you gather out your shoop [i.e., shop]' he answered 'Yes' and said that if the Masters got the day this time, we shall be poorly off, but we will try if we cannot master them.[59]

The suggestion here is that the lower-paid ordinary spinners like Sarah Taylor were not directly involved in the strike, but that the skilled millmen had shut down the factory by walking out. Further, they could command the support of their peers in other mills. Without a long tradition of trade solidarity or control of rates and conditions, a factory élite was none the less emerging united against the masters' insistence on treating them as 'servants'. The men seem to have held their ground, and after many recriminations they were acquitted and a compromise effected with Brinsley.[60]

A more carefully planned and run affair than the silk-workers' impromptu turnout was the artisan hatters' strike of 1806.[61] Here the men worked as journeymen in small workshops or as individuals at home, and the employers were either master hatters or middlemen who 'put out' the raw material and bought back the finished hats. The trouble began with a meeting of eight or nine hatters at Joseph Fowler's public house on Sunday, 30 March. A list of new prices was drawn up and three workmen appointed to deliver the lists to their employers.[62] At a mass meeting at Dane's Moss, a field about one mile outside town, the messengers reported the masters' refusal to agree, whereupon the men resolved to strike. Tavern meetings continued every Saturday night throughout the strike, and a seven-man committee was appointed to inquire as to the needs of the strikers' families, to write to other towns soliciting aid, and to set fines for men who refused to turn out. One of the men's most potent weapons was their ability to ostracise individuals or make a shop 'too hot' to work in. No one was to start work again until all strikers had been accepted back by their masters, and no one was to work for a master who took back a man who owed a fine.

It would seem that the strikers had some trouble keeping their forces together. After initially winning widespread support, they lost ground as the weeks wore on and men drifted back to work. Seven hatters' leaders (who worked for four different employers) were eventually charged with 'unjustly and corruptly' conspiring and agreeing not to work for their accustomed wages.[63] Samuel Allen, a prosecution witness, spoke of disunion in the trade, which was divided into four main groups: 'the Ruffers, the finishers, the Wool Hat makers, and the Stuff Hat makers'. His own section, the stuff hat makers, he said, had decided not to turn out and were satisfied with the old prices. He also told of dissension at the strikers' meeting over how to spend the funds collected from other towns. Allen and his mates did some work for the struck masters, and he later faced such ill usage that he had to leave his master 'and build himself a small shop to work in.'[64]

There were more reports of threats and intimidation, James Whitehead, for instance, charged that Joseph Wood 'came past him as he was at work on Whitsun-Tuesday [27 May] and called him "muck"' and further abused and struck him. Thomas Challoner endorsed Whitehead's story in court and said he himself had been knocked down and beaten and had had the windows of his house broken. Solomon Warhurst, residing in Marple but working for Macclesfield masters, was visited by four turnouts who told him to 'give over' his work and read out to him the new price list. He then inquired about the fines, and 'they said they had left two or three Men to shoot those who took any more work in.'[65]

The defendants' case was based on an appeal to traditional notions of labour relations. The hatters' solicitor, Mr Cross, opened by stating that the alleged offence was a matter of legal but not moral guilt, and that it could not be considered a conspiracy. Since no single man could advance his own interest in regard to wages, he argued, there was 'a necessity of treading nearly on the law.' The men were only after 'fair dealing'; they asked only for the same rates already paid at Stockport. Alluding to the indictment which referred to the men as 'servants', Cross objected to the use of the term: 'In the factories, men [are] retained for a term; — These men [are] under contract, and therefore no servants — no more than a taylor [is] a man's servant.'[66] At the heart of the defence was the men's attempt to elevate customary practice and morality over the recent parliamentary acts. They persisted in a vision of themselves as free agents, craftsmen paid for their product, not employees paid for their labour.

The employers responded by contending that the old prices were generous, that a man who worked eleven hours a day might earn 25*s* to 50*s* a week, and that wages 'generally advance by good times'.[67] They blandly denied any knowledge of the Stockport prices, and said they had not met with other masters or made any agreement among themselves. Judgment went against the men, and they were sentenced to twelve months' imprisonment at Chester Castle.[68]

These two cases are particularly instructive, since information on how strikes in this period were conducted, outside the large cities and the mining districts, is fairly rare. Overall, the evidence here, fragmentary as it is, reflects a period in which the old legal and moral systems were overlapping with the new. There was uncertainty as to which laws applied, and how they were to be interpreted. In the absence of clear, accepted precedents, one senses that the demeanour of the employers and workmen (their language, resort to physical violence, and reputation for reasonableness), their 'character' or past record in the community, a general feeling as to whether social order or property rights were threatened, and the experience and views of individual magistrates figured largely in verdicts and sentences.

The irony here is that the millmen of the spinning factories and the journeymen hatters in their small shops were invoking similar principles and images in defence of their status as skilled workers, not to be reduced to mere 'servants' of large entrepreneurs bent on supplying the new mass market. Yet no one was prepared to acknowledge, much less to act on, the unity of interests implied in the strikers' common language. Trade consciousness and sectionalism were to keep the workers' struggles tightly compartmentalised until the free trade 'crisis' of the mid-1820s forced the silk-workers to make some tentative gestures towards co-operation between millmen and outworkers, and even between themselves and workers outside their own trade.

The years of the French Wars brought prosperity to the protected silk trade and a temporary *détente* between workmen and masters. French exports suffered badly from blockades at sea and disruption of the economy at home, and a valuable opening was offered to the British producers. In Macclesfield weavers' wages rose to unprecedented levels, and some masters even paid bonuses for work quickly completed. A diligent worker might earn 18*s* a week or, with the earnings of his family and apprentices, even as much as £2 or £3. Factory wages were lower, but the work was steady. Thanks in part to this continuing prosperity, the old system of participation by the weavers in regulating their branches of the trade remained in effect. Mutually agreed price lists were respected, and in 1807 a lengthy list of rules and orders governing apprenticeship was signed by representatives of twelve leading manufacturing firms and by sixteen elected representatives of the weavers. This agreement, put forward by the weavers to counter 'the alarming multiplicity of fugitive boys and girls' entering the trade, proposed to set up 'our ancient established rules . . . (as in London allowed)' as a means of stopping 'connections and disturbances' in the town. These regulations continued in force — at least in the larger and more respectable shops — until 1815.[69] But the appearance of control of the trade by the master weavers was largely illusory. The trade boom rather than fealty to the 1807 List held the masters to the agreed prices. Behind the façade of trade regulation the erosion of the apprenticeship system and the dilution of skilled labour went on.

On the whole, Macclesfield was not as hard hit as Lancashire and Stockport by the 1812 slump in the cotton trade, though a few local cotton mills were devastated and cotton-spinning never recovered its place in the town's economy after the war. High food prices did bring distress to workers in all trades, and there was a food riot in the spring of 1812, coinciding with the height of the Luddite disturbances elsewhere. Several shops were ransacked and the Cumberland Militia and Macclesfield Volunteers, under Captain (and millowner) J.S. Daintry, were called out to subdue the crowds.[70] This conflict was a prelude to worse times to come.

By 1815 the harsh effects of post-war readjustment were eroding the economic well-being of all workers, artisans included. The price of provisions remained high, returning soldiers swelled the labour pool, and the demand for English silks dropped. The result was a bitterly defensive response by the silk-workers and an equally stubborn offensive by the masters. The era of good feeling was no more.

The weavers had a host of grievances: the masters proposed that they work at 25 per cent under 'book prices'; when the men offered a compromise of 1*d* less per square yard, the masters refused, 'introduced looms into their manufactories and laid out all kinds of allurements to entice our apprentices from us'; furthermore, they recruited 'all kinds of persons' to become weavers.[71] John Ryle, admitting that women, boys, and girls did the weaving in his factory, said, 'It is work which the others can do, and they are as much entitled to do it as the men.'[72] The master weaver, as a result, suffered both in his pride and his pocket-book; as one explained, 'To put a good aspect on the factory proceedings, they keep the most profitable part of our business inside their own manufactories, while the father of a family, living in a tolerably large house, having poor rates and taxes to pay, commonly receives the refuse or the most unprofitable part of the work'.[73] He might have added the common weavers' complaint that, after installing looms in their mills, the masters withdrew work from outdoor weavers during slack periods, to keep their own plant in use.

This dispute, which lasted sixteen weeks, dealt a severe blow to the old apprenticeship system, and the employers now began to employ large numbers of handloom weavers inside the mills. These factory weavers were paid at a lower piece rate than 'outdoor' weavers (or a deduction was made for overhead costs). In addition they were required to pay a weekly loom-rent, as journeymen did in small shops. Some of the factory weavers were now hired by yearly contract, as 'servants', a practice abhorrent to the outdoor weavers not only as an infringement of the worker's independence but because it meant they could no longer work in the mills for brief periods when necessary to supplement their income.[74] It was an all-out effort by the employers to bring the higher-paid branches of the trade down to the level of the less-skilled, more dependent factory weavers, and to obliterate the master-weavers' claim to be arbiters of rates and conditions of work. The effort succeeded. The weavers accepted lower rates, the List of 1807 was set aside, and the weavers' committee which had been empowered to enforce the List was broken up.

The confrontation of 1815 engendered a deeper sense of antagonism between the factory-owners and the master weavers. Afterwards each side developed its own mythologised view of events. For the weavers the years before 1815 became a golden age when 'wholesome rules and regulations . . . kept a perfect system of regularity and a proper understanding between the masters and journeymen.'[75] In the employers' version the halcyon time came after 1815, when, they claimed, there were no trade disputes and prices could be agreed informally and amicably.[76] In retrospect the weavers concluded that the masters' goal in 1815 had been 'to break us up entirely, and to have a predominant power over us, and give us what they thought proper, and do as they liked with us.'[77]

After 1815 a formal association of the masters became active. When questioned about it, the employers' representatives denied that it sought to regulate the trade in any way; they said its 'chief object' was to combat pilfering.[78] Before giving out any work the masters now compelled the weavers to sign a declaration stating, 'I do not belong to any committee or associated body of weavers; and . . . no committee or associated body has had any power over me whatsoever.'[79] Through such gestures the masters demonstrated their power, and they could punish insubordination both directly and through intimidation. When asked if a workman would not face dismissal if he lodged a complaint against his employer, Henry Critchley replied cagily, 'That is a very difficult question to answer . . . I should not think at all the worse of a man for summoning me before a magistrate.' He then added, 'There are men who would discharge them, I have no doubt.'[80] Work was withdrawn from at least one of the weavers' representatives who testified before the parliamentary inquiry of 1818, and in 1823 the Home Office was told that twenty-six complaints of violations of the Factory Acts had been withdrawn when the workers who made them were threatened with dismissal.[81]

In defence of their aggressive new policy the employers argued in 1818 that the silk trade was being drawn away from Macclesfield to Manchester and other places 'where the wages were lower'.[82] This claim set off a long period of complicated and technical wrangling about wage-rates and prices. The millowners said that an industrious weaver could earn anywhere from 15*s* to 31*s* a week under the new system, and that few were unemployed or on relief. The weavers retorted that wages varied widely from employer to employer, but that the average was not more than 14*s* to 17*s* a week — especially if allowance were made for time lost between jobs and setting up new work in the loom. One case was cited in which boys and girls were paid as little as 2*s* or 1*s* 9*d* per cut (i.e., seven yards) for work which had fetched about 5*s* in 1813.[83]

There continued to be more looms at work outside factories than in, but the weavers' bargaining position had deteriorated.[84] The owners of small mills, too, were hard pressed by new conditions which favoured big capital. Some tried to survive by price-cutting and other dubious practices, while others joined the weavers in supporting a return to the old system of strict price regulation, fearing that unrestrained competition would tend to drive small men from the industry. As Clive Behagg has pointed out, such co-operation should be seen, not as evidence of class collaboration, on either side, but rather as a pragmatic, limited alliance in the face of a perilous and shifting economic environment.[85]

Hard times continued and the workers' protest flared up again in January 1817, but this time in a new form. With the memory of the weavers' defeat still fresh, Macclesfield artisans were ready to join other labourers to move beyond intra-trade negotiation to broad political solutions. An advertised public meeting in the Town Field drew about 2500 people for the purpose of considering 'the cause of our present distress, and the proper means to remedy the same.' A local silk-weaver took the chair, introducing several 'itinerant orators', who presented the assembled inhabitants with a detailed accounting of political grievances and demands. Beginning with a denunciation of 'the late unjust and unnecessary wars', these speakers went on to attribute the country's ills to oppressive taxation and extravagant expenditure. They also condemned the large standing army, 'Placemen and Pensioners', the national debt, and 'that most obnoxious Law, the *Corn Bill*, the most pernicious Law ever made by a British House of Commons.' The only remedy was a thorough reform of the system of parliamentary representation. As a finale, the crowd heard an attack on the officials of the borough of Macclesfield and various servants of the Crown, with special attention to 'the villain, villain, villain Castlereagh'.[86] A petition embodying these points and addressed to the Prince Regent was signed by 2000, and another, directed to the House of Commons, by 4200 men and boys — almost two-thirds of the male population of the borough.

Clearly this new radical ideology had travelled southward to Macclesfield from Manchester and Stockport. Similar ideas were spreading throughout the northern industrial districts as part of the first wave of popular agitation for reform (and against the Corn Laws). In March 1817 when the 'Blanketeer' protest marchers from Manchester reached Macclesfield on their way to London, they were warmly received. The local press admitted that in spite of their 'tattered habiliments and forlorn aspect' and 'the desperate looks and language' of their leaders, they were offered food and lodging in many homes.[87]

John Corry, writing in the same year of 1817, called the mass meetings, 'the most singular . . . event[s] which occurred in this town since the commencement of the present century.'[88] They heralded a new style of protest, both more political and less confined to purely local issues than anything seen before. Large public meetings, presided over by well-known and respected working men were to become familiar occurrences in the 1820s and 1830s. It was as if the workers, stung by the defeats of 1815, had resolved to move outside the workshop, the tavern club-room, and the magistrate's court to establish a public, political presence in the town. And it was not only the lower orders who were politicised. By 1817 a local 'King and Constitution Club' claimed a membership of about a hundred, 'comprising the property and public worth of the town.' Modelled on many other such clubs throughout the country, it aimed to counteract 'the progress of Revolution'. The Club's banquet for the king's birthday, in June 1817, featured loyal addresses by Dr Davies, headmaster of Macclesfield Grammar School, and the Revd William C. Cruttenden, who ventured the hope that 'improvement in the circumstances of the Artizan . . . would enable him to pledge the permanence of the Constitution, if not in wine as his superiors did, at least in the wholesome English beverage of ale.'[89]

But the turn towards politics was at this stage only tentative and experimental. Simultaneously, struggle continued on the economic front. In 1818 a parliamentary select committee, summoned in response to silk-workers' petitions, collected evidence on many aspects of the trade. The workers called unanimously for extension of the Spitalfields Acts to the rest of the country, while most of the employers asked for a free market in labour and in raw silk with continued tariff protection for wrought silk.[90] The committee, chaired by Peter Moore, M.P. for Coventry, proved sympathetic to the workers' viewpoint and recommended an extension of the Acts, but its advice went unheeded. In fact, Moore's bill for extension, introduced in 1819, met with such a hostile reception that he had to withdraw it.[91] The inquiry seems to have aroused the doctrinaire free-traders in Parliament and bolstered their efforts to sweep away the Acts — which they succeeded in doing five years later.

The early 1820s brought a few years of relative prosperity in many trades and a temporary relaxation of strife. For some workers wages rose impressively.[92] But the silk-weavers and spinners generally lost ground; while the pace and complexity of their work increased, the rate of pay diminished. Thanks to improvements in the jacquard loom, crêpes, velvets, and elaborately figured goods could now be widely produced outside Spitalfields. A new influx of migrants, many of them cotton-weavers displaced by power looms, assured an oversupply of labour, and the depression of wages more than offset the drop in food prices since the immediate post-war years.[93] Employer John Brocklehurst estimated that a weaver in 1824 earned about 16*s* 6*d*, and a throwster only 11*s*, for a sixty-two-hour week.[94]

The silk-workers' situation was worsened again by the crisis of 1826, a turning-point in the history of the British silk industry. In March of 1824 an act of Parliament, put forward by William Huskisson and supported by Ricardo and the free-trade enthusiasts, had drastically reduced the duties on imported raw and thrown silk. This measure had the hearty approval of the silk manufacturers, but to their dismay Huskisson's act went further and substituted a duty of 30 per cent for the absolute prohibition against the importation of foreign wrought silks. This latter provision went into effect in 1826, and the French manufacturers were quick to take advantage of it.[95] The anger and alarm of the trade was increased by Peel and Huskisson's patronising tone and obviously imperfect understanding of the economic and technical details of the industry. In his speeches Huskisson made sweeping comparisons with the burgeoning (and unprotected) cotton trade, and suggested that the less impressive record of the silk trade was attributable to 'that chilling and benumbing effect, which is always sure to be felt . . . when we are rendered indifferent to exertion by the indolent security of a prohibitory system.'[96]

News of the act had touched off an immediate reaction in Macclesfield, with factory workers now replacing the independent artisans as ringleaders of the protest. Forty-five millowners joined in proclaiming an increase in the working day from eleven hours to twelve. On 5 April 1824 the men turned out to roam the streets, breaking windows and entering spinning-mills to bring out more workers. By evening some ten to twelve thousand people had gathered in the Market Place, and a committee of employers sat negotiating with a deputation of workmen in the Macclesfield Arms as stones came crashing through the inn windows. Mayor Thomas Allen addressed the crowd, to no effect, and both local and Stockport troops were called out. A band of 300 rioters stationed themselves in the Churchyard and held off two cavalry charges with paving stones. After suffering many casualties the Yeomanry drove the men out with pistol fire, and more troops arrived from Manchester the next day. Community feeling on this occasion seems to have favoured the men. After several compromise offers had been turned down by the workmen, the employers finally conceded the eleven-hour day, and the few workmen arrested seem to have been released without punishment.[97] This victory stiffened the millmen's sense of unity and opened the door to future co-operation between them and the artisan weavers who had so long stood aloof from the factory 'servants'.

Later in the year the weavers themselves suffered a serious setback at the national level. After a protracted campaign, led by Huskisson and supported by Peel, the Spitalfields Acts were finally repealed.[98] This defeat induced the silk-workers, who had earlier shown themselves indifferent to the cause, to join in Francis

Place's effort to have the Combination Acts repealed. Place achieved his goal in late 1824, and the result was the emergence into the open of many trade societies which had been operating in semi-secrecy, as well as the organising of new unions, in Macclesfield as elsewhere. There was also a flurry of local strikes, as if the workmen were flexing their new muscles.[99]

But trade unionism had by no means obliterated trade consciousness. Employers and workmen still presented a united front to the Government in denouncing the evil consequences to be expected from exposing the trade to foreign competition. The wholesale merchants began curtailing their orders in late 1825, in anticipation of cheaper French goods to come. So, even before the full effects of Huskisson's legislation were felt, the number of silk-workers employed dropped, earnings fell by more than half as many were working 'short time', and destitution was widespread. The year 1825 was one of disastrous slump in both the cotton and silk industries; unsound speculation, glutted markets, and bank failures throughout the North all led to full-scale panic in 1826.[100] A special local relief fund raised £4360 in Macclesfield and a further £3000 from London, to which was added £1000 from the Prince Regent. In January 1826 soup kitchens had to be opened and free bread distributed. In the spring of that year serious bread rioting took place, with troops again called in from Manchester to patrol the town and protect property. In May a mob tried to burn a cotton mill which had installed power looms, and a strict curfew was imposed. All through the year class tension and fear were in the air; when Sir Walter Scott stayed in the town in November 1826 the people at his inn pressed him not to travel at night, 'As the general distress of the manufacturers had rendered many of the lower classes desperately dangerous.'[101]

A new general union of weavers, embracing both 'undertakers' (i.e., master weavers with shops) and journeymen (both in and out of factories) but led by the former, was inaugurated in February 1826. This new inclusiveness on the part of the master weavers indicates that they badly needed allies.[102] Admitting that past attempts to build a lasting union had failed, the founders nevertheless laid out their principles hopefully, and in non-inflammatory language:

> Brother Tradesmen,
>
> If there were none but honest men in the world; — if men always acted upon the principles of justice and truth, and did unto others as they would others do unto them, there would be no necessity for men to unite for their common protection and support; but since this is not the case and because there are Manufacturers, who, if it were not for the liberal examples of others and being in some measure compelled by their servants, would never give what might be termed a fair price for their work — In this case it becomes necessary that we should unite, in order to keep these men up to the legal prices of the town — But this is not all, we have our trade to guard . . . moreover, a correspondence has been entered into with London and other places and a share has been obtained in the Trades Newspaper . . .[103]

The fourteen rules that follow this preamble — with its mixture of appeal to old-fashioned morality, Christian resonance, and tentative gestures towards a supra-local connection — are based on London models and call for limited apprenticeship, election of delegates from each shop to a central committee ('men of sober habits' were preferred), and the regular collection of dues.

To the elected leadership of the Weavers' Committee, composed almost entirely of respectable master weavers, fell the uncomfortable task of securing some real improvement in a trade ravaged by a decade of setbacks and losses, while keeping in check their own unruly, desperate, and increasingly radical following. The union's general policy was to support strikes deemed serious and justified and to confine public protests — which were to be non-violent and respectful of authority — to the two issues of restoring regulation in the trade and re-establishing protection against foreign competition. At a crowded public meeting on the silk duties (one of many over the next few years) held at the National School the chairman had a difficult time restraining a vociferous group who wished to give the proceedings over to radical political speeches. Several men tried to rush the platform amidst an uproar of shouting, clapping, and hissing, but the petition was finally approved.[104]

In March 1826, only a month after the weavers' union was launched, the news came that Parliament had declined to reconsider the matter of the silk duties and a crowd of several thousand young workmen and women (many of them unemployed) paraded up and down the Market Place arm-in-arm, whooping and whistling. By eight in the evening dozens of street lamps and windows had been broken, the Angel Inn attacked, two aldermen 'tripped up' and robbed, and several food shops looted. On the next afternoon the crowd re-formed, in a less belligerent mood, and for a while contented itself with 'tossing around a dead rat'. Repeated drives against the mob by the mayor and constables cleared the streets by nightfall. On this occasion the Weavers' Committee 'to a man' volunteered and served as special constables. An open letter headed 'Brother Tradesmen' and published in the *Courier* deplored the 'ungrateful conduct' of 'rash and inconsiderate youth': 'We, the Committee of the Silk Weavers, hasten to express our entire disapprobation of the Riotous Proceedings of last night, at a time when our more wealthy neighbours have used every exertion to alleviate our distresses. . .'[105]

But it was not only idle youths who were straining against the moderate and limited programme of the union. In the wake of the rioting a meeting of several hundred weavers gathered to discuss the Corn Laws and was addressed by several local radicals. These men, who do not seem to have held any office in the union, appear frequently in the next few years as unofficial organisers and advocates — turning up whenever there was trouble in a shop, or in court, or at mass meetings. One John Yearley, identifying himself as a native of London and 'a freeman of that city', who came to Macclesfield from Spitalfields with a wife and five children and was now 'ruined with debt', delivered a passionate denunciation of Huskisson and his works. Several less emotional speakers attacked the Corn Laws as a monopoly, suggested that the silk trade could better meet foreign competition if food were cheaper, and warned against the possibility that unscrupulous masters would try to lower wages if the Corn Laws were repealed. The meeting, which ended on a more moderate note, expressed criticism of the recent rioting and urged that a repeal petition should be taken round the shops.[106]

In addition to its indefatigable petitioning, the Weavers' Committee became involved in several large strikes and many smaller disputes, acting sometimes as a kind of watchdog over the behaviour of its own members. In one case, for instance, a master weaver named Mottershead was warned by letter that he must dismiss two of his four apprentices immediately. The extra apprentices themselves were told that they were 'illegal', and could expect to find no employment after their time was out, as they would be blacklisted. Mottershead's two journeymen were induced to leave his shop until he conformed to the union's directive, and he complained to the magistrates: 'It was absurd that a set of jackanapes should set themselves up as dictators to a body of men who had their own choice of conduct.'[107] Mottershead was caught between opposing philosophies and changing social roles. Apparently for some artisan/masters the principles of free trade accorded better with their sense of pride, personal ambition, and independence than did customary defensive strategies of the craft.

Ambivalence of one kind or another characterised the weavers' situation throughout this period. In a strike of November 1826, a group of artisan-weavers displayed all the force of their newly articulate radicalism, but in the service of very old-fashioned principles of 'fair dealing'. The men's complaint was that Mr J.W. Powell was paying his weavers at below the usual rates, and that when several put out a handbill against him he withheld silk so that they could not finish the work in their looms.[108] The ringleaders then called for a general weavers' boycott of Powell, and took their case to the mayor's court. Here the local magistrates dithered about problems of jurisdiction while cries came from the crowded courtroom, 'You have power to act. There is a precedent. . .'

When the mayor suggested taking the case to the county, a voice cried out, 'The [Arbitration] Act says *any* justice in the County may hear and determine the case.' Heeding their own advice, the weavers turned to the Revd John Browne, J.P., vicar of Prestbury, a parson of the old school, well known for his sympathy for the lower orders. Daniel Powell, son of the defendant, appeared before Browne and immediately antagonised everyone by his haughty and truculent manner. To Powell's excuses about difficulties with suppliers causing the delay in completing the work, Browne commented, 'I think it *ought* to be put out of the power of a Master to keep a man back from his work, when his family is famished.' After more technical discussion, the weavers asked if William Adam, a migrant from Paisley who had become popular among the town radicals and was known as the 'weavers' advocate', might come in. Over protests from Powell's people, Browne agreed readily: 'Oh Adam, come forward, you are a sort of Counsellor, I presume, without a wig.' Adam conducted a lively prosecution, accusing Powell of 'humbugging' the weavers. Browne finally agreed to put the case to arbitration (with Adam as one of the two arbitrators), after a summation in which we can almost see the good parson shaking his head over the mysteries of industrial life. The Act, he thought, seemed to assume that the parties could agree, but clearly they could not. This was 'excessively silly': 'certainly all persons have the right to govern their manufactories as they please; and if they say they will not employ a man who wears a blue coat . . . it's all very well'; but this was a contract — and after all, the men would be subject to imprisonment if they did not finish the work.

Mr J.H. Powell himself appeared towards the end of the proceedings and drew from the reverend magistrate a final burst of moral eloquence:

Solicitor's clerk:	But it's notorious, if a weaver had full work, he be drunk three days in a week.
Revd Browne:	. . . the Act was passed to prevent the rich man harrassing the poor man.
	. . .
Mr Powell:	Well, well, the men are doing the worst thing for themselves; there are seven of them, and they shall never have employment so long as we have a warehouse in this town.
Browne:	Pooh, nonsense; it's very silly of you to say so. Why make yourself so obnoxious? Were I you, I would not for the sake of my own respectability and comfort do so.
Powell:	Is it not a hard case that. . .
Browne:	But is it not harder for the poor man?

After many delays and misunderstandings on both sides, the arbitrators found for the weavers and awarded them cash compensation. Though the Powell case was a weavers' victory, it could hardly be called a triumph for the union.

In another strike, in which the union played a much more active role, the men had a limited degree of success. Mr Thomas Hall, employer of two hundred weavers, announced in October 1827 that he would henceforth pay lower rates for some types of work. His men then stopped the work they were engaged on and turned out. Hall prosecuted them vigorously; he got warrants for the arrest of the leaders and ten were sent to the House of Correction for one month. The men held out, and the full weight of the union was placed behind them. The town was plastered with handbills saying that collections were being taken for them in Spitalfields, and mass meetings were addressed by the leaders of the Committee.[109] The burden of speeches by John Foster and John Smith (venerable unionists who had been delegates to the Select Committee of Parliament in 1818) and other Committee-men was that the men must trust and support the union. Thomas Cope asserted that the recent decline in the weavers' status was mostly attributable to 'the unnecessary and ruinous system of individual competition' and 'the cowardice and disorganisation of the weavers themselves', which allowed the masters to lower the prices to match each other. Radicals Nicholas Lynch and the ubiquitous William Adam 'addressed themselves more to the passions of the assembled multitude' and were much applauded. A long list of resolutions were passed, declaring Hall's treatment of his men 'not in the spirit of the Trade', pledging support to the strike, promising to uphold union rules, and urging that the union be extended 'throughout the United Kingdom'. Finally the meeting voted to thank the Macclesfield *Courier*, the *Trades Free Press*, and the *Bolton Chronicle* for advocating 'the cause of truth', and criticised the hostile attitude of the *Herald* (a new paper in town, financed by the Brocklehurst family). By calling upon all working men to boycott 'any shopkeeper, publican, hairdresser or other person who shall take in the *Herald*' the union was employing exclusive dealing, a tactic widely used by Lancashire radicals.[110]

After a strike lasting about two months, the agreed compromise was greeted by the men with mixed feelings. Most returned to their work, and Hall promised to use bona fide apprentices in the weaving of cheap handkerchiefs and to pay union rates for better grades of work. But he refused to take back several of the strike leaders, and they had to be supported by union funds until they could find new employment. The union engaged London and Manchester solicitors to advise about possible appeal of the 'illegal' imprisonment of strikers.[111]

Strikers could be effective in keeping renegade employers like

Hall in check, but, as the radical reformers had been teaching since 1817, more complex problems would require political solutions. By 1827 at least one element of the labouring classes was suggesting that the trades should unite and address the Government with one voice. In January 1827 'incendiary' handbills, signed by 'The Operative Weavers' and addressed to 'the hatters, tailors, shoemakers, silk-twisters, small-ware weavers, cotton-spinners, and other trades in Macclesfield', had appeared.[112] It is significant that this bold move should have been undertaken by operative (i.e., factory) weavers; they would naturally have been less fastidious about joining forces with 'servants' and minor craftsmen than were the master weavers. The silk-twisters had a serious new grievance of their own, which brought them readily into line with the weavers' petitioning efforts. Because of the very poor state of the trade, spinning mills were now closing down, and the spinners turned to the weavers' perennial remedy, protective duties. In May 1828 a meeting of millmen declared that though food was as dear as in 1825, their own earnings had been reduced from 20*s* to 10*s* a week. The relatively high wages mentioned reveal that these 'millmen' were no ordinary spinners but the skilled (male) élite of the factory work-force. (Spinners' wages were said to have slumped from 11*s* to 6*s* in this same period.) A list of unemployed mills, containing a total of 10,000 dozen spindles, was read out — and two of these had already gone bankrupt.[113] Apparently this rather hesitant effort was an *ad hoc* affair; as far as we can tell the weavers were still the only Macclesfield trade to have moved beyond trade clubs and strike committees to a more durable form of trade-union organisation.

And the weavers, in spite of some assistance from the 'very formidable union' of Lancashire silk-weavers, still had their difficulties; they tended to look backward, tormented by the memory of much better days in the 1790s and 1810s.[114] When they took to the streets under the Committee's direction in 1829, the scenario was straight out of eighteenth-century Spitalfields:

> Processions of the populace were formed, headed by bands of music, and the most grotesque exhibitions, intended to illustrate the sentiments and condition of the operatives. Men, dressed as mourners, carried black flags, as emblems of their position. A weaver and his loom were borne in a cart, with a red herring suspended just beyond reaching distance of the

> hungry man's mouth. Others carried small loaves on poles, trimmed with black crape, and knives and forks, also covered with the same material . . . [Next day] another loom was borne through the streets, with a superscription in large characters, 'silk machinery to be sold by Mr. Huskisson'.[115]

Even their victories went against the tide, and were too soon swept away. A general turnout of weavers in the autumn of 1832 succeeded in establishing a price-list for the town, but the big employers took advantage of the depressed state of the cotton trade and began putting out work at lower rates in the country districts. Some firms went so far as to set up warehouses outside the town. Thus history repeated, in a smaller compass, the very process by which some sectors of the silk trade had deserted London and spread outwards to Cheshire so many years before. This latest blow left the weavers demoralised and badly split — between those who wanted to capitulate to the lower prices and those who insisted on holding out for a price list.[116] An even worse calamity, in the same year, was the ominous introduction of the first power-looms for bandanna weaving into the mill of Brocklehurst and Co. Power-weaving never entirely displaced the hand process in the silk industry, but its appearance marked the decline of the handloom weavers as the chief spokesmen for the artisan point of view and the weightiest, most respectable section of the town's labouring population.

Another parliamentary Select Committee on the silk trade, summoned in response to almost continuous petitioning by the trade since 1824, met in 1831/2. On this occasion John Brocklehurst for the Macclesfield masters, and John Prout, Thomas Cope, and David Rowbotham for the Weavers' Committee painted a uniform picture of desolation and distress. According to Brocklehurst, thirty out of seventy-one spinning mills in the town were standing empty in July 1832, and those spinners who still had work were earning less than half the hourly rate of 1824, as well as working short time. Weavers' earnings, he said, had sunk to 6*s* or 7*s* a week, without deductions.[117] For most workers there were long stretches of unemployment and no alternative sources of income: 'a weaver or millman in general knows nothing of agriculture; in and around Manchester and Macclesfield the land being chiefly grass land, but little labour is required to keep it in order'.[118]

John Prout, a weaver of thirty-four years' experience, corroborated the employers' testimony and spoke for the most respectable and moderate section of the artisans. He was careful to point out in his testimony that the crisis was undermining the 'peaceable and loyal disposition of the people; at the last public meeting that was called to memorialise His Majesty's Ministers . . . the people would not have "praying" inserted in the petition; but I took care to have it inserted.'[119] Another artisan witness, David Rowbotham, expressed his concern that the weaver should be able to 'maintain his proper rank in society'.[120] He illustrated the decline in the weekly income of his family workshop between 1823 and 1832 in tabular form, as follows:[121]

March 1823

		Oz. silk worked	Gross earnings
D. Rowbotham	(age 40)	18	28*s*
Apprentice	(19)	16	24*s* 6*d*
Journeyman	(40)	12	27*s*
Journeyman	(?)	12	26*s*
Journeyman	(?)	12	26*s*
Wife	(30)	12	23*s*
	Total (earnings per oz. worked, 1*s* 10½*d*)	82	154*s* 6*d*

Deductions: Journeymen's wages, quill-winder, rent, taxes, coal, candles: 85*s*

Net earnings: 69*s* 6*d*, to maintain a family of eight

March 1832

		Oz. silk worked	Gross earnings
D. Rowbotham	(age 49)	20	8*s* 3*d*
Daughter	(20)	30	12*s* 4½*d*
Son	(18)	18	10*s*
Journeyman	(21)	12	9*s* 6*d*
Journeyman	(18)	25	11*s* 3*d*
Wife	(39)	28	10*s*
	Total (earnings per oz. worked, 5½*d*)	133	61*s* 7½*d*

Deductions: 36*s* 9½*d*

Net earnings: 24*s* 10*d*, to maintain a family of seven

Rather than sacrifice any of his looms in time of crisis, the master weaver opted for the more intensive exploitation of family labour, and especially the labour of low-paid (and perhaps less skilled) female members.[122] It is not difficult to imagine Rowbotham's feelings, working up twenty ounces of silk for less than a third of what eighteen ounces brought him in 1823, and seeing his young daughter displace him as chief wage-earner in the shop. Crisis wrought havoc in the traditional status hierarchy of the workshop, the wife outstripping the husband, and the younger outstripping the elder journeyman. What was also involved, apparently, was a shift towards the plainer types of weaving, and Rowbotham had been forced to make use of suspiciously youthful 'journeymen'.

Both employers and master artisans were deeply disturbed, and both identified the same culprits — Italian and French competition. Parliament offered no relief, and Macclesfield had to content itself with whatever benefits it might eventually reap from its long-awaited enfranchisement. How satisfied the master weavers were with this political prospect can only be guessed; only eighty of them were found to be qualified for the voters' roll.[123] In 1835 two leading silk manufacturers were sent to Parliament, to carry on as best they could the defensive struggle of an industry which had already met its nemesis in free trade.

III

By the 1830s many workers were living better than they ever had before in Macclesfield, and the lives of the new masses of factory workers could certainly be compared favourably with the lot of the casual labourer of the eighteenth century. But at the same time there was, for many, a *felt* loss. The Hammonds sentimentalised the eighteenth-century domestic worker's situation when they wrote, 'He was not hopelessly and despairingly poor. He had some say in his own life . . . he was in short not quite disinherited from the old village economy in which a man did not merely sell his labour but had some kind of holding and independence of his own.'[124] Their analysis mostly ignores the fact that the old village economy could not have provided work for the post-1800 population, and that the largest sector of late eighteenth-century domestic labour (weaving) was actually a new creation, generated by the spinning factories and keenly vulnerable, in its turn, to the incursions of the factory system. But the Hammonds grasped a fundamental truth — to many workmen it seemed that liberty and security had been forcibly traded for uncertainty and powerlessness. A Macclesfield workman named Cosgrove, who had been set to work on the roads by the overseers of the poor in the dreadful year of 1826, summed it up; he had been brought before the magistrates for leaving his roadwork to go to the races with a friend: '. . . we are so oppressed by one beggar or another put over us to watch us, that one can't now-a-days blow one's nose *like another gentleman*! . . . I say we are [oppressed]; punish me as you wish, just like a soldier; aye you may flog me through the town, if that will do you any good. I am sorry I had ever anything to do with abolishing the Slave Trade, when I'm a slave myself.'[125] As for the women and children, uncertainty and powerlessness must have been a constant for many. If the factory offered a degree of financial independence for some, it also perpetuated women's subordination to skilled male labour. Whether working in the mill or at home, there must have been women who sometimes felt they were only the slaves of slaves.

E.P. Thompson argues that both employers and workers yearned to enjoy the benefits of two conflicting social systems at once — the old status-bound communalism and the new individualist capitalism.[126] Each group tried to impose traditional obligations upon the other, and each, for different reasons, viewed the vagabond, masterless labourer with trepidation. But the employers began with advantages of rank, wealth, and power; and they improved upon those advantages, while the skilled workpeople — collectively weaker and less free to react self-protectively to new conditions — lost ground. A hundred years had exchanged old Charles Roe, with his button-warehouse and copper works for the 'rich silk manufacturer of Macclesfield', whom Mary Howitt noticed at a country-house gathering in 1854 — 'a fat, jolly Conservative, whose work-people are emphatically *hands*, and who thinks "Mary Barton" a dangerous, bad book.'[127] Not such a radical transformation, after all.

It would be too much to say that a working class, or any other class, was 'made' in Macclesfield between 1750 and the early 1830s, but employers and workpeople emerged from each successive crisis somewhat more aware of their distinct interests than they had been before. And crises had come thick and fast between 1815 and 1832. The very pace of change was beginning to force the realisation that customary relationships would not, could not, be preserved. In the town's major trades ever larger numbers of workers were being employed by fewer, wealthier, and more powerful masters. An expanding national/international market brought both pressures and temptations for employers to abandon traditional trade practices, and the perennially overstocked labour market often gave them the means to do so.

The workers' main bulwark against exploitation, the newly-expanded and consolidated trade societies of the 1820s and 1830s, should be seen, not simply as reservoirs of trade particularism, but as evolving bodies, responding to profound changes in the economic environment. In their attempts to use traditional morality, customary practice, and some suggestions of the radical ideologues to reshape their relations with employers and with fellow workers across trade lines, the societies can reasonably be seen as 'a cultural expression of an emergent class'.[128]

But it must be emphasised that the outlook and programme of

the trade societies was limited and largely defensive. There is little evidence for the maturing of class consciousness. Both craft sectionalism and the vertical bonds of trade loyalty remained strong. It is true that after 1815 a sense of class conflict became embedded in popular memory. But at the same time, local expressions of political radicalism were based more on economic crisis and mass desperation than on principled opposition to the apparatus of local or national government, much less to capitalist property relations.

Gareth Stedman Jones has pointed to the importance, for the cotton masters, of inventions 'intended to break the hold exercised by the artisan over the method and pace of production.'[129] In silk, as has been shown, the same annihilation of the artisans' independence was achieved, without major technological innovation, through the combined effects of immigration, expansion of demand in the 'plain' as against the 'fancy' branches of the trade, the pressure of foreign competition, and the masters' introduction of factory-based weaving. The result, in the absence of either effective trade unionism or working-class political influence, was a consolidation of the employers' supremacy.

The new balance of class power was to last as long as the silk industry itself survived in Macclesfield; it was never overturned, even in the age of 'new unionism' and the 'labour aristocracy'. Badly crippled by the Cobden Treaty of 1860, the industry limped along until the First World War salvaged some sectors of it. Towards the end of the nineteenth century the silk-workers were still using their traditional weapons of defence, and, more often than not, losing. For most, the alternatives were submission or emigration. As for the employers, those who prospered never lost the spirit of aggressive paternalism. In 1880, William Coare Brocklehurst, the town's largest employer of labour and the inheritor of his father's parliamentary seat, called on his workmen to admit their latest defeat:

> Bring your list prices and your trade document and everything pertaining to your trade to the market place, make a grand pile of them and set fire to them; do your union up and I'll find you ale, and we'll have a jollification and an Indian dance.[130]

III

Standard of Living

Did the material conditions of life improve substantially for most of the population of Macclesfield with the advent of industrialisation? Many contemporary observers thought so. Yet even after it is accepted that the town's resources swelled to support a much larger population, that more infants survived and life expectancy for adults probably increased, and that many individuals and families undoubtedly 'bettered themselves' noticeably, the question of living standards has by no means been fully answered. This chapter will consider changes in the standard of diet, clothing, housing, sanitation, and other public amenities and will conclude with an examination of health, health care, and the relief of poverty. As with the riddle of class relations, the documentary evidence tends to be weighted towards whatever was perceived as socially problematic: for example, the written record gives far more attention to food shortages (and riots), workhouse rations, and the shortcomings of some retailers than to the normal diet of self-supporting families; and much of our knowledge of illness and medical practice comes from the annals of epidemic, accident, and death.[1]

To assess the material standard of working-class life it is necessary, as John Foster has written, to take into account 'the physical nature of the work itself, the relative sufficiency of the earnings received for it, and finally the combined effect of both on the larger structure of people's lives.'[2] To make precise calculations in the first two areas is difficult, indeed almost impossible, before 1850, and 'the larger structure of people's lives' turns out to be an almost infinitely elastic concept. The historiographical debate on the 'standard of living' during the industrial revolution has thus far concentrated on efforts to correlate wage levels with price indexes of commodities essential to the household economy (plus rent).[3] But Foster is surely right in taking a broader view, in pointing out that technical innovation often meant speed-up, fatigue and high accident rates for poorly nourished mill-workers (thus undercutting the advantages of steadier pay); that youth ended and old age began earlier than is expected today, especially in strenuous trades, so that an extension of life expectancy might mean only a prolongation of the period of dependency on one's grown children; that tuberculosis, 'the characteristic disease of overwork,' took life at twice the national rate in mill towns like Oldham in the 1850s, with women aged twenty-five to thirty-four dying at three times the national rate; and that the simple wages/prices equation hides a whole sub-world of 'secondary poverty' and the elaborate range of expedients designed to avoid or mitigate it.[4]

After making every allowance for the daunting complexity of the necessary calculations, there remains an inescapable central impression that grinding poverty was the circumstance of life for much of the working population throughout our period. Using wage and census data from Oldham (measured against the poverty guidelines established by Seebohm Rowntree [1901] and A.L. Bowley [1915], adjusted for mid-century prices), Foster concludes that about one fifth of all Oldham families would have been below the 'subsistence line' at any given time in the late 1840s.[5] The figure of about 20 per cent is actually lower than that arrived at for non-textile towns, and we can assume that poverty was alleviated somewhat in mill towns by the contributions of child labour to the family income.[6] Overall, the statistical picture is so bleak that the historian is challenged to explain how, in the face of such apparent likelihood of doom, so many managed to survive and even flourish.

How does Foster's assessment accord with the standard of living in Macclesfield before 1835? The evidence suggests a slow improvement over the preceding fifty years or so, with grave setbacks during hard times and for particular occupational groups displaced or pressured by economic innovation. While it is possible to imagine as much as half the population suffering distress, and most working-class families experiencing dire poverty at some time, the suggestion that 20 per cent or more of working-class families' wages would have put them below 'the subsistence line' cannot be made without some further explanation. Of course, high mortality rates at early ages are, in part, a reflection of poverty, but common sense indicates that there must have been economic cushions of various kinds, helping to assure the survival of the more fortunate or ingenious.

One important aid to survival was the existence of an 'underground' economy partly illegal and partly merely informal, side by side with the public or market economy reflected in wage and price statistics. The prominence of contemporary treatises on economic theory — in the years from Adam Smith to Ricardo — can too easily obscure the simple fact that not all economic transactions are cash transactions, a fact that becomes more important as we move backward in time, closer to rural life, and farther down the social scale. In eighteenth-century Macclesfield, no less than in Henry Mayhew's London, family incomes could be eked out by casual, sometimes illegal means. Take the 1767 case of two silk throwsters, both accomplished poachers, who lured their neighbours' geese away with bread; they used some of the birds in their own kitchen, gave some away, and sold the rest at less than market prices.[7] The pilfering of silk and other raw and finished materials created a flourishing black-market economy in the town. Clearly a multitude of such devices, changing with the times, hung on right through industrialisation. Millmen in the 1840s turned their free time and mechanical skills to profitable use in making mousetraps and other gadgets for their neighbours.[8]

The barter economy was also remarkably persistent, and not only as an expedient for the poor. In the 1820s some silk merchants would still accept payment in farm produce, and some weavers were partially paid in cloth. Even a forward-looking and prosperous businessman like Thomas Challinor, the town's leading cabinet-maker in the 1830s and 1840s, accepted payment in kind from customers who presumably could have paid in cash.[9] Services like baby-minding, housework, carting, gardening, and errand-running could be exchanged within the labouring population, or traded for food, a place to sleep, nursing care, and so on. In estimating, for example, the effect of alcohol consumption on the family budget we must not only think of cash wages but also remember that the price of a drink could be a song, a fiddle tune, a message delivered, or a lucky bet or turn of the card. However limited the total pool of material resources available, sharing and bartering could, and probably did, result in a significant redistribution of 'wealth' within the working-class community (especially within kinship groups). This redistribution process would have been controlled and shaped to some extent by the working class itself, through custom, peer-pressure, and inclination. The precise effect on the underground economy of population mobility, advancing urbanisation, the growth of the money-based factory economy, and the accompanying loss of face-to-face cultural relationships in the town can only be guessed at. But it is a question well worth pondering. Engels' famous comment that the Manchester workers' main recourse in hard times was their mutual aid and assistance from within their own community would seem to suggest that many struggled to keep traditional obligations (and opportunities) alive.[10]

I

The relationship of wages (or other negotiable resources) to the levels of staple prices and essential costs such as rent, if not a sufficient indicator of shifts in standard of living over time, is nevertheless a fundamental component of any such calculation. Unfortunately, in the absence of local wage series for even one occupation, much less a cross-section of trades, in this period, and with only fragmentary information on rent and food prices, we must be content with general impressions and informed estimates. Basing his conclusions on the consensus of local reminiscence, John Corry asserted that wages in Macclesfield before the great expansion of industry had been 'moderate but proportionate to the price of provisions,' with male labourers' weekly wages at about 7*s*, and the family wage at perhaps 10*s* to 12*s*. In the 1770s, brown bread cost five farthings a pound, milk a penny a quart, fine flour 1*s* a peck, butter 4*d* a pound, cheese 2½*d* a pound and prime beef 2*d* a pound.[11] Corry suggests a connection between the increases in food prices beginning in the late 1770s and the inflationary effect of high wages paid during the textile boom: 'the weavers earned high wages which they improvidently wasted; nothing that the market could afford was too good for them; and house-rent and provisions were raised to an extortionate height.'[12] Such indignation reflects the reaction of a conservative moralist to the first evidence of widespread comfort and prosperity in one section of the labouring class, but extra-local factors contributed to the pressure on prices as well — for example, the disastrous harvest of 1799 and the disruptions occasioned by war and large-scale migration.

The labouring population regularly sought to enforce customary price levels or the decrees (as popularly understood) of the county assize of bread. The first recorded food riot occurred in November 1757, when a crowd entered the house of Richard Pimlott at Butley and demanded that he deliver several loads of meal to Macclesfield and sell it at the price of twenty shillings a load (of five bushels). The intruders also seized ninety-six pounds of oatmeal and carried it away with them. Five Macclesfield men, Ralph Wright (carpenter), Fortunatus Bailey (butcher), John Oldham (whitesmith), Richard Fowler (silk-winder), and Edward Lloyd (apparently another silk-worker) were arrested. It is interesting to note that these men were artisans and textile workers — by no means from the lowest social stratum — and the magistrates were lenient. The only punishments recorded are fines of 6*d* against Wright and Oldham.[13] Richard Fowler seems to have been an active local militant, well versed in the traditional 'moral economy' of the crowd. In July 1762 he was arrested again, with three women and a man, for taking part in an assault on three farmers. The crowd gathered in the market-place and tried to force miller James Shepley to sell his oatmeal at 10*d* rather than 14*d* a peck. Later, on meeting a farmer who rebuked him for his part in the incident, Fowler said, 'Damn it, we go according to Act of Parliament and will regulate and fix the Market price.'[14]

Small-scale disturbances, sometimes no more than an anonymous letter left at the door of a particular offender, punctuated the second half of the century and broke out again during wartime shortages. Civil authorities displayed an uncertain, sometimes contradictory attitude on the question of price regulation. After the riots of 1757, for instance, a toll-free market was held in Macclesfield to encourage farmers to bring grain for sale at 'fair' rates. During the harvest crisis of 1796 the 'principle inhabitants' promised to observe various regulations for conserving grain and keeping prices down, and in 1800 the Corporation tried to tread cautiously, on the one hand assuring farmers that municipal authorities would stand firm against any attempts at violence or popular price-fixing, but also promising the labouring population measures to ease distress by reducing prices.[15] By 1812 or so upper-class sympathy for price-fixing had definitely waned, and generalised fear of public disorder dictated a harsh stance against rioters.

Food prices certainly rose steeply during the French wars, and local complaints were all the more bitter for the memories of prosperous times that had gone before. In a study of Kent, T.L. Richardson has noted a rise of 167 per cent in bread prices and 100 per cent in meat prices between 1790 and 1812.[16] In Macclesfield the wartime price of bread rose to 6*d* a pound, and many complained of poor quality flour that yielded sodden, ill-tasting loaves. Many years later one man recalled, 'Folks thowt it good if they got a loaf half barley and half wheat. It were when the French war were agate [going on] I reckon. They had to bake their bread at twice; first poo [pull] off one crust and then bake another crust.'[17] The demand for bread was always relatively inelastic, and poor families under pressure reduced their consumption of 'luxuries' such as meat, tea, and sugar first. For some, bread too became a rarity. A woman who had been apprenticed to a weaver in 1810 recalled a monotonous diet: oatmeal porridge, skimmed milk and oat cakes for breakfast; potatoes and buttermilk (sometimes with a little bacon) for dinner; and porridge for supper. 'We had no beer, tea, new milk, nor butcher's meat and no change on Sunday.' And in the worst of the war years, 'We had no tablecloths, nor knives and forks, nor plates. For dinner a large dish of potatoes was set in the middle of a clean table, and we all gathered round it, each with a basin of buttermilk and a spoon.'[18]

For the working population post-war recovery came slowly. Except for a sharp rise due to a poor harvest in 1817 the cost of living fell dramatically after the war. On average, prices of basic household commodities were approximately halved between 1812 and 1823, but the rate of improvement is difficult to estimate. In Macclesfield potatoes were cheaper in 1825 than in the 1770s, but meat was four times dearer.[19] In rural Kent consumption of meat did not return to its 1790s level after the war, probably because bread prices remained about 30 per cent higher;[20] in other regions depression of wages and unemployment would have had similar consequences. One authority, speaking of the Manchester area, pointed out that though the price of provisions had dropped by 30 per cent between 1815 and 1835, weavers' wages dropped by 60 per cent over the same period.[21] During the slump of 1831/2 silk weavers' wages in Macclesfield sunk to about 50 per cent of their average in the best years of the 1820s.[22]

It is probably safe to assume that for many working-class households, in the 1830s as in the 1790s, the core diet consisted of the familiar staples: potatoes, brown bread, milk, tea, butter, cheese, and only occasionally meat. In some homes this fare would have been supplemented by the addition of eggs, poultry, or vegetables raised in gardens or on waste ground, or by fish, game, and wild produce culled from the surrounding countryside. The Common was gone, but poor families on the outskirts of town still found forage for donkeys, cows, and fowl. Hares, rabbits, 'black game', and plovers were still popular items in the market-place in the 1840s.[23] Memoirist Adam Rushton remembered gathering abundant blackberries, bilberries, and raspberries in the lanes around Hurdsfield in the 1820s. His father, who alternated carting coal, lime, and stone for the factories in town with periods of farm labour, could always carve a family garden out of a backyard or bit of waste ground; the family was well supplied with vegetables, and they earned extra money by selling butter and potatoes to neighbours.[24]

The Rushtons' experience was far from universal; expanding population put steady pressure on quasi-rural, quasi-communal resources. The process of urbanisation is reflected in the changing structure of the retail market.[25] Wholesale operations expanded to serve a growing community of retailers. Authorities frequently complained that wholesale merchants were evading tolls by not trading in the markets and fairs, and thus deprived the Corporation of revenue at a time of expanding need for public services. By the war years, for instance, mealmen were commonly setting aside most of their flour and meal to sell directly to bakers and grocers, who were offered lower prices than those paid by the general public. Such dealers were denounced by traditionalist John Corry as 'a most unprincipled knot of extortioners', but they were the wave of the future.[26] In his study of Macclesfield retailing S.I. Mitchell contends that the town's growth was so rapid during the first quarter of the nineteenth century that both markets and shops benefited substantially; the tide was not turned against the market-place decisively until mid-century.[27]

Small neighbourhood shops of all kinds proliferated in Macclesfield. By 1825 a directory listed 124 bakers and 34 grocers, but there were as yet no butcher shops, because the Corporation still jealously preserved its ancient monopoly control over meat-selling.[28] Tolls were collected on stalls in the Shambles near the Town Hall, and no meat-selling was permitted elsewhere. Growing opposition by butchers eroded this system, culminating in a decisive victory for free trade in 1843.[29] More and more commodities previously produced at home, or hawked by stallholders and peddlers, were now handled by larger commercial enterprises. Bread, beer, clothing, boots, soap, candles and all sorts of household furnishings were regularly purchased in shops in the early nineteenth century. More exotic items like tea, coffee, loaf sugar, raisins, tropical fruits and spices, locally available since the mid-eighteenth century, grew more popular. Victuallers' shops specialising in ready-to-eat food were attractive to single workers, or families whose wives and daughters were busy at the mill. Bakers' shops provided facilities for baking and roasting dishes brought from customers' homes.[30]

The ill-famed 'truck system', under which employees were required to trade at company-run shops, does not seem to have been much used in Macclesfield. In some of the small factories tucked away in mountain valleys and hamlets employers did buy food and other necessities to resell to their work-people, but this seems to have occurred mainly in times when shortages were feared or bad weather prevented travel. Labour contractors who brought in gangs of navvies to work on the canal and later the railway ran 'tommy shops' where provisions were sold at exorbitant rates on short-term credit (paydays were monthly, and the navvies could not get credit at local shops).[31]

Taverns, pubs and beer-shops accounted for a sizeable proportion of the town's retail trade. Heavy consumption of alcoholic beverages was common throughout the period; drink must have been an important element of the adult diet and a significant item in most working-class family budgets. Drunkenness was a social problem of devastating proportions by the early nineteenth century; it posed a clear threat not only to public order but to family health and security. For the period 1830 to 1834 average annual per capita consumption (nationally) was 1.11 (proof) gallons of spirits and 21.6 (standard) gallons of beer; these official figures are probably low, as they do not reflect home and illicit brewing and distilling. Consumption was unevenly distributed by region, class, sex, and age, but the overall impression is clear.[32] As A.E. Dingle has pointed out, although strong drink had some nutritional value, this value would not have been evenly distributed among family members; furthermore, 'while drink was a significant source of energy, it was not a cheap source.'[33] Beer was almost certain to be a more expensive — and spirits a far more expensive — source of calories than food.[34]

The most popular drinks in Macclesfield were gin, beer and ale, with traditional specialities like frumenty (a fermented wheat porridge) and wine or spirit punches finding favour at Wakes and holidays. Every sort of transaction was sealed and every festive occasion celebrated with a drink (or several). Even at the local gaol, each newly incarcerated debtor was required by custom to pay a so-called 'Garnish Fee', used to treat his or her fellow inmates. If the unfortunate prisoner had no money at all, some garments were confiscated to pay for the drink; a special 'Gaol Song' was sung to complete the jollification.[35]

Hard drinking was not confined to men, and was hardly restrained by any religious or civil controls in the eighteenth century. Simultaneous with the beginnings of factory industry in the 1750s were complaints (mostly from employers) of a sudden increase in the number of alehouses, 'destroying the health, corrupting the morals and impoverishing the familys of Labourers and Manufacturers.'[36] It was proposed that licensing regulations be tightened and licenses limited to sixty, but enforcement, especially against small, out-of-the-way premises, was difficult. An example from 1765 will give some idea of the conditions temperance reformers were later to struggle against. Jane Walker (described as wife of Thomas Walker, absent) had been lodging with Jane Baker, single woman, for about a week when,

> on Sunday last in the afternoon the said Jane Baker asked [her] to go with her to Thomas Pownall who keeps a Publick House in Macclesfield aforesaid and there staid with the said Jane Baker drinking till about two of the clock in the morning following and then went to her lodgings and about six of the

> clock in the same morning [Walker] went with the said Jane Baker to the said Thomas Pownalls and staid there about half an hour and afterwards went to John Swindells's who keeps a Publick House . . . [Walker] saith that she was in Liquor on Sunday Evening and continued so untill the Time she was brought before the Magistrates.[37]

Towards the end of the century there were several campaigns to enforce the laws against serving drink on the Sabbath, but even after the evangelical-inspired temperance societies took hold, drunkenness remained a major source of fear and suffering. Local magistrates revived the old stocks as a deterrent punishment, but with little effect.[38] In the years 1823 to 1825 mayor Thomas Allen, a prominent Methodist layman, recorded in his journal prosecutions of twenty-eight cases of Sabbath-breaking (mostly connected with drink) and innumerable cases of drunken assault.[39] Francis Rushton, a silk-twister who died at the Golden Lion public house on 19 April 1823 after drinking thirteen glasses of gin in forty-five minutes on a bet, was a victim of an abuse which touched every class. Clergymen and municipal officials were among those brought to court for drunkenness. Mayor Allen sadly noted, on 12 June 1823, 'James Allen (my Brother) convictd of drunks on Sunday Eveng fined 5s and expenses.'[40] When the organised temperance movement got under way in Macclesfield in the 1830s there was always an abundant supply of 'habitual drunkards' to exhort and pray over, and there were constant, discouraged references to backsliding.[41] The prevailing fondness for drink must be evaluated, not only as a social and physical evil, but also in the light of the benefits (or supposed benefits) alcohol could confer, at a time when uncontaminated drinking water was scarce, and to be warm, dry, rested, and in a state of reasonable physical comfort were privileges not to be taken for granted.[42]

Another important component of comfort was clothing, and improvements of style, quality, and convenience in dress were among the first fruits of prosperity for all classes. Retail trade was not yet based on mass production, and clothes and household goods continued to be supplied on a bespoke basis; tailors and dressmakers and milliners flourished. At the turn of the century superior drapers like John Swanwick stocked fancy printed cottons — calicoes, lawns, cambrics — fine linens, velvets, light shawls, bonnets, lace-trimmed caps, and, of course, the myriad silks which were proudly worn as a Macclesfield trademark.[43] T.H. Worrall described Swanwick's as 'a very aristocratic and first-class tailoring establishment' which served the county gentry and supplied mourning silks and other funeral accoutrements to the local élite.[44]

In contrast to the more rural areas, where home-made clothes and household linens continued to be the rule, Macclesfield could boast an increasingly well-dressed labouring population. Though labourers and those engaged in heavy or dirty work could still be found in their rough smocks and leather breeches by the 1820s, artisans and mill workers invested their extra earnings in modest finery. Factory girls were quick to exchange shawls for bonnets, and to add Sunday dresses and fancy aprons to their wardrobes. A teen-aged male weaver, earning 17*s* to 18*s* a week in 1825, turned out in a blue jacket with gilt buttons, blue trousers, yellow waistcoat, grey stockings, shoes, silk-lined hat, black silk handkerchief, and plaid muslin neckerchief.[45] Like this boy, more and more workers disdained clogs, at least on special occasions, in favour of boots or shoes. A glimpse of the dress of the poorest class is found in the inventory of clothes sent with a woman transported from Chester for seven years in 1806: 'Three gowns, one on two off, five Petticoats 2 on 3 off, one Bedgown, three shifts one on two off, four handkerchiefs . . ., 4 aprons . . ., 10 linen Caps . . ., 3 pair of Stockings . . ., two pr of shoes . . ., one blue Cloak one Hatt.' This supply, meagre as it is, represents far more clothing than the poorest women would normally have owned at one time.[46]

Clothes were carefully tended and passed down in families, sometimes by formal bequest. One old Wilmslow woman remembered, 'Often a coat would last a lifetime. When my mother came home from church the first thing she did was to take off her gown, and I always do the same. She was married in 1818 and died in 1847. I had her wedding gown made up for my best. It was a print, lilac leaf on a white ground, and she said it cost half-a-crown a yard. In my grandfather's time persons often carried their shoes in their hands to church. . .'[47] A neighbour of this family was remembered as having attended church in his wedding clothes every Sunday until he died, aged ninety-three. The Methodist chapels in Macclesfield provided special sections of seats at the back, in dark corners, to accommodate those whose clothes were so shabby that they might be embarrassed to be seen.

For those who could not afford to buy tailor-made clothes, there was a brisk trade in second-hand apparel. The many recorded cases of petty thefts of caps, aprons, handkerchiefs, shoes and the like and the zeal with which the missing items were pursued testify both to the value placed on them and the ease with which clothes could be fenced or pawned in town. Drying laundry often vanished from lines or hedges, and coats and breeches were plucked from their pegs at lodging-houses while their drunken owners nodded. One dealer made a profitable business of cozening Grammar School boys of their spare garments.[48] When cheap ready-made clothes for the working classes first appeared in the early nineteenth century they were often purchased on credit from travelling representatives of the large Scottish firms.[49]

II

Another concomitant of industrialisation, the rapid physical growth of the town itself, brought the labouring population both losses and gains. On the one hand there were more jobs and more houses — houses better equipped, more solidly built, and easier to heat and keep clean than the old plaster, wood and thatch cottages. On the other hand, enclosure of common lands and other disused ground extinguished rights to pasture livestock, keep fowl, cut wood and turf, and so on. The extension of built-over areas meant fewer chances for gleaning and gathering, hunting, fishing, and bartering with farmers. Land was soon at a premium, not only for housing and industrial building but for commercial farming; proprietors became more vigilant and barriers against trespassing more formidable. House lots became smaller; even where open fields stretched away in all directions mill-owners and speculative builders crammed as many terraced houses as possible on to narrow pieces of land adjoining mills and warehouses.[50]

Only scattered examples of working-class rents are available for Macclesfield. We do know that few artisan dwellings yielded the £10 per year (4*s* a week) which would have qualified their ratepayers for the franchise in 1832. In the 'good' year of 1823 a three-storey house rented for 4*s* a week, and smaller houses for 2*s*.[51] By the 1840s, when pressure on housing had lessened, artisan families were paying about 3*s* or 3*s* 6*d* a week, and smaller houses brought 1*s* 6*d*; at this time roughly three-quarters of Macclesfield houses rented for 4*s* or less a week.[52] Of course, such figures cannot indicate precisely what most families paid, since they do not reveal the extent of shared dwellings, sub-letting, the taking in of lodgers, and other expedients for minimising rent.

In general, house-building seems to have kept pace at first with the growth of population. A building boom during the 1780s and 1790s nearly doubled the number of houses available and may actually have reduced the average number of occupants per house over that period.[53] Several of the town's main streets were paved for the first time during these years. Thereafter building proceeded in spurts, with rents rising in good times and houses standing empty during slumps. By 1825 most of the half-timbered, thatched structures in the centre of town had vanished, replaced by mill-owners' stone mansions, lawyers' offices, artisans' row houses, and modern shops with large bow windows. A survey undertaken in 1824 indicated that 1390 houses had been put up since the spring of 1821, and the surveyor remarked on the intense competition for housing, leading 'families to tenant the still damp, unfinished cottages.'[54]

A few streets were notable for the opulence of their dwellings, the centres of luxury in the eighteenth century being King Edward St (formerly Back St), and Jordangate, where 'Pear Tree House', the elegant Brocklehurst home,[55] faced 'Cumberland House', the home of eighteenth-century solicitor and town clerk, John Stafford. Park Green was a newer and only slightly less affluent quarter, dominated by the strikingly original house said to have been built for the Revd David Simpson.[56]

Some ancient streets lost caste as newcomers crowded in, and centuries-old slum quarters sank even further into degradation. Stanley Street (formerly Dog Lane), for instance, became notorious for the number of public houses in it. The popular Golden Eagle Tavern had once been the residence of Dr John Fleet, and the Old Lamb Inn had originally been a parsonage for St Michael's Church. In Derby St (formerly Barn St) the imposing home of mayor William Johnson (built 1775) became the King's Arms tavern. The Gutters, a slum area near the Shambles and a plague-spot since the seventeenth century, became even more dilapidated and pestilential.[57] Along Pickford Street and nearby lanes spaces between the old silk warehouses were quickly filled with cheap dwellings, and the area became a ghetto for the Irish poor. In notorious districts like the Dams, King St and Windmill Hill murderous free-for-alls were a regular feature of Saturday night carousing. Living conditions in these crowded streets and courts were appalling, but Macclesfield does seem to have avoided the worst horrors of urban housing, back-to-back building and widespread cellar dwelling.[58]

Even more than in larger cities, the proximity of wealth and poverty was a constant reality. The homes of the prosperous reflected the town's new wealth. John Corry regretted the fact: 'Luxury, the handmaid of wealth, soon insinuated herself among an opulent people, whose houses, furniture, and festive boards were adorned and supplied by commerce.'[59] Charles Roe had brought the first private carriage to town in 1770, and within a few years there were ten others, with innumerable light gigs and pony carts rushing through the streets. Whereas it had been customary in the eighteenth century to send to Manchester or Liverpool for fine furniture, musical instruments, and ornaments, by the 1830s an elegant house could be fitted out with local purchases. The town's leading cabinet-maker and decorator, Thomas Challinor, repaired carriages and supplied massive mahogany pieces, ornate mirrors, and heavy drapes and carpets for the silk-manufacturing magnates, but most of his customers were retail merchants, professional men, and artisans. The middle-class family wanted its pianoforte and inlaid card-table in the front parlour, its china dinner service, its dressing glasses and four-posters upstairs, and fringed drapes, wallpaper, and decorative borders in every downstairs room.[60]

For artisan families who wanted to live in respectable style but could not afford large single payments, Challinor offered furnishings for sale on a monthly or weekly instalment system. He also offered credit to reliable customers who were temporarily out of work.[61] By the 1840s Challinor was investing heavily in cottage property and had a new scheme by which, for a weekly sum, a working-class family could rent a furnished house; after paying for a set period the furniture became the property of the tenants. One silk-worker's family took a house containing a sofa, chest of drawers, 6 cane chairs, 1 painted table, 4 pictures, 1 glass, 1 fender and fire irons, 1 clock, 1 carpet, 4 chairs and 2 round tables,

1 painted dish, a tea kettle, 1 saucepan, 3 bedsteads, 3 chaff beds, bedding, a warming pan, and 'sundry other goods'. They made fifty-eight weekly payments of 7*s* 6*d*, which probably included 3*s* a week rent and a few shillings interest on the furniture, valued at £12.[62] In good times the silk-weaver's sitting-room presented a cheerful and cosy aspect; as journalist Angus Reach noticed, 'The eternal rocking chair stood by the fire; there were small prints hung upon the walls, mingling with shining pot lids, and placed around ranges of shelves filled with crockery. . .'[63]

Whether cheerfully or shabbily decorated, the workman's home was likely to be small and cramped. In a row of two-up, two-down labourers' or mill-workers' cottages like those in Parsonage Street, the front room opened directly off the street. This chamber, about 11′ by 11′, was used as a combined sitting-room, kitchen, and dining area. In the poorest homes it contained the only hearth. The second downstairs room, a scullery 8½′ by 6′, housed a staircase leading up to two bedrooms. A back door opened into a narrow yard with several privies serving a whole street of houses.[64] Three-storey weavers' houses were built to a similar plan (perhaps with slightly larger rooms and an additional hearth or two), with a third-floor loom chamber, accessible through a trap door in one of the bedrooms.

For those living in the poorest class of housing to keep up a decent standard of cleanliness was a continual struggle: 'soap cost 3*d* the half-pound, and none was ever used for the floor. [Housewives] scrubbed with a wisp of straw . . . [and] scoured with white sand.'[65] Eighteenth-century Macclesfield women proudly decorated their freshly scoured floors and doorsteps with patterns of red and white sand, and a pile of sand just inside the front door was used like a doormat for visitors to clean their shoes.[66] But such refinements were not for the earth-floored labourers' cottages, or for the overcrowded millworkers' houses and squalid backyard dwellings that replaced them. Dampness and the threat of flooding were other drawbacks to living in the low-lying tenement neighbourhoods. The River Bollin was poorly banked and in winter or during storms it regularly overflowed into cellars and courtyards. One of the town's worst disasters occurred in January 1839 when a violent hurricane and rainstorm caused a silk-mill reservoir to break its embankments and inundate the area from Mill Lane to Waters Green.[67]

The very worst housing of all was that provided by cheap lodging-houses. Living in lodgings or taking in lodgers was an economic necessity and dated from well before the time when overcrowding put space at a premium. Unmarried workers took lodgings if they were not living with their own families or masters, and this usually meant sharing a bed at an inn. Rental arrangements might be long term, or (more often) by the week or the night. Casual labourers like Samuel Siddal, a cordwainer down on his luck in the 1790s, alternated between sleeping in barns and taking a room at a tavern.[68] The free and easy atmosphere of such establishments, before Sabbatarian scruples intruded, is suggested by the man who told of stopping in the house of John Shufflebotham one Sunday morning for a glass of gin and gill of ale, which was promptly served to him by lodger Benjamin Tomkinson, a farmer.[69] Mixing of the sexes was common, especially in the larger inns, and drinking, gambling, and roguery went on without restraint.

By the 1820s and 1830s there was increasing concern about regulation of lodging-houses. Crowds of itinerant strangers came looking for temporary accommodation — textile operatives walking north to Lancashire and back again, Irish emigrants following the harvest southward, canal and railway navvies, and a growing population of wandering paupers, tramps, and fugitives. Squalid and disorderly premises inevitably attracted the attention of the constables, and later of the sanitary authorities.[70] The first inquiry by the Local Board of Health, in 1852, uncovered 244 lodging-houses, many of them dens of filthiness and disease. One landlord maintained four small, two-bedroomed cottages housing 188 people and served by 'the remains of what had been two privies.' Another house had three bedrooms, the first containing sixteen people sleeping on the floor, the second twelve, and the third used as a privy, 'the boarded floor being literally covered with human ordure.'[71]

These are the worst examples, assembled for sanitary reformers' propaganda purposes; it is more difficult to recapture a sense of the typical household. Rough averages of persons per occupied house (see Table III.1) can give only a very general picture. The data reflect times when new house-building failed to keep up with population growth (e.g. Macclesfield, 1801, or Hurdsfield, 1811 and 1821), or when there was a sudden burst of factory develop-

Table III : 1

Density of Housing Occupation, Macclesfield and District[1]

A: Macclesfield (Old Borough)

Year	Total Pop.	Occupied Houses	Persons per Occupied House
1801	8743	1426	6.13
1811	12299	2518	4.88
1821	17746	3008	5.90
1831	23129	4543	5.09
1841	24137	5021	4.80
1851	29648	6199	4.78
1861	27475	6236	4.40

B: Sutton

Year	Total Pop.	Occupied Houses	Persons per Occupied House
1801	1739	347	5.01
1811	2096	407	5.15
1821	2991	600	4.98
1831	5856	1111	5.27
1841	7035	1402	5.02
1851	7525	1644	4.58
1861	6756	1623	4.16

C. Hurdsfield

Year	Total Pop.	Occupied Houses	Persons per Occupied House
1801	528	108	4.89
1811	734	117	6.27
1821	1082	213	5.07
1831	3083	589	5.23
1841	3551	724	4.90
1851	4016	896	4.48
1861	3836	911	4.21

Source: Adapted from Census figures, in John Wootton, 'Macclesfield Past', *MCH*, 7 August 1880.

Table III : 2

Density of Housing Occupation, Other Locations

D: National (England and Wales)[1]

Year	Persons per Occupied House
1801	5.64
1811	5.66
1821	5.75
1831	5.60
1841	5.41
1851	5.47

E: Liverpool[2]

Year	Persons per Occupied House
1776	5.80
1801	6.78
1811	6.05
1821	6.25
1831	6.42
1841	6.95
1851	7.32

F: Nottingham[3]

Year	Persons per Occupied House
1779	5.50
1801	5.70
1811	5.20
1821	4.80
1831	4.60
1841	4.60

Sources:

1. J.H. Treble, 'Liverpool Working-class Housing, 1801-1851', in S. Chapman, ed., *The History of Working-class Housing*, p. 211.
2. Ibid., pp. 167, 211.
3. S.D. Chapman, 'Working-class Housing in Nottingham during the Industrial Revolution', in ibid., p. 155. The decline in density reflects the slump in the frame-work knitting industry and the spread of population outward to suburbs.

ment in an outlying district (Sutton and Hurdsfield, *c.* 1831). The figures, of course, do not reveal the pattern of distribution of housing resources among various social strata; nor do they tell anything about the size of rooms or the condition of houses. Abundant literary evidence, however, affirms that overcrowding and the growth of slums were acute problems by the 1820s. Magistrates condemned the only-too-common practice of unrelated adults sharing a bed. The presence of lodgers in a one-family house by no means indicated an extra bedroom.[72] At inns and pubs the abuse and the consequences could be even worse. In 1827 Charles Stubbs, fiddler at the Union Inn, was condemned to death for raping a maidservant who slept in the same room with him and his grown nephew.[73] Ann Boyle delivered herself of a baby (later found dead) in the lodging-house where she lived, 'the woman she slept with being asleep.'[74] In the Macclesfield workhouse adult paupers slept three to a bed, with no separate provision for the sick and dying.

A possible explanation for the paradoxical contrast between extreme examples of overcrowding and the reasonable occupancy figures shown in Table III:1 may be found in John Burnett's suggestion that even in poor neighbourhoods housing was underutilised during some phases of the family cycle. Young married couples and older couples whose children had left home, as well as better-off single workers of all ages, may have occupied a disproportionate amount of housing space, while large families and very poor families who had to share with lodgers or live-in relatives would have been badly crowded.[75]

A combination of indifference, inattention, and a general disinclination to any kind of public expenditure meant that public amenities were neglected by the Macclesfield Corporation until industrialisation was well advanced. As John Wootton put it, 'The sanitary regulation and municipal government of the town had not presented themselves as matters of much importance, compared with the commercial prosperity and pecuniary well-being of the inhabitants. . .'[76] In 1814 an act of Parliament made the Corporation commissioners of police, charged with improving the lighting and watching of the town, but 'the powers given by that measure were never put in force, and [the town] . . . was noticeable chiefly for its ill-regulated thoroughfares and an almost entire absence of any system of drainage.'[77] Until this time Macclesfield's only public lighting had been furnished by a few tallow candles or oil lamps. Convenience, as well as fear of rowdiness and crime, eventually dictated some improvement.[78] After several abortive attempts by a local experimenter to lay gas pipes in 1815, a private gas company was formed in 1818 and gas works built. In 1819 gas lighting was available (at 12*s* per 1000 feet and £7 7*s* per lamp per annum), and the Corporation erected a dozen gas lamps in the town centre.

By the 1820s local doctors and some laymen were beginning to be concerned about the town's high rate of mortality — especially infant mortality — and levels of disease. Intestinal diseases and fevers were said to be taking a dreadful toll in poor districts. Renewed public pressure resulted in a new Police and Improvement Act in 1824, which designated as commissioners the mayor, recorder, aldermen and capital burgesses, along with every male inhabitant who had occupied premises worth £50 annual rental for at least six months. One hundred and fifty individuals qualified under this scheme, but their reluctance to act is indicated by the fact that after the first few meetings it proved impossible to muster even half a dozen. The accomplishments of these unwilling commissioners were meagre, to say the least.[79] In nine years, three main streets were repaved and drained, and gas lighting slightly extended. This commission was finally swept away (not without protest from alarmed ratepayers) by the Municipal Reform Act of 1835, which created the borough. The inertia of the old Corporation was equalled by its inefficiency; the latter condition became something of an excuse for the former. There was an annual deficit of about 30 per cent in the collection of property rates in the early nineteenth century, and some property seems to have escaped taxation altogether.[80] Complaints about non-payment of poor rates were even more frequent.

Macclesfield was fortunate in having a natural water supply superior to that of most industrial towns, but piped water was at first available only in a few streets near the market-place. A by-law of 1769 set rates for the use of the Corporation water piped into private homes, on a sliding scale, from £1 for houses of £30 yearly rental to 2*s* 8*d* for houses of £2 yearly rental. Burgesses paid a few shillings less and innkeepers a few shillings more. There was an extra charge for every tap above one, or for using water for other than domestic purposes, and fines for sharing or wasting water.[81]

Better-off families were served by water-carters; the less affluent used public stand-pipes or the old town wells, or drew water directly from the industrially-polluted river and streams.[82] In the 1830s an act was passed regulating the town's water supply, and the drainage system was slowly extended and improved thereafter.[83] Thus by mid-century the exceptionally high levels of tuberculosis, rheumatism, bronchitis, and other diseases spread and exacerbated by foul water and dampness began to be checked. Reform efforts came too late to afford protection against the great cholera epidemic of 1832, and the town was hit hard. The disease recurred several times in following years.[84]

The authorities took no responsibility for the disposal of the piles of human and animal waste that accumulated in courtyards and streets. There were no sewers and only about half of all houses in the early nineteenth century had any direct access to privies — far fewer had individual privies.[85] Scavengers made ineffectual efforts to cart away some of the refuse, for those who could pay. A few public privies serving the congested tenement districts surrounding the largest silk mills backed directly on to the Bollin River. Before 1825 the only drainage was provided by open drains along some of the main streets. Slops percolated through the soil and accumulated in reeking, greenish pools in yards and cellars. In some courts privies could only be cleaned by carrying night-soil through one of the houses.[86]

III

Without statistical evidence for the eighteenth century it is impossible to trace precisely the advance or decline of health and mortality through the early decades of industrialisation. All that can be said is that a bleak picture apparently became slightly less bleak. Epidemics seem to have been fairly frequent in the eighteenth century; there were, for example, serious outbreaks of smallpox near Macclesfield in 1772/3 and 1776/7.[87]

The first few register entries for the newly-opened Christ Church burial ground (1776/7) are more detailed than usual and give some data on common causes of death in various age groups (see Table III:3). One is struck immediately by the fact that eleven (possibly twelve) of the twenty-two deaths recorded were of

Table III : 3

Causes of Death: From Christ Church Register, 16 January 1776 — 5 March 1777[1]

Sex/Age	Cause of Death	Sex/Age	Cause of Death
Female, 12 wks	Convulsions	Female, —	Measles
Male, 6 mo.	Tooth fever	Male, 9	Consumption
Male, 9 mo.	Weakness	Female, 16	Consumption
Male, 1 yr.	Tooth fever	Female, 24	Consumption
Female, 1 yr.	Measles	Male, 28	Consumption
Female, 1 yr. 9 mo.	Convulsions	Female, 29	Inflamm. of bowels
Female, 2	Fever	Female, 46	Consumption
Female, 3	Smallpox	Female, 48	Dry Gripes
Male, 3	Smallpox	Male, 53	Killed in a pit
Female, 3 yrs 6 mo.	Cough	Male, 57	Pleurisy
Female, 4	Cough	Female, 71	————

1. *Source:* Christ Church Register, CRO P84/1

children under five years of age. Consumption was, and remained through the period, the most common of deadly diseases and the great killer of young adults. Such a list for the 1820s or 1830s would probably not look very different, except that smallpox would have diminished, to be supplanted by other epidemic diseases like cholera and typhus, and the rate of infant mortality might have improved slightly (although in 1846, 214 of 825 deaths, or 26 per cent, were of children under one year old, roughly the same percentage as in 1776/7).[88]

Macclesfield, like other medium-sized towns, offered a hierarchy of medical services; the choices would depend largely on ability and willingness to pay, but also on preference; for more 'modern' scientific (and fashionable) as against more traditional methods. Until the opening of the Town Dispensary in 1814 the care of a formally trained doctor was a luxury beyond the means of most. At the top of the medical tree were a few 'surgeons' who had been trained elsewhere, at a university, in a large urban hospital, or under the private tutelage of some prominent physician in another city. Successful doctors occupied a high social position in the town. Along with the upper clergy, the best solicitors, and the Grammar School masters they formed a small professional élite, having some connections with the industrialists and merchants but distinct by virtue of their slightly more cosmopolitan air. Professional families were very likely to intermarry, and more likely to look for marriage partners outside the town, even outside the county, than were the millowners. The family of Dr Francis Newbold (mayor 1800/1, practiced in partnership with Dr W.B. Dickinson in Park Green) is described as 'one of the most distinguished in Macclesfield'. Newbold's son, the Revd Francis Newbold, M.A., became a fellow of Brasenose College, Oxford, headmaster of Macclesfield Grammar School, and inherited a landed estate through his mother's family.[89] Other distinguished physicians of the early nineteenth century were Dr Thomas Swanwick, 'the most important medical man in town . . . not an ordinary practitioner, but a consulting physician', and Dr John Birchinall of Park Green, a fervent Methodist, 'who always offered a prayer when attending the sick and treated the poor without fee.'[90]

One rung below the well-to-do physicians were a number of doctors who had simply served an apprenticeship under a local practitioner. Thomas Cockson, who described himself as a 'surgeon and man-midwife' in 1776, would probably have belonged to this group.[91] Next came the more numerous group of druggists and chemists who regularly prescribed and made up medicines and sold a variety of patent remedies and home medical manuals as well. The town's leading druggist, Charles Hadfield, with imposing premises on the market square, was used as a family physician by many.[92]

Even the druggists would have been too costly, or too intimidating, for some labourers' families, and many continued to rely on back-street herbalists, amateur doctors, neighbours, and time-honoured home remedies. A man known as 'Tommy Neild the Doctor', for instance, kept a shop in Barn St where he practiced as a barber and healer in the front room and pursued alchemy in a back chamber.[93] As late as 1849 a visitor to the market-place saw 'a quack, with his portable furnaces and retorts, distilling his remedies before a gaping crowd of onlookers.'[94] When T.H. Worrall suffered a bout of congestion of the lungs as an infant of fifteen months in 1830, an old neighbour woman was called in to apply leeches to his chest.[95] The difference between professional and amateur care may often have been a matter of style rather than sophistication of technique; Dr Fleet, who served the town Dispensary for many years in the 1820s and 1830s, was said to have used bleeding for almost any ailment.[96] In rich and poor families alike the retarded, the mentally ill, and the physically handicapped were tended at home. Blind, deaf, dumb and crippled beggars were seen in the streets and in the workhouse. With their limited technical resources doctors were called upon to treat a vast range of disorders. One small asylum served the whole county of Cheshire, and there were no other public facilities for special treatment.[97]

The term 'surgeon' became a rather loose label, suggesting some degree of professional and social distinction without making any specific claim as to qualifications. The most complete early directory, Pigot and Dean's for 1824/5, lists ten surgeons, one 'surgeon and man-midwife', six druggists, and two who claimed to hold M.D.'s (John Davies and Thomas Slack). Slack, who had been trained at the Manchester Infirmary, was undoubtedly better qualified than many of his colleagues.[98]

Quite apart from the cost, fear and suspicion of doctors must have kept many people from treatment. Local lore reflects an air of mystery and distaste surrounding medical men. Townspeople said that when the Jacobite rebels invaded the town and hanged a spy in the market-place, the body was bought for 4*s* 6*d* by an apothecary, who later gave the skin to a tanner to be sold as leather.[99] Corpses were sometimes kept at home for weeks, for fear of body-snatchers. Story-tellers remembered a widow who sat up every night for a week by the grave of her husband, who had died of an unusual disease. The dying man had resisted the doctor's request for permission for a post-mortem, and said to his wife, 'You know what sort of man the doctor is, and if he has set his mind on it he will *have me up*.'[100] When the body of an old woman disappeared from Christ Church yard suspicion immediately fell upon the local doctors.[101]

These attitudes of distrust were dissipated slowly, as health became more generally recognised as an ongoing public concern. In 1814 a group of prominent citizens, at the instigation of Dr Newbold, founded a Town Dispensary. Here, as in so many things, Macclesfield was following tardily behind its more urban counterparts; Stockport and Manchester had had Dispensaries for outpatient care since the eighteenth century and were already beginning to build public hospitals by this time. In response to a petition the mayor called a meeting in March 1814 to launch a fund drive for the proposed dispensary. Pledges for annual contributions were collected and this revenue supplemented by an annual fund-raising ball.[102] The Dispensary opened its premises in Mill St in May 1814, with Dr Thomas Slack appointed as physician at a stipend of £100 a year. Slack, a keen researcher, was somewhat notorious in town for maintaining a 'museum' of skeletons, human organs, and morbid growths. He used his collection as the basis for weekly lectures to medical students and other interested persons and occasionally offered public talks to raise money for charity.[103] Several other doctors served the Dispensary in a consulting capacity. Staff positions were much sought after, and when Dr Francis Newbold died in 1828 rival candidates advertised eagerly in the *Courier* just before the Dispensary Trustees' annual meeting. The trustees seem to have divided Newbold's duties; Dr. Kay was named physician and Mr Fleet appointed as surgeon.[104]

The annual meeting of dispensary subscribers in 1815 was told that 632 patients had been admitted in the first year, of whom 371 were cured; the total expenditure had been £350 12*s* 9½*d*. In the second year, of 934 patients, 628 were cured, and only £377 19*s* 7*d* was spent.[105] The post-war years saw a sharp increase in the demand for dispensary care. Clearly the free services were attractive, and the public's hesitation about using scientific medical facilities was breaking down. The typhoid epidemic of 1820 alone added 1500 fever cases to the institution's usual load. In the 1840s the Irish were widely blamed for bringing fever into the town.[106] During the virulent cholera outbreaks of the early 1830s slum dwellers, especially the Irish poor, suffered dreadfully. Worrall remembered walking through the Irish neighbourhoods as a boy and hearing the continual droning of prayers for the dead.[107]

Of course, the health histories of individuals and families are for the most part a closed book. The few incomplete examples we have may give at least some clues to the general picture. The experience of the Reverend David Simpson's family, for example, brings together many familiar elements, and illustrates how easy it was for wealth and poverty to be drawn together in a deadly intimacy. Simpson himself came from a family of seven children, three of whom died in infancy. His first wife, Ann, died young, probably in childbirth, but her daughter survived into adulthood. By his second wife he had a son who died at fourteen weeks, a daughter who died of consumption at eighteen, and a son who survived. In 1799 the second wife died of 'fever' at age fifty-three, and ten days later Simpson succumbed to the same disease, aged fifty-one. He was said to have contracted the fever while visiting a poor cottager's family during a bad outbreak of the illness.[108]

Families like the one which may have infected David Simpson probably had no better prospects for survival by the 1820s. One family from Staffordshire came to Macclesfield to work in the factories in the mid-1820s and lived in a 'miserable, wet, and dirty hovel, upon Bank Top.' First the children became ill with scarlet fever, then the whole family contracted measles. The wife and three children died within a year, and the family suffered their ordeal with only neighbours' help and no public relief at all.[109]

Fortunate were those families, like that of draper John Swanwick, who managed to avoid the traumas of early death and acute illness. Dr Samuel Stone attended the Swanwick family and visited the household frequently between 1791 and 1797. The most common occasions for his calls were digestive disorders of various kinds; dozens of prescriptions call for 'opening powders', or 'stomach powders', as well as cordials, emetic draughts, diuretic drops, syrup of rhubarb, and magnesia. Scattered notations of liniment, lotion, and ointment probably bespeak childish accidents. First Swanwick, then his wife, and finally their eldest son were inoculated against smallpox at a cost of £1 10*s* a visit. Stone charged about 2*s* for an ordinary house call, and several visits a month are recorded for these years. In 1791 the master was 'often ill with fever', and one illness in May 1793 required fifteen separate calls, mostly to prescribe 'strengthening draughts'.[110]

The Swanwick's story reminds us that even a healthy life, by the standards of the time, could be filled with discomfort. In less affluent families many of the Swanwicks' complaints would have been borne stoically, along with a host of other troubles — visual and hearing disorders, arthritis, chronic cough, toothache, imperfectly healed injuries, etc. — which were simply part of everyday existence.

The poor general health of children made them easy victims of diseases which might not otherwise have been fatal. Married women who worked in the factories were said to leave their infants with baby minders who charged 2*s* 6*d* a week and used 'immense quantities' of Godfrey's Cordial and other opiates to keep their charges quiet. In the 1840s several establishments specialised in the farming out of illegitimate children, who were 'not well attended to, and fed on a low diet.' The town's doctors estimated that about half the children who died had had no medical attention.[111] The surprising number of children who died in accidents — being run over by carts, burned by cooking fires, etc. — would seem to indicate inadequate minding and possibly listlessness or weakness as well.

Macclesfield had unusually high rates of rheumatism, pulmonary complaints, 'inflammations', and dysentery; the average rate of mortality in the years 1842 to 1848 was a high 33.3 per 1000 (excluding deaths in the workhouse).[112] More than 44 per cent of all deaths occurred at less than five years of age.[113] Life expectancy for 'the upper and middle classes' was 29 years, as compared to 23 years for 'the working classes'; in the much healthier environment of neighbouring rural districts the averages were 43 years and 29 years respectively.[114] Those among the poor who survived to adulthood were small in stature by today's standards: the average heights of thirty-seven adult male prisoners transported from Chester Castle (1811/12) was 5′6″, and of six females (1806 to 1812), 5′¼″.[115]

With grim irony, death actually bred upon itself. Provision for burial was one of the town's most dire sanitary problems. St Michael's churchyard was already badly overcrowded by the late eighteenth century, and the foundations of the nave were being used as a charnel house for bones displaced by newer burials. As the churchyard was situated on the brow of a hill, overlooking some of the town's most densely populated quarters, there was a constant risk of pollution of the soil and of water supplies. The erection of Christ Church, with its new graveyard, in 1775 provided an alternative, and Charles Roe recovered part of the cost of the building through the sale of grave plots.[116] The Methodists, Catholics, and Congregationalists all maintained separate burial grounds in the early nineteenth century, but these too soon became overcrowded. Not until 1866 was the situation alleviated by the opening of a municipal cemetery, after years of agitation and planning by the Local Board of Health.[117]

To sum up, it was not until mid-century, when the town's sanitary arrangements were substantially upgraded and population had levelled off, that the statistics of disease and mortality improved noticeably. Then at last the inexorable cycle of poverty, debility, contagion and premature death was challenged.

IV

For ten years after the passage of the New Poor Law of 1834, and in spite of the strenuous efforts of the Poor Law Commissioners and a succession of their local appointees, the town of Macclesfield successfully blocked all proposals to convert the town to the new system of poor relief and to construct a new Union workhouse. Sense cannot be made of the extraordinary unanimity and strength of this opposition without recalling, first, that during the two centuries preceding the new law the most prevalent and accepted form of poor relief in towns like Macclesfield was outrelief. Thus the workhouse test imposed by the new administrators at Somerset House ran counter to long-standing local tradition. Equally important, in the two decades before 1834 the town had undergone a series of trade crises which obliterated the traditional demarcation line between the sturdy, self-supporting working man and the helpless, dependent pauper. Respectable silk-workers, who could not have imagined themselves asking for public assistance in 1800 or 1810, found themselves without means to support their families. They might have to swallow their pride, but they would not bow willingly to the new tests and regulations.

The old system of out-door relief recognised a community responsibility to succour those who had fallen into unavoidable destitution, usually through illness, widowhood, orphanhood, or old age.[118] At all times female paupers far outnumbered males.

The age at which one was permanently incapacitated for work varied from trade to trade, and could be as early as forty-five; but given average life expectancies retirement was a remote prospect for most people.

The first workhouse in Macclesfield was set up in 1698, mainly for the purpose of housing poor children, who were to be instructed in button-making and spinning. Throughout the next century the Overseers continued to devote most of their attention to out-relief cases, making recommendations to the Corporation which granted 'pensions', or weekly payments to the elderly, and provided food, clothing, and medical care to many needy individuals who continued to reside in their own homes. Poor children were apprenticed, spinning wheels and looms provided for those who could work at home, bastardy money collected from fathers of illegitimate children, and weekly 'militia money' paid out to wives of serving soldiers. In 1782 Macclesfield agreed with the townships of Sutton and Rainow to co-ordinate their workhouse facilities to some extent. Of the two smaller houses, Rainow concentrated on providing for the elderly and Sutton took mainly young children. Each housed about thirty-five inmates. The Macclesfield workhouse, which could hold about two hundred, took mainly adult paupers, including transients. The workhouse diet seems reasonable by the standards of the time; the Overseers regularly purchased bread, beef, cheese, potatoes, onions, and milk, and occasionally sugar, tea, tobacco, and port wine (used as medicine).[119] Life in the workhouse in the eighteenth century must have been grim and monotonous, but bearable. As the population of homeless paupers swelled, severe overcrowding, dirt, meagre rations, disorder, and the constant threat of illness, eventually made workhouse life all but insupportable and the institution itself a symbol of hell on earth to many.

The effectiveness of private charity as a supplement to the Overseers' 'pensions' is hard to gauge. We do know that charitable donations administered through the Established Church were negligible; by 1834, after more than two hundred years of slowly accumulating bequests, the amount at the disposal of the incumbent of St Michael's was the interest on £1423 9*s* 0*d*.[120] Traditional disbursements to the poor, by the Church, the Corporation, or by private individuals formed a colourful part of community ritual, but probably contributed more towards a sense of holidaymaking and transient good feeling than they did towards the physical well-being of the needy. Occasions like the triumph of the Duke of Cumberland over the Jacobites, the Peace of Amiens, the Battle of Trafalgar, and the King's birthdays and jubilees were celebrated in style; on the jubilee of 1809, for instance, dinner was given by the Corporation to 1452 residents, including 200 orphans, and blankets and bread were distributed to the elderly poor. But such gestures could have no impact on the cyclical pattern of mass unemployment or the influx of Irish and other destitute immigrants that had rendered all the Overseers' efforts inadequate by the 1820s. Bitter comments from the poor about the bread distributions and soup kitchen experiments of the 1820s and 1830s decry the utter insufficiency of the relief offered, and also reflect a widespread distaste for that sort of charity.[121]

There was a hard core of what might be termed the 'professional poor', who could be extremely ingenious in combining pittances here and there from various public and private sources. Old Nicholas Stevens was a confirmed wanderer who used a military pension (he had lost an arm fighting in Jamaica in the 1730s) plus the proceeds of outdoor relief and begging to stock his peddler's pack. He described the half-yearly round which brought him regularly through Macclesfield:

> Having received his . . . pension — which was three pounds and eleven shillings and some odd brass — [at Liverpool] he set out with his wife for London and was near a quarter of a year on the road and when he came there he bought some thread Needles Buttons and other small wares and . . . he was in London about six weeks and went to the Parish he belong'd to and was there relieved with eighteen pence one time and one shilling another . . . he set out from London about sixteen or eighteen days ago and . . . came thro' Oxford, Birmingham, Litchfield and Newcastle . . .[122]

Frequent complaints of theft by householders who had offered food or shelter to wandering beggars show both a lingering tradition of casual private assistance, and a growing suspicion and reluctance to receive strangers, as the dimensions of the diaspora grew more frightening. Wandering beggars, odd-job men, wounded or discharged servicemen and their dependents, gypsies, and street entertainers were familiar figures in the eighteenth century. One traditional method of eliciting alms was to roam the county with a 'petition' describing a misfortune which had befallen the bearer — a barn-burning, the sudden death of livestock, etc. — and signed by a respectable patron (vicar or squire). Contributors' names, with the amounts they gave, would be added to the list. These petitions could be forged quite easily, and one sharpster in Chester turned them out for fourpence.[123] There were occasional cases, too, of vagrants feigning disabilities or making menacing overtures to would-be donors.[124] Vagrants particularly haunted the fairs and Wakes, and the Corporation's efforts to control or discourage them were unequal to the numbers.[125] There remained, of course, a clear distinction in the popular mind between these outsiders, fit perhaps only for the stocks or the House of Correction, and the new masses of unemployed poor, many of them respectable residents temporarily distressed, to whom the discipline and humiliation of workhouse relief was anathema.

Both the growing (though uneven) prosperity and confidence of the working-class community and the inadequacy of public provision for essential social services, meant that a large part of the burden of providing sick and death benefits and short-term relief for the labouring poor was taken up by their own clubs and societies. At the outset there was some pressure to bring benefit club activity under the control of non-working-class bodies, especially the Church. The Revd David Simpson of Christ Church was an eager advocate of clubs and established a Female Friendly Society in 1778 'for the cultivation of frugal habits and virtuous demeanour among the young women of the town.'[126] At the Angel Inn in 1792 traveller Robert Byng saw a 'grand dinner' held by 'old women of this town, who, having established a fund for the benefit of their helpless, their sick, etc., and for funerals, meet at this inn to settle their accounts.'[127] A society for the Relief of the Sick Poor existed in the 1790s. The Methodists also had a fund for the sick, and were sometimes criticised for restricting aid to their own members. They denied the charge, but many of their charitable efforts were channelled through their own institutions, especially the Sunday schools, and they may be said to have foreshadowed in some respects the more regimented style of relief-giving embodied by the 1834 law. Larger clubs, probably having their origin in the trade clubs, were founded and run by the workpeople themselves and proved immensely popular. By the end of the mid-1830s some clubs were expanding their sick benefit programmes to include medical care, paying surgeon's fees and offering members a kind of clinic service, as well as free medicine.

The burden of funeral costs was always a pressing problem for working-class families, and in 1831 specialised burial clubs, with weekly contributions of only one penny or less, were inaugurated in the town. At first these enrolled only persons over sixteen years of age. Later separate children's burial clubs were begun, but for many years it was customary for guests invited to a child's funeral to be reminded to 'bring their money', i.e., a small contribution towards the funeral expenses.

The assets of most benefit clubs were rather modest. In the early days, as with the trade clubs, most were loosely organised with no trustees or written rules, and with only enough cash in hand at any one time to pay for a single funeral (sick money was collected from the members as needed).[128] These informal bodies often proved vulnerable in times of severe hardship, just when their members needed them most. But overall the clubs' contribution to the well-being and security of working people was substantial. One Macclesfield club which had been in existence since 1796 had by, 1866, dispensed nearly £40,000 in sick benefits and £7000 in burial costs.[129]

A major crisis, driving hundreds who had previously been independent on to the poor rolls, occurred just after the French wars. By 1817 the poor rate was higher than it had ever been before — more than 4*s* in the pound (of rateable value). Sudden reversals in prosperity meant that spinners and weavers who had themselves been householders and contributors to the poor rate were forced to ask for relief. This galling necessity was made more painful when destitute artisans found that deductions for arrears of rates were taken out of their tiny weekly allowances. The parish officers were also hated for their petty and insulting exactions — refusing to allow a pauper who was ordered to haul coal with a wheelbarrow to borrow a friend's donkey to ease the task, requiring street-sweepers to work in the rain or forfeit their relief, refusing relief to any family (of whatever size) which had an earned income of 6*s* a week.[130] The Overseers, for their part, struggled against an avalanche of demands which far outstripped the resources available to them, and futilely tried one scheme after another to recover the massive arrears of rates — a perennial problem in good times as in bad.

Between 1821 and 1832 annual expenditures from the poor rates grew from £4208 to £8467, the number of families assisted annually went from 73 to 511, and the number of workhouse inmates rose from 69 to about 340. Still the help offered was not enough. In the worst years 'Committees on Distress' were formed to seek ways of supplementing the overstrained public treasury. By 1826 the level of relief offered had been greatly reduced, from 2*s* per head per week to only 10*d*, but none the less there were nine levies of the poor rate in the first three months of the year. The Committee estimated (perhaps with some exaggeration) that 15,000 people were out of work, with 10,000 seeking some form of relief.[131] To make matters worse, the Overseers stubbornly persisted in forcing on the unemployed a sense of moral culpability and subjugation: 'In general they require the able part of the family to break stones, sweep the streets, draw coals, and almost any superfluous work they can find for them.'[132] Bitterness and shame combined to produce a crescendo of protests; many weavers refused to break stones, saying that the rough work would damage their hands, and on one occasion the workhouse windows were smashed and the Governor hissed.[133] The assault on artisans' status was felt almost as heavily as sheer physical want. Weavers complained of having to sell their furniture and books and shrank from attending church because their clothes were ragged. One summed up his plight with wounded pride, 'I feel . . . that poverty does not necessarily infer degradation, because we may be poor from causes over which we have no control.'[134]

In good years a more normal state of affairs quickly reasserted itself. By early 1833, for example, the poor rate had already decreased by one shilling in the pound over the previous year's average. The workhouse, with a capacity of two hundred, held only eighty or ninety inmates, 'principally infirm persons and children'. The pauper children were sent to work in the mills, for wages of about 2*s* a week. There were 324 regular recipients of outrelief, generally a shilling or two a week, and only about fifty 'casual poor', i.e., able-bodied but unemployed.[135]

Soon after the New Poor Law went into effect trade declined badly and the workhouse was again overflowing. Yet no matter how dark the outlook became, the solid wall of opposition to the new law stood firm. From the painful results of attempts at regulating the silk trade in 1824 and 1826 Macclesfield as a whole had drawn the lesson that parliamentary meddling was only likely to make things worse. So, in the wake of unprecedented growth, sweeping industrial changes, and fearful periodic crises of destitution, the town still turned its back on solutions from outside and paused for a brief interlude of backward-looking communion. Old-fashioned clergymen and philanthropists condemned the new law as callous and impersonal; radicals hated the very idea of a 'Bastille' and the jumped-up clerks and beadles who would administer it; the helpless poor dreaded the new regimentation; the unemployed feared new assaults on their self-respect; the Benefit Clubs denounced heartless and bureaucratic usurpers of their functions; and ratepayers, large and small, saw nothing but extravagance in the new arrangements.[136] Whether all these sections of local opinion could have agreed on the more positive proposition that material welfare in the town had improved since 1750, or 1780, is very doubtful. Clearly industrialisation had brought a new level of comfort and security to many, including a sizeable portion of the working class. It had helped to create a new consumer economy, with at least some benefits and novelties for all. But the failure of public amenities to keep pace with the town's mushrooming growth, combined with the social evils that accompanied terrible overcrowding, meant that some of the labouring poor suffered as they never had before. Ironically, many of the town's poorer inhabitants were enjoying longer life-spans by the 1830s, but in circumstances of such squalid hardship as to make even the bare sustenance of the eighteenth century look faintly rosy.

IV

Social Order and Social Tension

If the precise measurement of material well-being evades the historian's best efforts, shifts in social relations — the bonds of authority, deference, influence, respect, rivalry, antagonism, or fear — can be even more elusive. As with questions of physical subsistence, patterns of social relationship reveal themselves most clearly when something unusual or traumatic occurs and individuals or groups are called upon to exercise power or influence which normally lies dormant. When votes are cast, or violence erupts, or court is in session, part of a town's social 'skeleton' is revealed; but more routine events — weekly market gatherings, the annual celebration of some ancient festival, thousands of daily interactions in neighbourhood pubs or at the domestic hearth — are the connective tissue, the flesh and blood of the social organism. While necessarily concentrating on the more public record, as revealed in documentary sources, the historian must be aware of the seamless backdrop to the drama.

Until the mid-eighteenth century most of Macclesfield's inhabitants were still closely bound together by face-to-face relationships; for the most part they lived in relative isolation from events in the greater world outside.[1] But on the very eve of industrialisation this state of affairs was disrupted briefly and violently by a military alarm, an invasion by the Jacobite army of Prince Charles Stuart during his sweep through East Cheshire in November-December 1745.[2] The Scottish rebels stayed only two days, billeting themselves in the houses of stunned and unwilling inhabitants and causing some offence by their boisterous behaviour and looting. One suspected spy was hanged from the railings of

Old Town Hall, but by and large the townsfolk were left undisturbed. Still, the invasion was felt as a profound violation of Macclesfield's privacy and security, so much so that its story has been indignantly retold in every local history of the town, and old men in the 1880s could tell exactly where their great-grandfathers had stood and what they had been doing at the moment when the rebel soldiers came into view.[3] When the Scots marched off to imminent defeat, calm and confidence were soon restored, but the brief shudder of panic which passed over the town in 1745 can be viewed as a kind of prelude to more serious tremors ahead. A less dramatic but much more significant invasion started in the 1750s; it brought thousands of strangers who came to stay and permanently altered the 'village' quality of Macclesfield life. New customs and institutions would be needed to regulate the conduct and dealings of all these newcomers, men and women who could not expect to know each other by sight, or even by reputation. Resistant to innovation but susceptible to gradual renovation, the pre-industrial social order was slowly stretched and pulled and kneaded into a new form.

This chapter will concern itself with three interconnected aspects of the social relations of Macclesfield. Each reflects the transition from village to town and the evolution of class relationships, and each is concerned with the distribution and exercise of social power. First, a consideration of the structure of political life, which for the most part is an extension of economic relationships and concerns. The persistence of a local oligarchy is attributed, in large part, to the mercantile élite's flexibility in embracing new sources of wealth. Second, an examination of the machinery for formal and informal control of criminal or disruptive behaviour; and last, a discussion of the social uses of leisure time. In both these areas there were adjustments, often hesitant and uncertain, to the new social realities of industrialisation and urbanisation; but change was clearly tempered by widely prevailing loyalty to pre-industrial customs and attitudes.

I

Eighteenth-century Cheshire was not very much exercised by political passions; the personalities and issues of national politics impinged on its local consciousness only rarely. The county had only one parliamentary borough, the City of Chester, whose two seats were firmly in the grip of the staunchly Tory Grosvenor family. The county representation was similarly monopolised by a few aristocratic Tory families. In the hard-fought county election of 1727 Sir Robert Cotton of Combermere, a Whig, was returned, mainly because of a successful campaign effort in the larger towns. But a Tory reaction soon set in, and Cotton lost his seat in the violent contest of 1734. In eight general elections and three by-elections between 1741 and 1784 Cheshire returned Tory candidates unopposed.[4] Pre-reform Macclesfield, though without a parliamentary representative of its own, harboured quite a few property-owners who qualified for the county franchise. In county elections, the town asserted its long-standing municipal independence by not being quite so decidedly Tory in its sympathies as the county.[5]

In the governance of the town itself, old customs and styles of exercising power persisted. Under the 'new' town charter of Charles II the officers of the Corporation were the mayor, two aldermen, and twenty-four capital burgesses, all elected annually by the freemen. The mayor and aldermen sat as magistrates during their term of office and for one year thereafter. In the eighteenth century the electorate normally included a large number of freemen resident outside the town, mostly prosperous merchants and farmers who paid for the privilege of trading freely in the Macclesfield market. But records of attendance at Corporation meetings show that the actual business of governing was in the hands of residents, and the trend through the industrialising decades was for the Corporation to be made up more and more of property owners trading from fixed premises in the town.[6] In the sixty years between 1775 and 1835 burgesses resident outside the town were elected mayor on only four occasions. During the same period the office was held on thirty-five occasions by men who can be identified as silk or cotton manufacturers, and several other mayors were professional men financially involved in the textile trade.[7] Gradually the gentry of the mill and warehouse replaced the gentry of the farm and market-place. Because it was so often the same families, even the same individuals, who moved from one role into the other, the transition was a gentle one, requiring no political upheaval.

Primitive in some respects, the political machinery of the old Corporation was serviceable enough for the major purposes of the town's social and economic élite. In particular, access to common lands and water rights was given over inexpensively and without fuss to new industry. Under the old regime both public funds and expenditures were minimal, and the Corporation was slow to flex its muscles or extend its grasp. Between 1750 and 1800 the mayor's regular disbursements increased from £229 to £360, and income, mostly from market tolls, water rates, and leases of public lands, just kept pace with the modest rise.[8] By the turn of the century, however, the Corporation by necessity had begun to branch out into separately funded improvement projects and had accumulated at least £1400 in debts. Ten years later the public debt had risen to £3300, raised in part on security of town lands, and an additional loan of £2673 was being negotiated with the firm of Daintry and Ryle. This money was used primarily for extension and modernisation of waterworks — a necessity for many new textile mills and dye-works.[9]

The Corporation's cordial relations with the respectable part of the community were further maintained through the creation of a small, loyal cadre of office-holders and public contractors. Patronage was dispensed in the form of supply and repair contracts, temporary employment on public works, and some dozen or more jobs, ranging from the lucrative post of coroner to appointments as inspector of meat, bread, and ale in the market, supervisor of 'moss' [i.e., peat] cutting, scavengers, beadles, and pig-catchers. Several of these posts might be held simultaneously by one individual, and municipal jobs were sometimes handed down in families.[10]

In the rather prestigious position of Borough Recorder there was a gradual shift away from county gentry toward local men, and the change brought a new spirit of liveliness and contention to elections. The Recorder was a solicitor who sometimes presided at Borough Sessions, made recommendations on patronage matters, and acted in general as legal adviser to the Corporation. Tenure was for life, or until an incumbent chose to retire.[11] The colourful recordership campaign of 1804 is a good example of a continuing preoccupation with local interests and rivalries as against issues of national concern, or ideological considerations. The candidates were James Abercrombie, a non-resident but well regarded in the county,[12] and John Harriot Roe, youngest son of the great industrialist Charles Roe. Abercrombie received considerable support in Tory circles and among those who distrusted John Roe's personal character. John Roe, who had lived for some years in London, had apparently offended family and friends by some misconduct, but pledged to reside in Macclesfield if elected and was contemplating marriage, which, it was hoped, would 'settle' him.[13] During the campaign William Roe of Liverpool, eldest son of Charles and head of the family, walked through town under an elaborate banner with a view of Christ Church on one side and 'Roe, and the Town and Trade of Macclesfield' on the other, leading a procession decked in blue favours and crying, 'Roe Forever'.[14] The opposition bombarded John Roe with broadsides and scurrilous verses and even commissioned a satirical play about him, but in the event loyalty to the name of Charles Roe, twenty-three years dead, prevailed.[15]

In this election the voters were the freemen of the borough, and the opposing camps tried to pack the voting list with last-minute creations. By polling time the electorate numbered 271, of whom 128 favoured Roe and 112 Abercrombie (with 31 not voting).[16] Most of the larger manufacturers supported Roe, though some important silk families, like the Brocklehursts, divided their votes. A few prominent individuals, notably John Ryle and attorney John Clulow, soon to succeed to the town clerkship, prudently declined to vote.

The town clerk, also elected for life, was the most active representative of the Corporation in day-to-day affairs. He was at the very centre of town life — the fulcrum of a great deal of patronage, legal manoeuvring, disbursement of town money, and political negotiation. The clerk often appeared in court on behalf of the Corporation, or prepared evidence for others to present, and his office was usually combined with that of coroner.[17] The fact that the clerkship was held by only two men between 1765 and 1830 added to the influence of the office. Peter Wright (who served from 1765 to 1804) and John Clulow (served 1804 to 1830) were fixtures in the public life of the town.[18] The contest over the succession to Clulow adds a footnote to the overall picture of traditional considerations of 'interest' and 'connection' prevailing over more modern party-oriented politics. On Clulow's death in 1830 the burgesses elected a young solicitor, Thomas Parrott —

favouring him over two extremely well-connected party candidates, Tory solicitor Thomas Grimsditch and Whig silk-owner William Brocklehurst. Parrott's advantage was that he had served in John Clulow's law office from the age of fourteen. He proved an astute advisor to the town, and served until 1879.[19]

Though party spirit, in the modern sense, was faint, there were some fitful attempts during wartime to muster patriotic sentiment as a binding element between social classes. From the pulpit of Christ Church the Reverend David Simpson preached influential sermons on the iniquities of Tom Paine, the atrocities of the French Jacobins, and the virtues of limited monarchy. Elements of traditional communal revelry and 'street theatre' were employed in Corporation-orchestrated patriotic celebrations, such as the festival which marked the defeat of Napoleon in 1814. An effigy was paraded through the streets and burned, while the town crier called for any Jacobin in the town to come and witness the destruction of his hero. Flags were flown from the factories, and white favours distributed to the populace.[20] There was some sporadic persecution of radicals by vigilante groups or drunken gatherings of Saturday-night patriots. Among the victims of popular ire were a mercer who had derided the Volunteers as 'Billy Pitt's Dancing Dogs', and a Chestergate merchant named Bacon who had his windows broken for his radical sympathies and was eventually driven to emigrate to America.[21] Said John Corry, 'No man even suspected of whiggism could live [in Macclesfield] without annoyance from the *canaille*, or dregs of the people who were instigated by opulent royalists.'[22] Corry, a devoted Whig himself, took a jaundiced and perhaps exaggerated view, but such instigation did come, for a while, from a King and Constitution Club founded in the 1790s. The mayor and magistrates, Volunteer officers, Anglican clergy, and nearly a hundred large employers and other Tory stalwarts signed the membership roster. But by the 1820s the wartime panic had dissipated and the Club dwindled into inactivity.[23]

Although peace brought an end to the noisier manifestations of nationalistic fervour, the events of the war and the economic dislocations which followed stimulated a deeper political awareness in the provincial population as a whole. There was a growing tendency to translate local economic grievances into matter for national political agitation. All classes in Macclesfield were more willing after 1815 to pay some heed to the various reform movements that were radiating outward from northern urban centres like Leeds, Bradford, Manchester, and Sheffield. In spite of frequent charges that the mass local reform demonstrations — some attracting as many as two or three thousand people — were manipulated and inspired by outsiders, it appears that there was genuine enthusiasm for the radical remedies proposed, at least in so far as they might possibly benefit the silk trade. The two-thirds of the male population of Macclesfield who, in January 1817, signed a petition calling for reform of the franchise, annual parliaments, and an end to the Corn Laws may have been following the lead of Manchester and Stockport, but they were also taking a first step towards finding a voice and a vehicle that could carry local complaints into the national arena.[24]

In late 1818, when preparations began for the great mass meeting to be held the following summer in St Peter's Field, Manchester, a Macclesfield committee was formed to collect signatures for the petition to be sent from that meeting, and to organise a local contingent to attend it. On 15 August 1819 'Orator' Henry Hunt stopped overnight at Macclesfield *en route* to Manchester and addressed a large crowd in Park Green. Sympathisers who could not follow Hunt to Peterloo turned out closer to home. On the night of 17 August a Macclesfield crowd attacked the residences of wealthy Tories, concentrating on the homes of the mayor, magistrate Rowland Gould, and members of the Yeoman Cavalry who had reported for service in Manchester, and inflicted a reported £1000 worth of damage. The Riot Act was finally read and the crowd was dispersed by the military.[25]

Radical organisation and activity in Macclesfield seem to have remained on an *ad hoc* basis right up to 1832. There is no evidence of an ongoing 'cell' or club of pre-Chartist reformers; yet there was clearly a radical element, and Macclesfield produced at least two early martyrs to the cause. Robert Swindells, a silk-worker, was imprisoned for selling radical pamphlets in 1824. Joseph Swann, originally a hatter then a bookseller and later William Cobbett's agent in Stockport, was jailed in 1819 and again in 1831 as a vendor of seditious literature.[26] Swann was blacklisted by local employers, and his family suffered greatly as a result of his activities. Because of the severity of his 1819 sentence and the harsh conditions of his confinement in Chester Castle Swann became a national hero of the 'war of the unstamped'.

By the 1820s radical ideas were regularly reaching the town through the visits of a succession of nationally-known speakers. Later a local Chartist committee existed for some years, under the leadership of John West, a weaver at Brocklehurst's mill. West, a native of Dublin who emigrated as a child, first to Manchester then to Macclesfield, was a veteran of the Factory Act and Anti-Poor Law agitations. A gifted speaker, he was invited to become a paid organiser for the Anti-Corn Law League but declined.[27] An acquaintance and fellow weaver, Timothy Falvey, did go to work for the League and rose to become a newspaper editor and prominent citizen of Southampton. John West went on to become well known in the Chartist movement and stood for Parliament in Stockport in 1847.[28]

Until the Reform Act severed the 'respectable' reforming elements from their base of support among the labouring classes, there seems to have been something of a 'united front' in Macclesfield. In 1832, for instance, a radical reformers' meeting was allowed in the Town Hall, with local dignitaries in attendance. John West roused the audience with a passionate call for reform combined with an attack on the Corn Laws. Within a few years, however, the *entente* between classes was a thing of the past, and the town fathers were quick to call on military aid or to enlist special constables when radical disturbance emanating from the working class threatened.[29]

In March 1831 the town had solemnly petitioned Parliament for its enfranchisement — pointing out that the ratio of representatives to population in Cheshire was only 1 to 68,875, as compared to a national average of 1 to 23,817. Macclesfield, 'the principal seat of the silk manufacture in England', with an unrepresented population of 31,000, clearly required 'the continual care and intervention of members of Parliament, for the protection, not only of the interests of the proprietors thereof, but also of the very numerous persons to whom those branches of manufacture afford employment.'[30] This was the familiar argument, used again and again from the mid-eighteenth century onward when asking any favour from Parliament for the silk trade. It was not entirely accurate to say that the town was unrepresented before 1832; at the time of the Reform more than five hundred property-holders of Macclesfield Borough were qualified to vote in the county election.[31] But what was wanted was a representative answerable only to the town and devoted exclusively to the silk interest. When the parliamentary franchise was granted, the terms of the reform measure brought disappointment to the radical working men who had petitioned and demonstrated so energetically alongside their employers. Under the £10 householders' franchise only 718 Macclesfield citizens qualified as voters.

Electioneering in Macclesfield, from the boisterous county elections of the early eighteenth century to the temporary disfranchisement of the borough for corrupt practices in 1881, always had an Eatanswill flavour about it. The first parliamentary election, in 1835, was the occasion of riotous carousing; the hustings, set up in front of the Town Hall, were almost torn down by drunken revellers, market-stalls were knocked over and plundered and shop windows broken and looted in the general mêlée. Special constables failed to prevent assaults on prominent citizens, mostly Tories, including two former mayors. One man later nostalgically recalled the turmoil of electioneering in the 1830s: 'flaming election addresses, . . . the excitement and bands of music, the fun, fighting, and frolic . . . the dinners, balls, and tea-drinking, with the good-humoured rows . . . . To see the Committee at work night and day, as if in a beleaguered town, receiving mysterious scouts and messengers . . . to see the paid Election agent, not caring a drop of his own ink what methods were used if only he could secure the return of his man.'[32] The practices of politics were more like a wild sport than a contest of ideologies or a solemn debate over the destiny of the town. Not surprisingly, Macclesfield divided its vote between a Tory and a Whig in 1835 (and in several succeeding elections), thereby choosing a pair of M.P.'s who were also the town's two leading silk manufacturers.

An examination of the parliamentary election returns for 1835 shows that Macclesfield voted strongly for silk, putting economic interest and personal loyalties ahead of party identification. In the town centre, where miscellaneous retail premises and smaller silk workshops predominated, the Tories were favoured by a small margin, but even here voters showed a marked preference for Ryle (Tory) and Brocklehurst (Whig), the silk manufacturers, over the second Tory candidate, solicitor Thomas Grimsditch. [See Table IV:1.] A generous Tory remarked of the new Whig M.P., 'John Brocklehurst was always sure to be elected on account of his being

Table IV : 1

Voting in the Parliamentary Election, Borough of Macclesfield, 1835[1]

Candidates:

John Ryle, silk manufacturer, Tory (elected)
John Brocklehurst, silk manufacturer, Whig (elected)
Thomas Grimsditch, solicitor, Tory

Electors voting for:

Macclesfield Town	
Ryle only	47
Brocklehurst only	65
Grimsditch only	19
Ryle & Brocklehurst	152
Ryle & Grimsditch	166
Brocklehurst & Grimsditch	102
Sutton	
Ryle only	21
Brocklehurst only	4
Grimsditch only	1
Ryle & Brocklehurst	44
Ryle & Grimsditch	23
Brocklehurst & Grimsditch	6
Hurdsfield	
Ryle only	0
Brocklehurst only	25
Grimsditch only	0
Ryle & Brocklehurst	6
Ryle & Grimsditch	3
Brocklehurst & Grimsditch	19

---

1. *Source:* 'The Poll at an Election of Representatives in Parliament for the Borough of Macclesfield in the Year 1835' (Macclesfield: J. Swinnerton, [1835]). Copy in the British Library. Seventy-two eligible voters failed to cast their votes.

such a large employer of labour. But he deserved to be elected . . . a very good man, very modest and . . . retiring.'[33]

The great factory masters, with the assistance of their stewards and solicitors and friendly publicans and tradesmen, brought a united community of dependents to the polls, just as the landed proprietors did in rural areas. In Sutton, a district where the Ryle family were the principal land-owners and employers, 88 per cent of the voters cast at least one vote for Ryle. In Hurdsfield, site of the vast Brocklehurst mills, 94 per cent cast a vote for Brocklehurst. Macclesfield, a pioneer in the development of the factory system itself, is also an early example of that system of political clientage with an industrial base which Patrick Joyce has found to be so widespread throughout the industrial North of England after 1850.[34]

If the town's first venture into Parliament was a cautious foray into unfamiliar territory, the reform of municipal government — carried out under the Municipal Reform Act of 1835 — was more like an invasion, engineered by metropolitan experts. There had been no local mass meetings calling for reform, and the old guard resisted change passively but stubbornly: 'The Old Corporation died quietly. In the year previous to its dissolution the burgess assembly met with dwindling numbers and no business was transacted.'[35] From 1835 the borough, now enlarged by the addition to it of parts of Hurdsfield and Sutton, was divided into six wards which elected a total of thirty-six councillors. These in turn chose one of their number as mayor, and also elected twelve aldermen, not necessarily councillors but similarly qualified. The Council appointed several committees — Finance, Watch, Waterworks, etc. — to handle the increasingly complex business of government. On the evidence of Corporation records, procedure became more formal and meetings more frequent.[36]

The new Corporation may have been more efficient, but it was actually less representative than its hoary predecessor. Those qualified to vote were all male owners or tenants of property of £10 rateable value who had occupied their premises for at least three years and whose rates were paid up. Under these terms about 800 individuals, from a population of about 33,000 in 1835, were qualified, and some men who had qualified as freemen of the old Corporation were now excluded.[37] The qualifications for holding the office of councillor were substantially higher than those for electors; one had to own or be tenant of property worth at least £1000 or with an annual rateable value of £30. Only 235 individuals qualified as potential council members.[38] The reform exhibits its designers' apparent confidence in the leadership ability and enlightened self-interest of a town's largest property-holders. Small merchants and craftsmen were effectively excluded from policymaking. In Macclesfield the result of the new dispensation, for many years, was extreme fiscal caution and inertia. Stella Davies finds the minutes of the first ten years of the new Council 'singularly lacking in incident'.[39] Indeed, in the absence of either strong reform sentiment or appropriate machinery for implementing change, the new Council was unlikely to introduce any significant innovations. Not until the 1840s did pressure from London, combined with persistent efforts by a small band of forward-looking local bureaucrats, begin to overcome the pervasive indifference of the Council.

D.C. Moore has described the typical provincial political community of post-Reform England as one in which 'the effective electoral unit was neither the class nor the individual.'[40] Voters, he contends, behaved instead as part of an 'interest' community, that is, a group of men who lived in close contact with one another, and either were associated with the same trade or followed the lead of the same large employer or land-owner. According to Moore, individuals might equally be bound together politically by 'somewhat less tangible ties of common political, economic, social, and religious interests.'[41] In such a system the ideal elector was not the free agent, but rather one who 'recognised himself as member of the community . . . [and] might thus be affected by the legitimate influences of the established leaders of the community.'[42] Moore's general model fits Macclesfield's political history — even before the Reform Act — well enough. In electoral politics, and to some extent in popular sentiment, it was a town which recognised a single, over-arching 'interest', the well-being of the silk trade, and which was inclined to look to a few industrial magnates for leadership. The steady development, from the mid-eighteenth century onward, towards increased municipal self-consciousness, confidence, and self-sufficiency should best be seen, not as a movement towards political democracy, but rather as the maturation of this distinct political 'interest', clamouring for representation at the national level.

Moore's insistence on deference as the key descriptive term, however, has the defect of obscuring tension and conflict which sometimes, especially in the context of local economic and political issues affecting the labouring population directly, took on the unmistakable appearance of class warfare. Peter Searby brings us somewhat closer to an understanding of the temper of Macclesfield politics in his account of Coventry, another borough whose over-riding interest was the prosperity of the silk trade, ensured by the preservation of the tariff. Here, too, popular politics were dominated by skilled artisans anxious to preserve customary price-lists and other traditional practices of the trade. As Searby shows, conservative instincts among such artisans can be seen, not simply in terms of deference to large employers (in fact, these were largely absent in Coventry), but as intrinsic to certain privileged and defensive strata of workers.[43]

A further difficulty with D.C. Moore's terminology is that it veils the machinery of coercion — the constant threat of legal sanctions, official violence, and informal communal reprisals against rebels and deviants — that was a backdrop against which social rituals of deference and loyalty were enacted. The next section will consider some of these devices for containing or suppressing social disorder and will concentrate in particular on the system of criminal justice and the employment of military force at the local level.

II

A majority of the 'respectable' residents of Macclesfield in the 1820s and 1830s would probably have felt that crime and violence in the town had increased over the preceding fifty years. The problem of assessing the seriousness of perceived threats to the social order or to personal security at any time during this period is particularly difficult for the modern historian because the early nineteenth-century definition of what constituted 'crime' is not necessarily our own. Over the last century and a half the professionalisation of law enforcement has, in a sense, multiplied crimes, sharpening the perception of anti-social behaviour at the same time as there have been intensified efforts to control it. J.J. Tobias makes this general point, and adds that nineteenth-century commentators did not usually categorise 'assaults, drunken misbehaviour, etc.' as crime.[44] Local historian John Wootton commented approvingly that only one murder had been recorded in Macclesfield for the first half of the century; yet the newspaper columns give abundant evidence of what might now be called manslaughter, especially in cases of wife-beating and the neglect and abuse of children. The formalisation of the whole process of meting out punishment for 'crime' was a long-term effort drawn out over the whole century. As early as 1820, Tobias points out, it was said that more attention was being paid to crime than in the old days: 'offences which in former times would have been ignored or dealt with on the spot by a ducking or a thrashing . . . were now . . . . being brought before the courts.'[45] In fast-growing industrial towns like Macclesfield petty offences — e.g., pilfering or misbehaviour by apprentices — could take on new and frightening aspects.

In a formerly close-knit community, where the guardians of public order could reasonably expect to know everyone either by direct contact or by reputation, the influx of weavers, factory hands, and casual migrants from as far afield as Dublin and London naturally aroused fear and suspicion. There were dark tales of profligacy and irreligion among the newcomers.[46] The young textile workers who hoped to share in the prosperity of the 1780s and 1790s seemed to their more settled elders 'the thoughtless captives of pleasure', their behaviour characterised by 'unseemly vulgarity, silly levity, and brutal sensuality'.[47] Much of this uneasiness can be attributed to generational conflict. The pool of young residents with no blood relatives in the town was growing just as the pseudo-parental relationship which had bound master and apprentice was disintegrating under new economic pressures.

The administration of justice in the provinces, at least until the eve of the nineteenth century, was primarily the responsibility of lay magistrates operating at the community level. They could expect little interference and less help from national or county authorities, and therefore they needed to tread carefully, respecting (and often reflecting) local prejudices and standards. Quinault has stressed both the inadequacy of resources at the disposal of local justices of the peace, and their isolation from the national government — circumstances which make understandable both the occasional incidents of panicky over-reaction to popular violence and the tendency of some magistrates to show a keen sensitivity to community opinion.[48] The Cheshire historian T.C. Curtis, writing of the seventeenth century, has concluded that the weight of community feeling was a major factor in determining the outcome of legal proceedings, not only at petty sessions but also at the county level.[49] Many of the influences which constrained the Cheshire magistracy in the Stuart period — for example, political and religious prejudice, the weight of kinship and friendship networks, and pressures from powerful economic groups (such as alesellers or large employers of labour) — still held sway in Macclesfield through the eighteenth century and into the nineteenth. Curtis concludes, 'It is evident that the law, and its precise letter, were not viewed in the depths of the country in quite the way that they would have been in King's Bench or the Inns of Court . . . . Local men regarded [the law] less as an unalterable score and more as a theme upon which they could improvise.'[50]

A local outlook prevailed on the bench, but that outlook became an increasingly narrow one. During the first quarter of the nineteenth century the Macclesfield magistracy was drawn heavily from the local élite of well-to-do manufacturers. This meant that in cases involving industrial disputes the ethos of the factory-master was likely to prevail, to the detriment of the artisan and small master. And, at a very rough estimate, it appears that as many as one fifth of the cases at Macclesfield petty sessions in the period 1823 to 1825 (the only years for which there are statistics) involved direct conflict between work-people and employers — over pilfering, neglect of work, short wages, and so on.[51]

The apprehension of wrongdoers in eighteenth-century Macclesfield was the responsibility of one constable and one or two assistants, who in turn relied heavily on information and co-operation from townsfolk. As Curtis puts it, 'The power of neighbourly opinion . . . was deliberately cultivated as a tool of detection.'[52] Even the types of punishment inflicted on offenders reflected the size and intimate nature of the community and the role of public disapproval as a deterrent. Public exposure and humiliation were important remedies against petty crime. Those convicted of petty theft or disturbing the peace might be confined to the stocks or flogged in the market-place. Both men and women were stripped to the waist for flogging and the sentences were generally carried out at noon on Market Day. Culprits were sometimes led through the streets imprisoned in an iron cage which fit closely around the upper body. The town ducking stool and the 'brank' or scold's bridle (a helmet-like iron contrivance which immobilised the tongue) were reserved for female offenders. These instruments of punishment, along with public flogging, remained in use until about 1830, and the stocks at least into the 1840s. The Church also tried, with considerably less success than the civil authorities, to mobilise public outrage against breaches of its moral code. In 1754 couples accused of fornication or adultery were still suffering the traditional punishment of being made to stand in full view of the church congregation draped in sheets, but by this date it is most probable that only a small portion of the community came under the direct influence of such ecclesiastical discipline.[53]

In addition to the machinery of civil and ecclesiastical justice there was a third level of 'policing' rooted in the mores of the community at large. This was the body of customary attitudes and behaviour expressed and enforced by the community itself — the living code which governed day-to-day intercourse. Such pressure could be exerted by parents on children, by neighbours or workmates on each other, and occasionally by mass direct action against someone who had incurred popular displeasure. A man who seriously annoyed his neighbours might find himself followed through the streets by a howling crowd beating on tin vessels, or a notorious adultress might be forced to 'ride the stang', as happened in Rainow village in the 1820s.[54] The informal moral code operated on a more continuous and direct basis than the institutionalised systems of social discipline, but inevitably its (perhaps diminishing) efficacy is difficult to assess.

There has been much scholarly debate about whether or not a sub-class of professional criminals emerged in Victorian Britain, and if there was such a class, what proportion of all crime can be attributed to it.[55] The overall picture is hazy, but it seems that there was some tendency toward professionalisation and increased specialisation in crime in Macclesfield. For some, serious crime was becoming a trade like any other, or at least a steady avocation. We hear more in the nineteenth century about 'bad sets', that is, established gangs or criminal families, specialising in burglary, highway robbery, cheese-stealing, horse thievery, and so on.[56] Early in the century it appeared to local observers that crimes against property increased markedly in times of economic distress; but by the later 1820s the depredations of footpads and gangs of professional thieves and housebreakers seemed to be escalating year by year — with no discernible relationship to economic crises. Newspaper accounts of crime proliferate steadily into the 1820s. No doubt editors were learning to exploit such news for its entertainment value, but the impression of a swelling crime wave was not entirely manufactured. And underdeveloped enforcement procedures were straining the Corporation's ability to maintain social peace.

In-migration and overcrowding created pressures which could transform harmless carousing into destructive rioting, and a population of rootless young workers meant an expanded market for prostitution and gambling.[57] Some neighbourhoods became notorious as the scenes of murderous brawls and vandalism every Saturday night. The slum quarters known as the Dams and the Waters were among the worst, and in Chester Road 'loose characters' carried the noisy revelry over into the Sabbath, to the intense annoyance of churchgoers.[58] In the mid-1820s there were 'nightly broils' in the streets near the new barracks, where soldiers mixed uneasily with the civilian population.[59] Juvenile crime also became a matter of concern in the post-war years. Unoccupied, unsupervised children were suddenly more visible — crowds of howling, dirty urchins beseiged arriving coaches, begging and harassing travellers.[60] The situation was beyond the control of the primitive constabulary, and citizens who complained too loudly were liable to find themselves appointed as special constables and asked to patrol their own premises and streets.

Prostitution, which in the eighteenth century was a rather casual trade, centred in the 'loose' taverns and boarding-houses, later took on a more organised aspect and was carried on in bawdy-houses (often managed by women) and by street-walkers. During Wakes and fairs there was considerable competition from visiting Manchester and Stockport professionals. Among the local street-walkers the trade was sometimes followed by several sisters from one family — or by several generations.[61] Many such families became outcasts, living on the fringe of society, and with long court records involving bastardy, drunkenness, assault, and theft; but some hardy individuals seem to have made the business pay handsomely — notably Sarah Boothby, the town's best-known brothel-keeper.[62]

Underlying much of the crime, poverty, and distress afflicting the town was the pervasive social problem of drunkenness. There is ample evidence that the scourge cut across class lines, but the poor were most likely to end up in court because of it.[63] The vast majority of petty offences — not only arrests for drunkenness, but most assaults, cases of disturbing the peace, vagrancy and some sexual offences — were connected with drinking.

In the eyes of the law, drunkenness (like every other category of crime which could apply to both sexes) was almost entirely a male offence. [See Table IV:2.] How much this sexual imbalance in the statistics of arrests reflects differences in behaviour, and how much is a matter of a disinclination to arrest women, is impossible to say. John Beattie, in an examination of records from Sussex and Surrey, finds that women were far less liable than men to be indicted for serious crimes. When they were involved in such crimes they were often the accomplices of men, and female violence was likely to occur either within the household circle or close to home. In sum, Beattie is inclined to conclude that the low incidence of female crime is attributable less to under-reporting or innate gender differences than to 'the restricted scope of women's lives and the training that shaped them to their social role.'[64] The Macclesfield evidence generally supports this view, but the percentages of female defendants are consistently higher than those he found, indicating that women were more likely to be involved in petty crime than in the major offences studied by Beattie.

Professional expertise developed simultaneously among both criminals and magistrates. During the war years local and county authorities began to try to keep more elaborate dossiers on wrongdoers, and special attention was paid to habitual offenders. But there was still the problem of inadequate resources for enforcement. Sentences, both harsh and mild, were sometimes clearly intended to be minatory. One miscreant might be plucked out of a crowd and made an example. On one occasion in 1828 a gang of rowdies threw acid on the silk gowns of women coming out of St George's Chapel. No one was apprehended on this day, but the magistrates retaliated the following Sabbath by arresting an eighteen-year-old lad, one of a crowd flying pigeons in one of the tenement districts during the hours of divine service, and setting him in the stocks for three hours.[65]

Table IV : 2

Some Petty Offences in Macclesfield, 1823-25[1]

Assault: 574 defendants		
	Male against Male:	331 (Irish: 5)
	Male against Female:	177 (Irish: 6)
	Female against Female:	54 (Irish: 2)
	Female against Male:	12 (Irish: 1)
Disturbing the Peace[2]: 172 defendants		
	Male:	148 (Irish: 9)
	Female:	24 (Irish: 0)
Drunkenness: 184 defendants		
	Male:	162 (Irish: 9)
	Female:	22 (Irish: 3)
Theft: 168 defendants		
	Male:	144 (Irish: 5)
	Female:	24 (Irish: 2)
Vagrancy & Begging: 181 defendants		
	Male:	144 (Irish: 46)
	Female:	37 (Irish: 17)
Neglect of Family or Bastardy (Male): 76		
Bastardy (Female): 14		
Other Sexual Offences:		
Male [Lewdness, Attempted Rape, Indecent Exposure]:		11 (Irish: 0)
Female [Street-walking]:		22 (Irish: 3)

1. *Source:* Compiled from Thomas Allen's Notebook, *c.* 15 March 1823 to 24 June 1825, Macclesfield Public Library. All statistics reflect the number of individuals appearing in court — not the number of convictions or the number of cases. The numbers of Irish refer only to those defendants with clearly identifiable Irish surnames.

   Only selected offences are listed here; the large category related to master/employee relations is excluded, as are market nuisances, and a number of miscellaneous offences ranging from bigamy (1) to deserting the Army (3).
2. Includes 'riotous' or 'disorderly' conduct.

The administration of justice was neither consistent nor impartial. Some offenders were treated lightly. For instance, it was still a common practice in the 1820s, as it had been in the eighteenth century, for local courts to accept gross undervaluations of stolen property, so that the charge could be entered as petty larceny and severe sentences avoided. Some magistrates bypassed the code entirely, and concluded a case with 'settled' or 'defendant admonished'.[66] Outsiders, however, especially Irish, Jews, gypsies and foreigners, remained the objects of special attention and persecution. In 1828 a young navigator was sentenced to a year in prison for stealing a shirt, although, as the *Courier* noted, 'The evidence adduced to identify the prisoner was very slight.' Not long before this a local man had been given the same sentence for beating his wife to death.[67] The harsh sentence of four and a half years' imprisonment for sedition and blasphemy given to Joseph Swann in 1820 was as much a reaction to his dissident reputation as a response to the particular offences cited.

Prejudice against and mistreatment of the Irish was endemic, and quite often the problem was not so much harsh treatment as the unwillingness of officials to take Irish complainants or witnesses seriously.[68] In 1825 an Irishman accusing an Englishman of assault testified that some law officers scoffed at the very idea of taking anyone into custody on the word of an Irishman. The newspapers commented, 'His native brogue excited considerable laughter.'[69] The Englishman was quickly acquitted. Indeed, the treatment of the Irish in court merely reflected widespread ethnic and religious prejudice in the town. The Tory *Courier* summed up the anti-Irish view in an editorial statement of 1826, 'The vices of falsehood and dishonesty — trickery and cheating — idleness and drunkenness, are so universal in Ireland, that the ordinary relations of society scarcely exist in the country.'[70] The point was driven home in dozens of columns of argument against Catholic emancipation. The first generation of Irish to settle in the town — the skilled weavers and spinners who came in the 1790s — were assimilated fairly calmly, and some became respected leaders in the local artisans' movement. But when this group was followed by ever-growing numbers of their impoverished compatriots, and hard times brought fierce competition for jobs, bigotry flared quickly. The *Courier* played upon this tension by using police reports of cases involving the Irish as a kind of comic relief element in its local news columns. Journalists' approximations of verbatim testimony, embellished with facetious description — a man charged with disorderly conduct would be described as 'a lazy, drunken-looking Patlander'[71] — became a regular feature. In contrast, what sketchy information there is on the proportion of Irish actually involved in crime, measured against a rough notion of the percentage of Irish in the total population (about 10 per cent in 1851), suggests that there was no truth to the popular picture of them as criminally inclined. [See Table IV:2.] If the most numerous categories of petty crime are considered, the Irish were over-represented only in vagrancy and begging, reflecting poverty and the fact that so many passed through town as transients.

In the eighteenth century the authorities only rarely resorted to imprisonment for minor crimes. The local jail was apparently a ramshackle affair, capable of holding only a few inmates at a time. It was used for short sentences and for housing vagrants who could not find refuge in the workhouse, and there were frequent complaints of its inadequacy.[72] The jail property was privately owned and leased for some years to a manufacturer, Samuel Lankford, who employed a jailer to oversee the prisoners.[73] After charges by town clerk John Stafford that inmates were being allowed to run about free, the Corporation transferred a number of them to a publicly-owned institution, known as the House of Correction in Dog Lane.[74] By 1790 the old jail-house was in such a dire state of disrepair that the Corporation initiated legal action to force the owner to undertake improvements. Most cases, including those that involved a sentence of hard labour, were sent to the House of Correction at Knutsford, and the most serious offenders, including all those awaiting transportation, were assigned to Chester Castle. Informal pressures and penalties were a constant feature of the penal system. For instance, five Macclesfield prisoners were held at Chester Castle an average of seventy-seven days before being brought to trial in 1832; the delay alone worked a severe hardship on any working man or woman with a family to support.[75]

During much of the period law enforcement was entrusted to a single constable, with occasional part-time assistance. The constable was forced to rely heavily on informers and the support of private citizens. Night-watchmen, stationed at several posts around the town, also supplemented the constable's efforts. As the population grew, and with it the incidence of crime, it was sometimes found necessary to resort to temporary citizens' patrols. Private associations of property-owners were formed to reward zeal in capturing law-breakers, and vigilante groups walked the streets after dark in times of unrest. During the Luddite scare of 1812, for instance, a 300-member corps was organised, serving in rotation, with ten groups of six men patrolling the streets each night.[76]

Like most small provincial towns, Macclesfield remained suspicious of the concept of a permanent, professional police force. Though the London force was organised in 1829, a combination of fiscal caution and fear of oppression blocked local efforts to reform the constabulary. The Municipal Corporations Act of 1835 provided the first impetus toward change; under its provisions the town was obliged to appoint a Watch Committee which, in turn, would appoint 'fit men' to act as constables, these to be paid out of the rates. There was to be a chief constable, with four day officers and two night officers under him, and four part-time officers for duty on Saturday nights and special occasions.[77] These men were to be provided with uniforms modelled on those of the London force. This was the core of the modern police force — though the idea continued to generate hostility for many years.[78]

Before the creation of a professional police force the town's only recourse in times of crisis, or seeming crisis, was to call on the military. The mayor of Macclesfield on several occasions appealed to the Lord Lieutenant of Cheshire for such aid, and a troop of cavalry or company of militia would be sent. After several instances of serious rioting in the years 1817 to 1819 and some difficulties occasioned by the need for billeting troops in private dwellings or lodging houses, the Corporation in 1820 agreed to pay rent for a temporary barracks for the troops in times of emergency and built a permanent barracks a few years later.

To supplement the strength of the county military forces a troop of Macclesfield Yeomanry and two volunteer foot regiments were organised. Originally formed in response to the supposed threat of French invasion in the late 1790s, the Yeomanry operated with varying degrees of efficiency — often exciting more hostility than it quelled and becoming the special object of reprisals from the rioting population. The foot regiments, the Macclesfield Volunteers under Col. Davies Davenport of Capesthorn and the

Macclesfield Loyal Foresters under silk throwster Jasper Hulley of Macclesfield, were a creation of the Tory faction and enjoyed the patronage of the Established Church.[79] The Revd David Davies, headmaster of the Grammar School, acted as military chaplain, and Volunteer reviews were occasions for ultra-patriotic oratory and declarations of devotion to the royal family.[80] Enthusiasm waned after the Peace of 1802, however, and both units were disbanded temporarily in 1805.

During the disturbances of 1812 panic and rumours of revolution again reached a high pitch. Government informants, like John Lloyd, clerk to the magistrates at Stockport, described a climate of extreme tension; apparently relying on hearsay, Lloyd wrote of Macclesfield that it was 'a nest of illicit association'.[81] But the spies seem to have exaggerated. The reports which reached the Home Office directly from Macclesfield indicate that the town strongly preferred to rely on local vigilante patrols rather than endure the continued presence of troops. Innkeepers and butchers made complaints about billeting, and the mayor asked that troops be redeployed to surrounding villages, which, he said, were the real hotbeds of disaffection.[82] F.O. Darvall's contention — also supported by the work of George Rudé and Eric Hobsbawm — that Luddite violence was a variable phenomenon, locally based and for the most part locally motivated, is also true of wartime political and economic violence in Macclesfield.[83] The rioting that occurred in the town in April 1812 was short-lived, and the crowd, after engaging in some window-breaking and looting of food shops, turned to settling scores with a few unpopular employers and magistrates. All accounts of the disturbances suggest that the bulk of the participants were local people — for example, they knew very well how to elude the pursuing cavalry by ducking down narrow alleyways or leading the horses into impassable stony fields.[84] Purposive mass violence often gained its limited objects: for example, in the 1811 break-in at the town jail, aimed at destroying records, or the radical demonstrations of 1812 and 1819 when crowds assembled to rescue prisoners taken into custody by the military.

Sometimes the course of a riot revealed divergent tendencies within the working classes, as in March 1826 when Parliament's latest failure to alleviate distress in the silk industry set off four days of vandalism and random attacks on prosperous-looking citizens. The handloom weavers' Committee joined shopkeepers and other small masters in asking to be sworn in as special constables. The outburst was finally quelled, with the help of troops from Manchester. Yet only two months later, in May, a more serious, disciplined outbreak of violence occurred, with more class solidarity in evidence. On 2 May a crowd of 2000 to 3000 gathered outside Mr Waters' cotton mill in Crompton Road, where about 130 power looms had recently been installed and a troop of Yeomanry was standing guard. Windows were smashed, the soldiers stoned, and the door to the mill forced open. Thirty special constables soon arrived, followed by the mayor and a troop of cavalry. The angry crowd was subdued with difficulty and three youths captured in the mill — with only one loom slightly damaged. On the following day there were rumours of impending attacks on other power-loom mills in the vicinity. A partial curfew was imposed and some millowners distributed firearms to their servants. The Revd W.C. Cruttenden, a magistrate, addressed a large crowd in the market-place and induced them to disperse quietly. The 2nd of May disturbance was clearly motivated by widespread fear of worsening unemployment, compounded perhaps by hostility to the recent-immigrant cotton-workers employed in Waters' mill. On this occasion there was no active popular opposition to the protest and no published disavowal by the Weavers' Committee.[85]

It is by no means apparent that the threat of military intervention acted as an effective deterrent to violence; once rioting had begun, however, the troops successfully prevented its spread on several occasions. Even an escalation of military force could not always guarantee that working-class rebellion would be extinguished. In 1829, when there was a violent turn-out of weavers protesting low wages and high food prices, a company of Grenadier Guards and the 80th Regiment of Foot were stationed in the town. The troops were armed and special constables sworn in to assist them, but these preparations did not keep the turn-outs from smashing windows and invading several factories. Later, when a Guards unit from Manchester and a company of Foot from Stockport were brought in the violence abated, but the strikers went on to hold parades and demonstrations for two more days.[86] Again, in 1832, a very violent weavers' strike lasting for seven weeks resulted in complete victory for the men.

Authorities expressed some doubts about the reliability of locally recruited troops, and this is hardly surprising. They came mostly from the poorest sections of the population and often had ties of kinship or friendly sympathy with local rioters. A majority of those serving in both the regular forces and the county militia were paid substitutes for those who had been balloted; thus, most of those serving from rural districts in hard times were actually unemployed textile workers or labourers from the larger towns.[87] The term of service for the county militia was five years, and men between eighteen and forty-five were eligible (with several exempt categories).[88] An alternative form of service was the local militia, in which the term was four years and men eighteen to thirty were eligible. There were always more volunteers for the local militia, but this poorly-trained corps was of little practical use — the County Lieutenancy cautiously recommended that the annual exercises of the local militia be cancelled in 1812, 'owing to the disturbed state of the Country.'[89]

Recruiting officers took full advantage of economic distress, but one eighteen-year-old expressed a prevalent attitude when he said that 'he still had three days a week work and that was better than "listing".'[90] Eligible men who could not afford the substitute payment — usually about £30, paid in instalments[91] — sometimes clubbed together, paying a few pence a time into a kitty which would be given to any member whose name was picked. He could then either keep the money and serve or use it to pay a replacement.[92] Wives of serving men received a small weekly allowance administered by the Overseers of the Poor.[93]

Like the later hostility to the New Poor Law Bastilles, a generalised dislike of the idea of a standing army was common at all levels of Macclesfield society. After Peterloo, Sir John Leicester, a keen supporter of the military in Cheshire, tried to promote a second infantry troop for Macclesfield, but nothing came of the proposal. John Ryle, speaking for the propertied interest of the town, said that there was no further danger.[94] The establishment of a permanent barracks in 1826 did nothing to enhance the popularity of the military. There were frequent complaints of rowdy behaviour by soldiers and dark tales of both heterosexual and homosexual offences (leading to blackmail and other unsavoury consequences).[95]

It would appear, then, that the increase of crime and violence accompanying industrialisation in Macclesfield was largely a matter of petty offences — spawned by overcrowding, poverty, ethnic prejudice, and the new geographical mobility. When the problem, already beyond the control of the antiquated enforcement machinery available to the Corporation, was exacerbated by periodic outbreaks of politically motivated violence, the military was called in to defend property and class privilege. Military force filled a temporary vacuum in local police capacity and taught some hard lessons, although there was always a good deal of ambivalence about its use, even among the town's élite. Unquestionably the growing military presence in the town and county during the first decades of the nineteenth century, reinforced by an increasingly employer-dominated judiciary, weighed heavily on working-class efforts at self-assertion and political expression. And when the military receded, its place would be taken by the new police force. Still, it is as difficult to see any serious degree of 'Prussianisation' of provincial English society here as it is to detect an insurrectionary element in the Macclesfield riots of the 1820s. There was no question of a breakdown of local or national authority; in Macclesfield on the eve of Reform the barricades were nowhere in sight.

III

As was the case with changes in the political and peace-keeping machinery of the town, transformations in social activity occurred piecemeal, without sharp breaks or wrenching attacks on past practice. There was a constant intermingling of older customs with new elements; generally speaking, the round of public recreations and festivals continued in its traditional pattern. But surface continuities masked some distinct shifts in economic and social relations. Events often retained their time-honoured form, but under new auspices; the annual 'walks' and tavern dinners of benefit clubs, fraternal organisations, and chapel societies, for example, preserved most of the features of the old artisans' guild holidays.[96] In the cornerstone-laying ceremonies for the New Town Hall in 1823 new social groupings, the Methodists, the Masons, and the King and Constitution Club, joined the members of the Corporation in a procession through the streets. To the accompaniment of a band playing patriotic tunes they passed through a triumphal arch and ascended a platform. There they watched as the Worshipful Master of one of the Masonic Lodges performed the ancient ritual of spreading corn, oil, and wine on the cornerstone, while pronouncing a benediction.[97]

Urbanisation meant the disappearance of communal open spaces previously used for pastimes which had tended to bring townspeople of various social levels together in easy intercourse. Among the old sports and gambling games which had afforded some opportunity for the mingling of classes, bowling was one of the most popular. In the early eighteenth century bowling greens dotted the county, and members of the gentry and clergy joined merchants and farmers at play. Cock-fighting and bull- and bear-baiting also attracted large crowds, until public disapproval began to drive them underground in the early nineteenth century.[98] In 1789 the Macclesfield magistrates, at the prompting of the Crown, resolved to refuse a licence to any publican who encouraged mountebanks, persons travelling with an unlicenced show or lottery, cock-fights, animal-baiting, or illegal horse racing — but all these diversions hung on.[99] The more disreputable traditional pursuits seem to have moved outward from Macclesfield to small villages and rural areas, away from the vigilance of Corporation authorities.[100]

It was said that the Reverend John Browne of Prestbury, the kindly magistrate known as 'the weavers' friend', was so fond of the old sports that he had the greatest difficulty making his way to church on Sunday past the bear-baiting outside a local public house.[101]

Folk customs harking back to ancient agricultural rituals naturally lost some of their force in an industrialising setting, or they were adapted to new conditions of life. The old Cheshire practice of soul-caking (probably traceable to a Roman harvest/fertility rite), wherein a troop of mummers wandered singing and begging from door to door on All Hallow's Eve, fell prey to the confusions of town life; there were stories of 'soulers' harassing potential donors, or of brawls between rival troops of singers and unseemly carousing in public houses.[102]

As some recreations linked with the rural past began to fade, others were reorganised on more modern lines. The Macclesfield Hunt, in existence for seventy years, was broken up in May 1825, the 'increase of operatives and the great decrease of country having rendered such a measure necessary.'[103] Devoted members were obliged to turn to one of the larger and more gentrified county hunts. The old open-field horse-races were likewise replaced by an official Macclesfield Race Meeting, a three-day event with stewards, judges and substantial prize-money. Beginning at the Wakes in 1828, the races became an annual event, drawing spectators from a wide area. Small-scale agricultural competitions, like the popular flower shows, usually devoted to one species only and held in public houses, were taken over by committees and societies. There was a move in 1828 to amalgamate several of these groups into one Floral and Horticultural Society.[104]

Wakes and fairs were the festive high points of the year. As the town grew, these too became more elaborate and commercialised, the province of professional hucksters and entertainers. Barnaby Fair in June and the Wakes, in October, were important regional trading fairs, accompanied by unbridled drinking and gambling — perhaps a prize-fight and some horse-races in the town field, all enlivened by wandering troops of musicians and acrobats. The fairground in Waters Green was filled with stalls offering cheap toys, candy, fruits and nuts — and the ribbons, scarves, and combs that hopeful swains presented to their sweethearts (the courting couples called these tokens 'fairings'). Half a dozen bands blared in competition with each other and with side-show barkers offering glimpses of genuine wild beasts from Africa, giants, dwarfs and living skeletons, or a marionette show for only a penny. The more affluent could visit a large wooden booth serving as a theatre, where a programme featuring three murders and a ghost, a pantomime, and several comic songs was performed by 'London actors of great eminence'.[105] The crowds of young workers and farmers with six months' savings in pocket and a mind to enjoy themselves naturally attracted pick-pockets, fortune-tellers, card-sharps, and prostitutes from several counties.[106]

It proved easier for professional entrepreneurs to take over and transform traditional pastimes like Wakes or horse-races than it was to stimulate support for commercially-based cultural novelties. For example, several attempts to open a permanent theatre in town met with only meagre success. A wooden playhouse built in Chestergate in 1770 attracted some notable travelling companies; but the enterprise foundered, thanks in part to the hostility of local clergy led by the Revd David Simpson, who thundered against playgoing from his Christ Church pulpit. Working conditions were dismal enough for the visiting actors. One described a 1795 performance of *The School for Scandal* starring the beautiful Harriet Mellon thus: 'The dressing rooms were the stalls of a stable, and the roof so bad, they had pattens and umbrellas to walk to the wings; the people in the pit called for blankets to keep them from catching cold.'[107] The Theatre Royal in Mill Street, reopened for several years in 1811, and refurbished and opened again in 1824, tried to offer programmes varied enough to appeal to every taste. A selection from Shakespeare might be followed by a comic song, an acrobatic display, a 'Laughable Farce', a hornpipe, and a pantomime to close.[108] Every member of the struggling proprietor's family would be pressed into service, and visiting artists were given glowing publicity (anyone who had ever played in London was announced as a star of the metropolis), but audiences were thin. Between dramatic performances the building was let out for pugilistic exhibitions, amateur concerts, and scientific shows. There was regular — and cheap — competition from travelling circuses and performers like one Ingleby, Senior, 'the Emperor and Father of All Conjurors', who promised to smash a watch into twenty pieces and restore it again, and to catch a bullet fired by any gentleman's pistol in his mouth.[109] A serious Choral Society, founded in 1816, faltered on until at least 1826 — though attendance was poor; and an amateur Thespian Club flickered briefly into existence in the mid-1820s.[110]

Douglas Reid has described the conjoined influences of urbanisation, evangelicalism, commercial considerations, more efficient policing, and the emergence of an artisan subculture of respectability in subduing 'carnivalesque' elements in the older popular culture.[111] Both Peter Bailey and Hugh Cunningham, in studies of leisure and industrialisation, acknowledge the subtle complexity of this process, and the surprising tenacity of customary pleasures. As Cunningham puts it:

> There is no 'vacuum' in the history of popular recreations. In the first place many 'traditional' sports and customs survived much longer than one might suppose, sometimes after their demise had been celebrated. Secondly, recreations which were threatened in one form could evolve; in particular a number

> of sports, previously dependent on the patronage of the rich, learned to survive and even grow when that patronage was withdrawn. And thirdly, and most important, new forms of recreation were being created and invented. The outcome was an efflorescence of popular leisure . . . which begins to make intelligible the virulence of the campaign that was mounted against it.[112]

Both the gradual commercialisation of leisure activity and the proliferation of clubs and societies contributed to a drawing apart of the upper and lower classes into separate social spheres. Leisure pursuits, always quite sharply segregated by sex, became more segregated by wealth and social status. While the small master might continue to mingle with his journeymen and apprentices around the tavern banquet table, the owner of a large factory was more and more likely to socialise with his own kind. Macclesfield's élite enjoyed an increasingly elaborate round of balls and private parties; their daughters' gentility was enhanced by the attentions of dancing and music masters imported from Liverpool, and their sons could gain polish by participation in a select Conversation Society, founded in about 1800. Members of the Society gathered to debate such questions as, 'Whether very Extensive Dominions at a distance from the Ruling State will probably be of service or disservice to such states', or 'Whether the Hypocrite or the openly Profligate be the worse character'.[113]

In what might be called the middling ranks — the social level occupied by tradesmen, small masters, and the less successful professional men — the organised activities associated with Church and chapel tended to be especially attractive. For the more secularly inclined, the Masons' lodges, by the early nineteenth century, began to take over some of the functions of the old masters' associations and guilds. Several lodges had been started up and then extinguished during the eighteenth century, but the Masons did not become well established in Macclesfield until the 1790s.[114] Like the chapel societies, many lodges had as their basis kinship or friendship groupings, and there are indications that some lodges were differentiated by occupational level. For example, Lodges 107 and 189 in 1799 had memberships composed mainly of artisans, while the majority of members of Lodge 454 were merchants or innkeepers.[115]

For the working classes, as has been shown, the pub was the

pivot of male social interaction. Each had its special character and its place in a hierarchy of inns, taverns, and lowly beer-houses. There were grand establishments like the Macclesfield Arms or the Angel Inn, catering for well-to-do travellers and civic balls and dinners; lesser hostelries like the Bull's Head and the Queen's Head, the favourites of visiting merchants and traders in the market; and others that served particular trades. The Irish had their favourite houses, as did the soldiers and the navvies. Fiddlers, ballad-singers, those who were fond of dancing, the confraternities of gamblers and petty thieves and prostitutes — each group had its chosen gathering places. The Hen and Chickens and the Swan with Two Necks were known for their radical atmosphere, while the Old King's Arms, kept by John Cruttenden Lea in the 1830s and 1840s, was notoriously Tory. Lea would not serve either Irish customers or Irish whiskey, and it was said that when he was once offered a note from (Whig) Brocklehurst's Bank over the bar he exploded, 'Tak it off. I'll have nowt o' Brocklehurst's here.'[116]

Many employers and clergymen, and others as well, were alarmed at the lure the pub culture exerted over the working classes. An ambitious undertaking, promoted by upper- and middle-class patrons anxious to undermine the pubs' influence and provide 'rational entertainment' for the respectable working classes, was the Macclesfield Society for Useful Knowledge, founded in 1835. Patterned after the Mechanics' Institutes established in so many northern cities during this period, it aimed at drawing together a number of small self-improvement classes that had already been initiated by skilled workers in Macclesfield. Such self-generated activity, the organisers argued, should be brought under the control of an over-arching Institute, with the sponsorship of 'influential gentlemen'.[117] Advocates of the Society urged the need to keep teen-age workers off the streets at night, and hoped that opportunities for direct social contact would reduce barriers and misunderstanding between classes.[118] One letter-writer to the *Courier* in 1835 expressed the hope that the Society could provide a counterweight to the 'convivial societies' so prevalent among the working classes.[119] Among the attractive features of the new institution was a library of two hundred volumes, the first public provision of reading matter for the working classes in Macclesfield.[120] Still, from the outset the Society had to struggle against the indifference of many employers and the suspicion of many working men. As in other Mechanics' Institutes all discussion of politics and theology was strictly banned, and the 'introduction of infidel principles' was specifically interdicted.[121] But there were persistent charges that the Society undermined religion. It proved difficult to raise the necessary annual operating budget of about £150, and by 1837 only 211 students were registered. Evidently the Society never reached large enough numbers of working men, for long enough periods, to make any appreciable difference in class feeling.

It should not be surprising that one of the most popular features of the Society was its library. Advances in literacy, due largely to the Sunday schools, had created a hunger for printed matter of all kinds. The appearance of a local newspaper marked a certain coming-of-age in the town's public life. Macclesfield's first paper, the weekly *Courier*, brought out its inaugural issue in February 1811. Published by bookseller and printer Jonathan Wilson with the backing of two attornies, a cotton-spinner, and an ironmonger, the *Courier* adhered to Tory principles. Though the cost was high, 6½*d* for four pages, it enjoyed a reasonable success at first. Setting its columns of national and international news, mostly culled from metropolitan papers and official reports, against anecdotes of the proceedings of the mayor's court and reports from the local markets and auction-rooms, the *Courier* helped readers to place Macclesfield in a larger context. Even a political opponent like John Corry could concede the paper's substantial contributions to general knowledge and to 'the mutual convenience and advantage . . . of all persons engaged in public business.'[122]

The taste of the lower classes for information in printed form was encouraged by hawkers of unstamped almanacs and pamphlets (some used the ploy of 'selling straws and giving books'[123]), prints and broadsheets (sometimes pornographic in nature). Religious societies competed with this tide of illicit reading matter by distributing thousands of inexpensive tracts, sermons, cards, and pictures. Still, in unsettled times there was suspicion of the stimulation a book or newspaper might bring — be the publisher ever so Tory. During the disturbances of 1812 a local cotton manufacturer confided to his diary, 'I am aware I shall be greatly misled, without care, in paying too much attention to newspapers.

I never subscribed a farthing towards one in my life, and I perceive it is a captivating thing since the country has been in such agitation, and murders and depredations committed . . . [people] have become so fond of hearing and reading news that they have ventured to take a glass in the Bar of an Inn, to see a favourite paper . . .'[124] The diarist was far from being alone in finding cause for trepidation in the march of Progress.

V

The Evangelical Revolution

The most profound and noticeable change in the cultural landscape of Macclesfield between 1750 and 1830 occurred not in the social or political sphere but in religious life. In the 1750s the town, with a population of more than 5000, supported only one church and two tiny Nonconformist chapels (a legacy of the seventeenth century). But, as John Corry noted approvingly, by 1817 there were ten well-established places of worship for a population of 14,000 — several of them rivalling the venerable Anglican Church of St Michael in size. This effervescence of spirituality, which critical contemporaries were inclined to see as an outbreak of vulgar 'enthusiasm', was given lasting institutional form through earnest teaching and preaching, both within and outside the Anglican fold.

The religious revival chronologically paralleled the rise of the new factory-based industrial economy, and the shaping influence of evangelicalism is reflected in the educational, philanthropic, and political developments of the period. Yet the precise nature of the relationship between religious and socio-economic developments in the making of modern class society in Britain remains obscure. It will be the purpose of this chapter first to trace the growth of the Wesleyan Methodist Society and other religious bodies offering a challenge to the Establishment, then to consider in detail the personal and social consequences of evangelicalism in the life of the community, and finally to assess the impact of religious revival considered as one factor in the complex process which brought the town, by slow stages, from an agriculture-based village to a modern commerical urban centre. In all of these themes the story of the growth of Methodism will occupy centre stage. The whole of the period considered here fell within the 'heroic' expansive phase of the Society's history. East Cheshire was one of the areas which embraced John Wesley's teaching earliest and most fervently, and in Macclesfield, where Wesley preached many times, it was the Methodists who reaped the largest share of the new harvest of souls.

Without detracting from John Wesley's creative dynamism, it can be said that the new teaching filled what almost amounted to a spiritual vacuum. The diocese of Chester was enormous and poorly served.[1] Of its many eighteenth-century bishops, most held other appointments to supplement their relatively meagre income, and two were non-resident, as were many of the lower clergy. The sprawling parish of Prestbury had only one third as many Anglican chapels as there were townships. When Wesley first came to Macclesfield in 1745 he found a community in which the Established Church was slumbering — comfortably, perhaps, but rather ineffectually as far as most of the population was concerned.

Macclesfield St Michael's, a parochial chapel, was better served than many Cheshire churches, perhaps because its incumbents were closely bound to the will of the town's leading residents. There was a prime curate, appointed by the mayor, and an assistant curate, elected by the Corporation. Customarily the two curates divided the duties, preaching at alternate services. These unusual arrangements resulted in some conflict when an evangelical 'party' grew up in the town. But before the storm of controversy broke more than one of the local clergy resembled George Slater's picture of the archetypal Cheshire vicar of the old school — corpulent and convivial, always ready for an Irish jig or a hornpipe with the servant maids at Harvest festival, a good schoolmaster, not particularly religious but beloved.[2]

A series of undistinguished incumbents held the office of prime curate of St Michael's through the eighteenth century.[3] The best known of these was James Roe (served 1756 to 1765), elder brother of industrialist Charles Roe. A likeable, well-educated man of moderate attainments, he was tolerant but entirely conventional in his views. He was also a pluralist, almost by necessity, as the living of St Michael's was worth only fifty guineas a year in his time;[4] still, after his appointment he always resided in the town. Roe was suceeded by John Burscoe (served 1765 to 1773), a shadowy individual who had previously been assistant curate for more than thirty years. Burscoe filled his new post inconspicuously, in contrast to his successor, Thomas Hewson (served 1773 to 1778). Hewson, a rather unpolished cleric of irascible temper, was a jealous guardian of the perquisities of his office. It was his misfortune to inherit as his young assistant the popular, controversial David Simpson (appointed 1772), who was to do so much to foster evangelical, and particularly Methodist, influences in the town. John Lingard (served 1778 to 1799) seems to have satisfied a bishop and Corporation anxious to avoid enthusiasm and innovation. Lawrence Heapy and William Cruttenden Cruttenden, who served between 1800 and 1847, filled their office with somewhat more energy than their predecessors. Both were zealous Tories and active in town affairs, but they had little success in stemming the tide of Dissent.

By the mid-eighteenth century the fabric of St Michael's Church, which had reached a state of considerable dilapidation, was being repaired and extended. But even so, the church could have provided accommodation for only a small proportion of the town's population, even if it had been full for every service, which was far from the case. For poorer inhabitants pew rents would have posed an obstacle to attendance. Pews were held on a kind of lease arrangement and could be transferred from one owner to another with the approval of the congregation. Only about a quarter of the available space consisted of 'free sittings', towards the back of the church, for servants and the labouring population.[5] While the new Methodist and Dissenting congregations could by no means afford to do away with charges for seats, they did offer more free space and a sliding scale of charges, varying with the level of social aspiration (or ideology) of each chapel. [See Table V:2.]

I

Between 1750 and 1830 Methodism, a novel system of belief and practice developing within the Anglican communion, gained many of its followers from the emerging industrial middle and working classes.[6] Its origins as a sub-group within the Established Church, its increasingly centralised and authoritarian national structure,

Table V : 1

Membership of Macclesfield Nonconformist Chapels, 1829[1]

Macclesfield Township:	
Sunderland Street (Wesleyan Methodist)	700
Broken Cross (Wesleyan)	50
Parsonage Street (Methodist New Connexion)	250
Bunkers Hill (Primitive Methodist)	90
King Edward Street (Unitarian)	100
Townley Street (Calvinist)	300[2]
Roe Street (Indep. Calvinist)	300
Chester Road (Catholic)	1000
Common Street (General Baptist)	106
Dams Street (Particular Baptist)	20
Mill Street (Society of Friends)	40
Total number of members:	2956
(Total population, at 1831 Census: 23,129)	
Sutton:	
Brunswick Chapel (Wesleyan)	550
Langley Lane (Wesleyan)	60
Hollin Lane Chapel (Wesleyan)	50
Lane End Chapel (Methodist New Connexion)	60
Total number of members:	720
Hurdsfield:[3]	
Wesleyan Methodists	550
Baptists	60
Catholics	120
Unitarians	7

1. *Source:* CRO, QDR, Miscellaneous Documents Relating to Nonconformists (3 boxes), 'Returns of Nonconformists, 1829', estimates gathered by William Lockett, Constable.
2. There may be some confusion here between 'membership' and attendance; the Townley Street Chapel itself was only claiming 61 members in 1830; see [W. Urwicke, ed.], *Historical Sketches of Nonconformity in Cheshire* (London: Keat & Co., 1864) p. 64.
3. It is not clear from the source document whether these rough figures for Hurdsfield refer to chapels located there or to residents, who may also have been counted as part of the membership of Macclesfield chapels.

Table V : 2

Attendance at some Macclesfield Churches and Chapels March 1851[1]

	Morning	Evening
St Michael's Church (Anglican)	465	343
free sittings 439, other 1,232	150[2]	
	615	
Christ Church (Anglican)	350	400
free 600, other 1,000	300	150
	650	550
Sunderland Street (Wesleyan)	339	507
free 342, other 532	161	
	500	
Brunswick Chapel (Wesleyan)	470	700
free 300, other 700	280	
	750	
St Alban's Church (Catholic)	737	688
free 600, other 140, standing room 300	253	192
	990	800
Park Street Chapel (Methodist New	255	424
Connexion) free 400, other 800	136	110
	391	534
Fence School, Hurdsfield (Methodist New	72	260
Connexion) free 250, other 600	314	
	386	
Primitive Methodist Chapel	150	200
free 182, other 168	180	
	330	

Table V:2 continued

Townley Street Chapel (Independent)	260	255
free 150, other 500	40	
	300	
Roe Street Chapel (Independent)	195	238
free 132, other 500, standing room 250	55	
	250	
General Baptist Chapel	90	200
free 100, other 400	70	
	160	
Mill Street (Quaker)	37	21
seats 230		
King Edward Street (Unitarian)	70	200
free 100, other 250	80	100
	150	300

1. *Source:* P.P. 1852-53, LXXXIX, 'Census of Religious Worship, 1851', enumerators' returns for Macclesfield Township; copy in CRO, Mf 11/1.

   For purposes of comparison with Table V:1, only those congregations which were in existence before 1835 are listed here. Many congregations complained that attendance was lower than usual because of bad weather, special programmes put on by rival chapels, etc.
2. The second figure in all cases indicates Sunday school children.

and its predominantly conservative political stance inclined the Connexion towards social quietism; at the same time its association with Dissent, its stress on personal salvation and personal improvement through education, and its social welfare projects stimulating local chapel initiative exerted an opposite pull. Only through a close analysis of this inner tension, and the schisms which resulted from it, can the genesis of those familiar Victorian figures, the Methodist factory-master, the Methodist trade-unionist, and the Methodist radical, be understood.

In East Cheshire, as in many other areas evangelised by Wesley, Methodism first took hold in the outlying districts, away from the institutional strongholds of Anglicanism and the prying eyes of Church authorities. Rural prayer meetings like those conducted by itinerant preacher John Bennet of Chinley at the home of Mary Aldersley in Higher Hurdsfield became the nucleus of the first Methodist groups in the area. Worshippers walked from great distances to attend these gatherings, and travelled even farther, into neighbouring counties, for the chance of hearing Wesley himself. The occasion of Wesley's first visit to the Macclesfield area, on 8 November 1745, was probably an invitation to preach to the modest conventicle in Higher Hurdsfield.[7]

The founder of Macclesfield Methodism was George Pearson, an uneducated tailor whose sons and grandsons were to become magnates of the new silk industry and mayors of the town.[8] Pearson was converted in 1746 and in 1747 walked to Manchester to hear Wesley and to persuade him to return to Macclesfield. A few days later Wesley preached outdoors near Pearson's house on Waters Green and authorised Pearson to become a Methodist Class Leader. Wesley himself did not visit again until 1759, when he had considerable difficulty subduing the unruly populace who gathered to hear him. He noted in his *Journal*: 'Abundance of people ran together, but wild as colts and untamed. Their noise quite drowned my voice at first but in a while they were tolerably quiet, and before I had done all but four or five lubberly men seemed almost persuaded to be Christians.'[9] The early class meetings organised by George Pearson were also beset by disruptive mobs, who occasionally broke his windows and threatened to burn down the house.

In Wesley's train came other revivalist preachers like John Oldham, who conducted a prayer-meeting in 1762 and produced a huge outpouring of that emotional zeal which so readily aroused the suspicion of the orthodox clergy. Oldham's hearers gave out 'loud and bitter cries' and 'shouts of gladness' and remained praying and weeping through the night.[10] The 'Divine Visitation' lasted eight days and resulted in forty conversions. Oldham's was only the first of several such revivals and camp meetings (sometimes led by American preachers) to sweep the town in the next few decades; after the first flashes of exultation subsided there would be some 'falling away' of souls, but many stayed on as new recruits for the local chapels.

The first public meeting-place of the Macclesfield Methodists was a converted stable on the eastern edge of town. Then, in about 1750, a cottage was rented on a forty-year lease in the names of Pearson and Elizabeth Clulow, wife of a baker and mother of John Clulow, solicitor and Town Clerk. She was only one of a number of pious and strong-minded women who became pillars of early Methodism throughout England. Neither her husband nor her son shared her strong formal commitment to the Society, but John Clulow the younger remained close to the Methodists and represented them professionally on many occasions. An elder son, William, likewise sympathetic to the Society, became a solicitor in London and drew up John Wesley's will as well as other documents establishing the legal framework of the Connexion.

As the Methodists grew steadily, not only in numbers but in worldly prosperity, popular violence against them abated. By 1764, largely through the generosity of a well-to-do sympathiser, Alderman John Ryle, whose mother was an early member of the Society, they were in possession of their own meeting-house in Commercial Road.[11] By 1779 they were ready to construct a much larger building, known as 'Wesley's Chapel' in Sunderland Street. This stark, graceless building, crowded between silk factories and warehouses in a narrow street off Waters Green, remained the 'mother church' and main bastion of Macclesfield Methodism, and had to be considerably enlarged within only a few years. From the start all of the dozen or more trustees of Sunderland Street Chapel were leading factory-owners, substantial merchants, or prominent professional men.[12] In 1787 Wesley found 'a people still alive to God, in spite of swiftly-increasing riches', and he warned them of the pitfalls.[13] Beside uplifting accounts of poverty meekly borne there were to be more and more Methodist memoirs and obituaries in which worldly success and godliness were comfortably intertwined. One of many Macclesfield examples is the story of Joshua Thorley (1748-1848), who rose from poor widow's boy to wealthy grocer, Steward and Trustee.[14]

The Chapel itself was rapidly paying off its debts and improving its facilities. The Wesleyans adopted the Anglican practice of collecting pew rents, and the income from this source alone was about £40 per quarter in the 1790s, rising to about £60 in the 1820s. There was growing attention to the outward trappings of respectability, and a small dark section of seats (called the 'Nicodemus Corner') was set aside at the back of the chapel to accommodate those whose shabby clothes might have embarrassed them before the other worshippers.[15]

Macclesfield became part of the earliest Wesleyan circuits in the North-west, and by 1770 was the head of its own large circuit, extending into Staffordshire and Derbyshire. The circuit claimed 1380 members by 1782.[16] At the turn of the century small meeting-places dotted the surrounding countryside — reaching to the remote hillside farms of Billinge Brow, and to hamlets like Pott Shrigley and Broken Cross. Chapels had also been established in nearby towns, at Bollington, Congleton, and even Prestbury, on the very doorstep of a decayed parochial authority. By 1814 Macclesfield was the head of a district comprised of nine separate circuits.

The expansion of itinerant preaching brought a succession of young and ambitious preachers to the town, among them some who were destined to become central figures in the national history of Methodism. Jabez Bunting the iron-willed president of Conference who became known as 'The Methodist Pope', was appointed to the circuit as a young man in 1802 and chose a bride from Macclesfield.

As important as the Wesleyan preachers to the success of evangelical revivalism was David Simpson, a lifelong Anglican, but with strong 'Methodistical leanings'. Simpson was a commanding figure, even as a young man — a compelling preacher, an energetic philanthropist and patron of popular education, a leader in civic life, and a staunch protector of the rights of those Nonconformists whose teaching he found compatible with Anglican doctrine.[17] His career reflects the heart-searching and uncertainty that the Wesleyan challenge to traditionalism produced in many individuals. Tutored in his youth by schoolmasters of various Nonconformist tendencies, Simpson as an adult shared to a large extent the outlook and theology of Wesley. He was apparently introduced to Methodist ideas and practices at St John's College, Cambridge, where he met Charles Whitefield and other 'enthusiasts'. He experienced conversion at the age of twenty-four, while still at college and under the influence of the Revd John Berridge, a fellow of Clare Hall and a strong evangelical who eventually became an itinerant, and the Revd Theophilus Lindsey, a St

John's alumnus, who later became a Unitarian.[18]

Simpson's ordination followed, and he spent a brief unhappy period as curate in Buckingham, where he met intense hostility to his evangelical doctrines. Still chafing from his inconclusive trials at Buckingham, he removed in 1773 to Macclesfield to take up the post of assistant curate at St Michael's and was soon embroiled in similar controversies.

Simpson found in his superior, the Revd Thomas Hewson, an implacable foe. By custom the two curates divided the duties of the church, but Hewson soon expressed his resentment and disapproval of Simpson by excluding the younger man from preaching. This breach of tradition caused an uproar in the congregation, followed by negotiations and a promise from Hewson that Simpson would be readmitted. The promise was soon violated — causing a noisy mob to follow Hewson to his home after the service. No permanent solution was forthcoming, and Hewson's supporters eventually submitted a list of complaints against Simpson to the Bishop of Chester, who replied by temporarily suspending Simpson from preaching.[19] The young curate's defiant response was to travel around the district speaking and conducting prayer meetings wherever he was welcome — in his own parlour, in cottages, or in the spacious dining-room of industrialist Charles Roe's house. The dispute was never settled; it ended only when Roe offered to finance the building of a new church expressly for Simpson and any who might defect with him from St Michael's. Christ Church, an imposing classical-style building which could seat 1500, was completed in 1775 at a cost of £6000. John Wesley called it 'the most elegant I have seen in the Kingdom.'[20] Simpson officiated there from the beginning, and Charles Roe formally presented him with the living in 1779.

Simpson's ministry represented an exceptional example of cooperation between Methodism and the Establishment. Christ Church is the only Anglican place of worship in Cheshire where Wesley is known to have preached; he occupied the pulpit on several occasions at Simpson's invitation. Simpson himself, in an extraordinary display of ecumenical spirit, sometimes conducted his regular services on Sunday morning and then accompanied his congregation to the Methodist Chapel in the afternoon.[21]

While not a creative intellectual, David Simpson was what might be termed a serious populariser. His writing style was clear and attractive, and he could easily hold an audience through lengthy, didactic lectures and sermons on his favourite subjects, which included abuses in the Anglican Establishment (especially absenteeism), the evils of slavery, the interpretation of dreams, the efficacy of smallpox vaccination, and the horrors of deism and Jacobinism. An effective polemicist, he could also be a generous opponent; for example, in his anti-radical sermon, 'Strictures on Religious Opinion', he is careful to concede that Doctors Price and Priestley are well-meaning though mistaken men. He adds that Price, whom he had heard in London, 'had the happiness of mankind much at heart.' As for his own political views:

> If it be enquired whether I myself see no need of a reformation? — I ingenuously answer I do. — And whether I am *perfectly* satisfied with the constitution of this country both in church and state? — Certainly not . . . . But I see no defects of that magnitude to render it advisable to convulse the kingdom, and to plunge ourselves into civil war, for the sake of them. Many things, in my judgment, might be altered for the better. And I doubt not but such melioration of the state of things will gradually take place.[22]

Simpson saw himself and his sympathisers as a social vanguard, striking a new passageway between bloodthirsty, infidel republicanism and lazy, selfish Toryism. In his sermons he stirringly contrasted the dynamic virtue of men like Charles Roe with the sinfulness of the idle rich.[23]

In spite of his departure from strict orthodoxy both Simpson's primary loyalty and his personal prestige were firmly anchored to the Church. To the end of his life he continued to debate inwardly the merit of breaking with the Establishment. Local Methodist historians have insisted that he died in 1799 convinced that he should formally associate himself with Methodism. His death is said to have occurred just twelve hours before he had planned to preach a farewell sermon at Christ Church, announcing his resignation from the living.[24]

In the face of Simpson's overwhelming popularity with rising elements in the community — the more liberal manufacturers and tradesmen, some of the trade clubs, and a considerable segment of the labouring population — his adversary Thomas Hewson was increasingly isolated. The climax of their dispute — which showed elements of the generational conflict so noticeable in the evangelical rebellion — came at a time when Methodist achievement had reached a first plateau in Macclesfield. In 1774 John Ryle became the town's first mayor to identify himself as a Methodist; he walked at the head of his inaugural procession accompanied by Hewson, Simpson, and John Wesley himself. Still, like many respectable Methodists, Ryle remained a dutiful Anglican as well. In company with Charles Roe he endorsed a petition of 1205 leading citizens calling on the Bishop of Chester to intervene and restore 'peace and harmony'.[25]

In 1778 Thomas Hewson reported to his bishop, 'The number of Methodists is greatly increased in late years . . .'[26] He probably counted all the worshippers at Christ Church as deserters to Methodism. Clearly the opening of the new church, the institution of regular Sabbath-day meetings by the Wesleyans, and Hewson's truculent stance, had hurt St Michael's badly; only about 150 were receiving the sacrament there each month, and only about 300 attended at Easter. A decade later even the Church's official estimate acknowledged about 500 Methodists in town, and almost 500 other Dissenters.[27] But now, with Hewson gone, attendance at St Michael's was restored somewhat, to about 300 to 500, rising to 600 to 700 at holidays. Attendance figures, of course, are only a very rough guide to relative memberships.[28] And they can indicate nothing of the nature of individual commitments; the rapt convert takes up the same space as the squirming infant or a fellow who snores through the sermon. The Methodists may well have attracted proportionally more of the former than the latter; but it is difficult to know. Furthermore, since it was still common for Methodists to attend both chapel and Anglican services, these attendance estimates must be seen as overlapping quantities. But clearly the Church was suffering. An official estimate of five hundred worshippers in regular attendance at each of the town's two Anglican churches in 1821 represents a sharp decline from the numbers communicating in the 1770s, if the rapid increase in population during the intervening decades is taken into account.[29] The more resolutely the Methodists moved towards a clear break with Anglicanism, the more far-reaching was the damage to the Church. For Macclesfield the parting of the ways was a gradual process, well under way by 1800, gaining momentum thereafter, and complete by the mid-1830s. Mass defections to the Methodists posed not only an ideological and political threat to the

Established Church, but a serious financial one as well. In a municipal chapelry such as Macclesfield the Church's chief sources of income were burial fees, pew rents, and an annual tax known locally as the 'church ley'. The last two were particularly vulnerable as the Methodists became more and more estranged from the Church. (Because of the severe overcrowding of the old churchyard at St Michael's, burial fees had become a negligible source of income there, and a very lucrative one at Christ Church.) The Anglican clergy's bitter attacks on irregular Methodist practices such as performing baptisms and the 'churching' of women in private homes, were partly inspired by the loss of the 'surplice fees' or special charges for such services.[30]

The growth of the chapels proceeded, with occasional setbacks, during the turbulent and poverty-stricken wartime and post-war years. And the force of the spiritual awakening set on foot by Wesley and his followers was such that many more were touched by it — in field meetings and revivals, chapel festivals, Sunday schools, or simply through contact with friends and relatives who were converts — than ever became duly enrolled members of any chapel. By 1830 it would appear that Macclesfield conformed to W.R. Ward's general description of the balance of religious forces in the industrial North — that is, roughly equal memberships for the Anglicans, the Catholics, and the Protestant Dissenters.[31] In Macclesfield the numbers favoured the Methodists over the Catholics (who were stronger in the big industrial cities) but together these two groups accounted for more than twice as many adherents as the Church could claim. [See Table V:1.] Still, the combined membership figures are not so very impressive when set against the total population, even if its youth-biased age structure is taken into consideration and it is assumed that only adult members were counted. Fewer than one in eight of the town's inhabitants were formally attached to a church or chapel.

The very task of assigning an individual this or that religious label can be a dubious undertaking. The tendency of church historians to concentrate on denominational studies has obscured the fact that, for many people, spiritual progress was a matter of experiment, with advances, side excursions, and retreats, frequently overstepping the boundaries of denomination or chapel. Even the supreme moment of 'new birth' or conversion might be a recurring experience, with periods of doubt or indifference intervening. The unusually eventful religious odyssey of printer and pamphleteer Joseph Nightingale, for instance, began in an Anglican home and moved to Unitarianism during his period of apprenticeship, and from there to 'infidel' beliefs under the influence of Thomas Paine. Then, after a period of suicidal depression he turned to Methodism, next to deism, and again to Methodism when he was nine years as a preacher, ending his life once more as a Unitarian.[32] This is an extreme example, but few converts remained unswervingly faithful throughout their adult lives, and fewer spent all their lives in one denomination. Prospective members sometimes sampled various offerings before making a commitment. Methodist stalwart Joshua Thorley, for instance, as a youth often went to Townley Street Independent Chapel, where he enjoyed the preaching, and at the same time occasionally attended Methodist services.[33]

At the local level the broad outlines of denominational or connexional history tend to break down into more intricate configurations. Separate groups co-operated now and then, sharing premises or even preachers and working together in umbrella organisations like the Bible Society. Parents might send their children to a popular Sunday school run by one chapel, while themselves attending services at another. Many kept up the practice of occasional attendance at Anglican services (especially at major holidays), while simultaneously pursuing a deepening commitment to a Dissenting Chapel or Sunday school. When the Churchwardens counted Nonconformists in the town in 1754 (ten years after Wesley's first visit), they did not deem it necessary to mention the Methodists as a separate group; Society members were still considered, and considered themselves, entirely within the fold.[34] And long after the Wesleyans had started down the path which led so inexorably (in retrospect) to separation, many continued to hope for complete reconciliation. As late as 1824, when the new Brunswick Street Chapel was opened by Jabez Bunting, the service of the Church of England was used there 'in respect to those many members converted under David Simpson, who venerate the Church of England liturgy.'[35]

The road from the Methodist chapel could lead outward and upward socially, as was the case for the Revd Melville Horne, who began as a Wesleyan itinerant, served as a missionary in Sierra Leone, officiated for some years at Christ Church, Macclesfield, and ended his career as a fashionable Anglican preacher in Manchester. For some families Methodism was simply a revolving door: John Ryle the Methodist mayor had a son who became Anglican Bishop of Liverpool, and the Roe family likewise returned to orthodoxy after only one generation of chapel-going. Still others who became discontented with the organisation or theology of official Methodism might succumb to the lure of one of the smaller schismatic or competing fellowships which were more radical in doctrine, democratic in governance, and plebeian in style.

No doubt one of the secrets of Methodism's early success was its flexibility; it insisted on no rigid catechism of belief and extended a welcome to believers of widely varying temperaments, from the rationalist to the naively superstitious. Some chapels even lent their pulpits to colourful visitors like the fiery American evangelist Lorenzo Dow, who toured the North in the years 1805 to 1807. The uncontrolled emotionalism of camp-meeting revivals drew criticism from both Methodist and civil authorities, but the chapels were ready to gather in the more serious converts.[36] The lore of local Methodism includes many instances of pre-Christian folk belief grafted on to the 'official' theology. Stories of ghostly apparitions and portenteous dreams abound in chapel histories, and Macclesfield had its share. A mysterious dog is said to have appeared miraculously one night, to guard the chapel funds on a journey through robber-infested woods; and in another tale George Pearson returns after death to discuss with his relatives the disposition of some of his effects.[37]

For some years the Methodists succeeded in holding all these disparate tendencies together in a unified Society, but eventually the strain began to tell and fissures appeared. A comparison of the chapel membership figures in Tables V:1 and V:2 indicates that by 1830 or so the peak period of Wesleyan Methodist expansion had been reached. The big gains thereafter were made by newer chapels, some of them breakaways from Wesleyanism and others remnants of Old Dissent, reanimated by the general revival. Macclesfield Methodism experienced all the schisms and realignments which shook the Connexion nationally in the uncertain years after Wesley's death. The secession led by Alexander Kilham in 1797 quickly resulted in the formation of a New Connexion group in Macclesfield. They founded Lord Street Sunday School in 1820 and met for worship in the school for many years before opening Park Street (or Parsonage Street) Chapel in 1836.[38]

The Macclesfield New Connexion opened a second Sunday school, the Fence School in Hurdsfield, which proved very attractive to poor parents from the back streets of the textile workers' districts.[39] Almost as many girls as boys attended, and applicants were so numerous that some had to be turned away, after vetting by a teacher. The School offered cheap, practical elementary education for the labouring population. Secular subjects like arithmetic were taught, and a library of more than 150 books, borrowed at the rate of five or six books per child per quarter, was maintained. The teachers ran the School without formal participation of trustees or other representatives of the chapel at large (a system which brought occasional conflicts and accusations of waywardness).[40]

The New Connexion congregation was apparently drawn from a somewhat lower social level than that of the Wesleyans, and finances were a constant problem. Yet Park Street Chapel tried to preserve its democratic, self-sufficient stance, calling on the national or circuit leaderships only in emergencies. By April 1826 the circuit was forced to point out that, 'in consequence of our embarrassed circumstances as a circuit we cannot possibly support a married preacher, unless conference will allow us the wife's quarterage.'[41] The group entered the decade of the 1830s burdened with debt and unpaid arrears of class money, and in 1839 circuit leaders were still lamenting 'the present languid condition of some of our societies.'[42]

Some of the working-class parents who sent their children to Fence School in the 1830s may have themselves attended a Primitive Methodist rather than a New Connexion chapel. The Primitives, who made a special appeal to labouring people, counted their formal beginning from the great field meeting led by Hugh Bourne in 1807 at Mow Cop, Staffordshire, not far from Macclesfield. Their first serious attempt to proselytise in Macclesfield was in 1819 and from that time forward Bourne and other itinerant preachers visited frequently, speaking anywhere they could draw a crowd. The Primitives, with their emphasis on uninhibited lay preaching, extempore praying and testifying, and fervent singing provided a compelling spectacle; as one preacher described it, 'As soon as I had done preaching, there was such an outpouring of the Spirit! — Sinners were crying out on every hand! . . . some were singing and praising God . . .'[43] They preached at all hours, all days of the week, and they probably initiated the early morning weekday prayer meetings for factory workers which proved so successful that the Wesleyans soon adopted them.[44]

By 1820 the Primitives could claim 172 members locally, organised into twelve classes served by six local preachers and eight class leaders. Their chapel membership was much more socially homogeneous and much less prosperous than that of the Wesleyans. Macclesfield Primitives were predominantly artisans, and the upper and middle bourgeoisie were conspicuously absent from their ranks.[45] The faithful were so poor that money was a perpetual problem. In 1830 Beech Lane Primitive Methodist Chapel was opened, but its travelling preachers had to walk from town to town, and its Sunday school had to buy twelve Bibles in loose sheets, because bound ones were too expensive.[46] The outburst of faith generated by a public 'coming to God' was not always easy to sustain, and there was a high turnover of membership among the Primitives. In 1836, 260 joined the local chapel, but in the same year 128 either left or were expelled, died, or moved away.[47]

Women took a conspicuous part in all the work of the Primitives, and the novelty of hearing travelling preachers like Ann Brownsword, Ann Stanna, and Elizabeth Dakin drew large crowds.[48] To judge from the memoirs and obituaries Primitive Methodism must have had a particularly strong appeal for Macclesfield women of the lower class. A typical story is that of Mary Fearnley, a member and Sunday school scholar who died 'triumphantly' in 1820, aged sixteen. She was 'fully resigned to God', in spite of her 'trial of deep poverty' and after three weeks' illness 'strongly requested her mother not to run into debt on her account, for that a small piece of bread with water daily, would . . . be sufficient for her.'[49] Even more than other Dissenting groups, the Primitives were concerned with assuaging the anxiety and guilt sick and dying members felt, not only about their chances for Life Eternal, but also at not being able to work or perform household duties, to earn their keep and help sustain their families.

The older Dissenting denominations, tracing their ancestry in an unbroken line to the Reformation, maintained a far more dignified, intellectual style of worship. But in some cases they, too, were beneficiaries of the religious awakening kindled by the Methodists. King Edward Street Independent Chapel, founded in 1672, claimed a following of five hundred worshippers in 1715, but experienced a rapid decline through the eighteenth century.[50] From 1772 to 1779 it came under the influence of a new pastor, the highly eccentric John Palmer, who had studied under Joseph Priestley and 'imbibed' Unitarian views at Warrington Academy.[51] The result was a split in the chapel, with the Calvinistic Trinitarians forming their own congregation and King Edward Street continuing as Unitarian. The Trinitarian Independents who withdrew from King Edward Street worshipped for a while with the Wesleyans, then subscribed towards the cost of bringing preachers to address them in private houses, and later accepted an offer from David Simpson to meet in a schoolroom connected with Christ Church. But even before the high tide of wartime panic, Macclesfield was decidedly inhospitable to Nonconformists who dared to proselytise. The numbers attending their prayer meetings increased steadily and by 1785 the Independents could raise 12*s* to 14*s* a week to pay a minister from London, but their trials continued:

> We hired a room; prejudice in the town rose high against us, and we were removed to several places, one of which was a barn in Mill-street . . . we were only permitted to worship in said barn three Sabbaths, and turned into the streets. After that we got an old silk shop . . . and were turned out of that place.[52]

In 1787/8, with the financial assistance of the prosperous Mosley Street Independent congregation in Manchester, the local Independents built Townley Street Chapel, a simple structure with no galleries, vestries, schoolrooms, or pews, at a cost of £400. Five ministers occupied the pulpit in the first fourteen years of the chapel's existence. The war years, with xenophobic feeling running high, were a time of discouragement; members were taunted in the streets with cries of 'Jacobin' and 'Calvinist', and threatening mobs gathered outside the chapel.[53] In 1803, during a lull in the bigotry, they opened a Sunday school, which flourished, as did the chapel itself in the next two decades. Although the congregation numbered only about fifty at this time, 160 pupils were enrolled almost immediately (the figure rising to about 500 in the 1820s).

Parents were apparently quite willing to put aside any religious scruples they might have in favour of getting competent instruction for their children.[54]

According to the Managers' publicity material the Sunday school was a philanthropic venture whose purpose was to teach 'poor children' to read the Scriptures; further, 'the most deserving part of them are given *Religious Tracts* and other books calculated to improve their morals.'[55] But the additional weekday classes offered by many Townley Street pastors must have attracted a middle-class clientele as well. The Presbyterians made a speciality of pedagogy in this period. The high standard of education they demanded for their own clergy produced a pool of qualified schoolmasters, and meagre chapel revenues meant there was always a need for ministers to supplement their incomes.

But ecumenical ventures could be unsettling, even to old-established Dissenting bodies. Because of their special concern for education the Independents played a leading role in the large nondenominational Macclesfield Sunday School — modelled on the famous Stockport Sunday School, the biggest in England — founded by the Methodists in 1796. A prolonged struggle for control of the school between Anglicans and conservative Wesleyans on the one hand and the more militant Dissenters on the other resulted in the withdrawal of the Anglicans. At this point (1815) an Independent, the Revd R.S. McAll, was appointed Chaplain to the school. In the face of continued recriminations about his role (he was accused of turning the school into an unlicenced meeting-house for worship), a group of supporters raised money to build a church for him. The shareholders of this establishment, St George's Church, opened in 1824, made it a condition of tenure that no doctrine contrary to the teachings of Anglicanism be preached, and McAll accepted this condition. But when McAll left in 1827 a strict Calvinist, the Revd G.B. Kidd, was invited to fill the vacancy. Having failed to meet with the Trustees' approval, he soon withdrew, taking much of the congregation with him. While Kidd's group built Roe Street Independent Chapel, those who stayed at St George's renounced Independency and petitioned for their church to be consecrated by the Bishop of Chester in 1834.

Others of the Old Dissenting chapels were passed by, or very nearly so, by the revivifying force of evangelicalism. For these, exclusiveness took precedence over expansionism, and they paid the price. The Quakers, with a meeting-house in Mill Street built in 1705, had numbered eighty members in 1715 but declined over the century. The Macclesfield Meeting continually worried about Friends who forfeited their membership by 'marrying out' of the Society.[56]

The Baptists re-established themselves precariously in Macclesfield, after a long hiatus, through the work of the Revd W. Marshall in the 1810s. He preached at first in rented premises, in one of the old abandoned buildings of Charles Roe's copper foundry in Calamine Street. By 1823, with the help of some Derbyshire Baptists, Marshall's group was able to purchase this building and convert it into a simple chapel. Still, at this time the congregation consisted of only eleven members, and the next few years saw much division and faltering. Several ministers came and left, and the congregation split in 1826. Strictness of doctrine and ethical hair-splitting produced frequent expulsions, but at least a tiny Baptist cell managed to survive through the nineteenth century. It may well have had influence beyond its numbers, because the Baptist clergy and lay preachers were indefatigable outdoor evangelists in the surrounding rural villages.[57]

Perhaps it was partly because of the energy and proselytising zeal of the smaller local chapels that Macclesfield people never succumbed in any numbers to the allure of extreme or outlandish sects. Unlicenced 'ranting' preachers, Mormon missionaries and the like visited the district occasionally, but the chapels united in condemning such people as vagabond charlatans, who deserved to be restrained by the magistrates. The respectable clergy does not seem to have felt threatened by them, and they were always the objects of popular curiosity. Adam Rushton tells of a surprise appearance at his Sunday school of a 'wild-looking', bearded wanderer who proved to be a devotee of the prophetess Joanna Southcott. The man was allowed to speak his piece, and the disapproving teacher then calmly led a discussion of the merits of the points he had made.[58]

Unique among the denominations because of its ethnic base and its profound alienation from the dominant culture, was the Catholic Church. Nearly extinguished after the Jacobite troubles, it was restored to life almost overnight by the Irish immigration. East Cheshire harboured a handful of English Catholics through the eighteenth century, thanks to the protective influence of several aristocratic Catholic families, notably the Falconbergs of Sutton. By 1790, when the first Irish workpeople were arriving in Macclesfield, the total number of Catholics in the area was about thirty 'of no rank', according to the incumbent of St Michael's.[59] The town was soon established as a mission and was assigned a resident priest. Ten years later the number had grown to about ninety, and the congregation, with financial assistance from well-wishers in Ireland, was quietly amassing money for a chapel. Deliberately unobtrusive in design, this building consisted of a first-floor schoolroom, with the church itself above (perhaps to protect the worshippers from intrusion and harassment). Father John Hall, who was to be a familiar and much-loved figure in the town for the next half-century, arrived to take charge of the Macclesfield chapel in 1821 and found a congregation of about three hundred — 'chiefly Irish weavers' — which was to grow tremendously under his care. [See Table V:1.] After the Catholic Emancipation Act of 1829 Father Hall could extend his pastoral efforts considerably. He encouraged the foundation of several new chapels in the area and personally served seven towns in addition to Macclesfield; his weekly labours covered a circuit of some seventy miles.[60]

Whether Catholic, Baptist, or Independent, all the struggling Nonconformist groups — like the Wesleyans before them — went through a period of meeting in makeshift premises, perhaps a silk workshop, a schoolroom, or a warehouse, before they could muster support for a permanent home.[61] The chapel building was both a haven from interference and persecution and a symbol of respectability, solidity, and status in the community. It implied a degree of seriousness and permanence no amount of street-preaching or cottage evangelising could convey.

II

How did the new religious life offered by evangelicalism in its many forms affect the individuals who were drawn to it in such impressive numbers? James Obelkevich has suggested that Methodism, even in its early period, provided a kind of 'artificial community' — re-creating through the social network around its chapels and schools some of the values of the older pre-industrial village.[62] Through its close attention to personal spiritual experience, the emotional outlet provided by its gatherings, both large and small, for prayer and worship, the practical support and conviviality it offered newcomers to the Society, and the consolation it provided in times of stress and loss, Methodism responded to the tensions and upheavals of an industrialising society. On a smaller scale, the other Nonconformist groups functioned similarly.

If the spiritual awakening kindled amidst the mass fervour of a field-meeting or in the intimate intensity of cottage prayer-sessions was solemnised by formal membership in a chapel, the new member could become drawn into an absorbing round of activity. In a period when the older community, with its relatively simple structure of social, political, and religious roles, was expanding geometrically, the chapels provided new means of achieving distinction in the eyes of one's neighbours, new offices to fill, new methods of self-improvement, and new ways of acknowledging gradations of status while binding participants together in a surrogate community. Local Methodist histories abound with accounts of Sunday school anniversaries, tea parties, Love Feasts, and outings. Charity sermons, a fund-raising device featuring recitations, a concert of sacred music, and a stirring appeal by a visiting preacher, were popular highlights of the chapel calendar. The chapels, whether they acknowledged it explicitly or not, were building an alternative social milieu to that of the Establishment. For the most dedicated and pious, able to negotiate all the rungs of the new ladder, they even offered the possibility of easier entry into the ranks of the clergy — at a time when, among other obstacles, attendance at Oxford or Cambridge was still a requirement for Anglican ordination.

Quite apart from the inner sense of security and self-worth which a chapel member might gain from the theology of direct, personal experience of holiness, there was a new sense of importance to be gained through chapel work. The chapels, in contrast to the Anglican Church or even the new trade and benefit clubs, gave a great many lay people a great deal to do. Adam Rushton, for example, as a newly converted and eager young Sunday school teacher was busy from 7 a.m. to 9.30 p.m. each Sunday with classes and services.[63] Such activity appealed strongly to energetic individuals seeking both personal recognition and a comfortable niche in an increasingly impersonal community. Among the Wesleyans, for example, the most ambitious might aspire to becoming a Steward, Trustee, or Lay Preacher. Those preferring the more intimate relation of teacher and counsellor might become Class or Band Leaders, or take a Sunday school class. All of these functionaries filled in for each other on occasion, and all were involved in subsidiary activities like sick-visiting and committee work.

A Class Leaders' Meeting exercised sweeping administrative powers within each chapel. They heard accusations of immorality, including dishonest financial dealings, and had the power to expel or suspend members. They also settled minor doctrinal disputes — sometimes cross-examining ministers in response to complaints from the congregation, and they made arrangements for the frequent Watch Nights, Love Feasts, anniversaries and other special events.[64] A Local Preachers' Meeting concerned itself with drawing up the monthly plans of preaching for chapels in the immediate area, examining candidate lay preachers, and disciplining those who failed to fulfill their obligations or fell prey to 'heterodox sentiments'. The Preachers' Meeting could be surprisingly lenient in its disciplinary measures; apparently a delicate balance had to be struck between enforcing good conduct and retaining much-needed volunteers (who could always find another chapel down the road). In one 1832 case Brother Goodwin, who had neglected a preaching assignment in Langley, returned to Macclesfield where he 'sauntered about the Town . . . went to a spirit shop and purchased Rum . . . rambled about till 2 in the morning' and created a disturbance at the home of a widow. He was rebuked but not suspended.[65] The sense that one's every move was under such close surveillance may have been a stronger deterrent than threats of punitive measures.

Financial management of the chapel was in the hands of the Trustees, who met quarterly to consider major expenditures (e.g., support of the full-time preachers, money paid to the Circuit, and repairs to the Chapel), and two Stewards who oversaw the collecting of weekly class money (the famous penny-a-week system, later borrowed by many Victorian trade unions) and the distribution of the tickets indicating that a member was paid up and in good standing, without which one could not gain admission to many chapel functions. Two Poor Stewards took charge of distributing donations for charitable purposes.

The activism of the new Dissenting groups appealed especially strongly to adolescents and young adults. In memoir after memoir there are similar accounts of intense spiritual struggles, beginning at a young age, sometimes almost in infancy, characterised by agonising doubts and deep yearning for salvation. Then an electrifying conversion experience occurs, most often between the ages of sixteen and twenty-one; for young men this momentous personal commitment often came just as they finished an apprenticeship, completed their schooling, or in some other way began to break loose from parental restriction and protection.

A particularly vivid account of this typical spiritual journey was left by John Boothby, a farm worker born in Macclesfield in 1739. He began to be troubled by religious questions at about the age of six, under the influence of his mother, but joined his friends in mocking the Methodists until, when he was fifteen, he attended one of their meetings out of curiosity. He experienced a profound reaction and wrestled with himself for twelve months without coming to God. The next crisis came when he was twenty-three, struggling to support a wife and three children (two of them sickly) on a wage of £8 a year which he made as a servant in husbandry to his father. At this time, he says, '[I felt] the plague of my own heart . . . the depravity of my own nature . . . . I saw new sin mixing itself in all I did.' But, ignoring the jeers of friends and relations, he turned to the Lord: 'The Powerful Presence of God descended upon me; my soul was so abundantly filled with divine Love, that, for a time, I knew neither where I was, nor what I did. When I came to myself, I was quite another man; the light of the moon was sevenfold (Isaiah xxx:26). When I came down from the mount, I felt myself as weak as an infant, but nevertheless I possessed a constant peace and serenity.' The tale has the standard triumphal ending; Boothby became a long-standing member of the Methodist Society and a Class Leader, and converted his wife, seven children, and fifteen other relatives.[66]

John Birchenall's conversion occurred earlier, at the age of sixteen. He had just left school and was assisting at his father's cotton factory, while groping towards a decision to embark on a medical career, against his parents' wishes. Mental and spiritual pressures built up to the crisis point:

> I became pensive and meditative. A crowd of religious impressions were awakened, under the influence of which I sought guidance and relief in the means of grace . . . . One night, after retiring to rest, a giddiness seized me, with a sense of swooning. I imagined I was going to die; I knew I was not prepared to stand before God.[67]

He turned away from the secular pursuits which had delighted him in his student days — gave up reading his favourite classical authors and abandoned his music lessons: 'half-frenzied, half-paralysed, I got through the avocations of the day; but the midnight hour was again to be passed, and it might be the hour of my doom.' After days of praying and crying out to God, 'in a twinkling of an eye my burden was removed, my distress was at an end, my heart was filled with love and peace and joy.'[68] Birchenall went through several more cycles of depression and exaltation within the next few years, until at last he 'found himself', both as a doctor and as the most effective Methodist Class Leader the town ever knew.

Six of Charles Roe's children were seduced into Methodism, much against his will, by the combined influence of his second wife, Mary Stockdale, who had been a Methodist in London before her marriage, his niece, Hester Ann Roe, and his protegé, David Simpson.[69] Of the six, Robert seems to have clung most tenaciously to the new faith, in defiance of his father's wish that he be ordained in the Church of England. From the beginning, he says, 'I was my mother's darling, and went under the general appellation of a pious young man which filled me with pride and carelessness.' He became a wild youth and suffered conscience-stricken dreams. While at Brasenose College, Oxford he became involved with Wesleyanism and underwent a conversion experience there at the age of twenty-two, rejecting the counsel of friends who derided the Methodists as 'a parcel of Coblers and Tinkers, etc.,' and asked him, 'What good will your College Education do you, if you ramble after *them*?' In 1777 the College authorities refused him the testimonial necessary for ordination.

In the next few years he drifted, visiting Macclesfield several times and falling under the spell of David Simpson's preaching. On one occasion, after he had been to a Methodist meeting with his sister Margaret and cousin Hester Ann Roe, he returned home to find that his father had forbidden him the house: 'He said my cousin had been the ruin of all his children.' There were many attempts at reconciliation, but Charles Roe was obdurate and Robert unyielding: 'The family are very kind. But my father gave me pain by joking me about Miss . . ., and seemed wishful I should approve of her as a wife; but what are ten thousand pounds to me without grace . . . . He said you are honest but too nice Robert.'[70]

As it turned out, Charles Roe disowned his sons Robert, Charles, and Joseph. Charles the younger eventually abandoned Methodism and became a prosperous alderman, and Joseph, too, devoted himself to business and served as mayor, 1791/2. One Methodist historian summed up Charles Roe's attitude thus, 'He was a man of imperious temper, and though far from indifferent to evangelical religion, was much more anxious for the temporal interests of his family than he was for their spiritual and eternal welfare.'[71]

The basic elements of these stories, the revolt against parental influences, an experience of loss of identity followed by rebirth and new-found strength and maturity as a 'child of God', are reproduced again and again in evangelical memoirs. In the autobiographies of women, who apparently formed a slight majority of Society members in the early decades, the pattern is similar, with more stress on resignation and a 'helpmeet' role.[72] Typical of these is a memoir of Rachel Bower, born in Macclesfield in 1747, who lost her father as a young child. She was raised by a God-fearing mother who distrusted the Methodists and shared the common view that they were 'the filth and offscourings of all things', a set of ignorant persons led by 'illiterate and designing' preachers. Rachel, an earnest child, worried about her unfitness to die and was deeply frightened by a serious bout of illness at the age of nine. At twelve she began to attend Methodist meetings, and for years tried to reconcile her own spiritual yearnings with her mother's censure. She 'found peace' when she was twenty and eventually married a devout man who, her obituary says, helped to curb her 'irritable' temper. In December 1805 she died, after a lingering, painful illness which had confined her to her bed for a year. The couple spent her last days praying together. At the last, she cried out, 'I wish I could sing', and he replied, 'Thou wilt soon be singing above.'[73]

It would not be too much to say that, for many rank and file members of the chapels, the major function of religion was to provide a comforting and reassuring antidote for personal anxiety. On a short-term basis piety was periodically stimulated by accidents, epidemics, and natural disasters. In 1778, for instance, an earthquake which occurred during a Sunday service in September produced a flurry of conversions. The collapse of Clayton's cotton factory in 1791, which caused the death of six people, brought forth similar results, and two more accidents in 1798 induced many more to repent. Typhoid and cholera epidemics also evoked an outpouring of spirituality. The chapel's task was to translate this fleeting impulse into a more lasting commitment.

The main vehicle for doing so was the weekly class meeting, in which a dozen or so chapel members met with a Leader who cross-examined them closely on the 'state of their souls'.[74] Members were encouraged by a highly supportive and intimate group atmosphere to reveal any matters which might have troubled them over the past week, and to share any significant religious experiences or insights. For those who had 'grown in grace' and sought a more intense and frequent communion, there were smaller units (usually five or six members) called 'bands'.[75] So that members would feel completely free to share personal details, and in order to create a close bond of shared experience and concern, bands were segregated according to sex and marital status.

In a period when the shadow of death was a looming reality, year in and year out, in so many homes, the Methodists understandably stressed the themes of patient resignation to loss and exulttant acceptance of death. The death-bed experience formed the centre-piece of many a Methodist tract or sermon. The vogue for this kind of literature was so pronounced that for several years the Macclesfield Wesleyans produced as a Sunday school fund-raising project an annual pamphlet called *A Record of Happy Deaths.* J. Wright, the editor, recounts with a kind of macabre enthusiasm repetitious tales of the deathbed scenes of all Sunday school scholars and young teachers who have died during the previous year. Without exception these exemplary young people expire secure in their faith, exhorting the visitors who flocked round their beds not to grieve but to rejoice at their sure salvation. In spite of the stilted language and suspect uniformity of the narratives, the stories do reinforce the image of chapel folk trying to re-create a sense of communal solidarity, offering ritualised consolation and mutual support in time of personal crisis.[76]

Naturally, denominational literature emphasises spiritual 'success stories', but there is also evidence of another kind, showing that for many the tension between contradictory or warring elements in their personalities was a lifelong condition. The story of David Simpson's unresolved dilemma of choice between his position as an Anglican clergyman and the fuller, warmer, freer spiritual atmosphere offered by the Methodists is a case in point. Another prominent Macclesfield figure, who associated with Methodists all his life but whose effort to resist the dominance of an earthly parent took the form of avoiding conversion, was John Clulow. His Methodist mother was an imposing figure who tried to overcome her son's deep ambivalences by sheer force of her will. When he was eighteen she sent him on the rounds of the circuit with a particularly inspiring preacher, a plan to which young John at first readily assented. But they had not gone far when the young man disappeared, only to turn up drunk in a pub, surrounded by disreputable friends. Later in life John Clulow gained a reputation as a drinker and a brawler, but he also stood by the Methodists, serving them faithfully as a lawyer and contributing generously in his mother's memory. It is said that he insisted that his house be used for Methodist class meetings, though he would never attend them but sat in a nearby room, smoking and gambling or talking business with his cronies, while the faithful worried and prayed over the state of his soul.[77]

It is striking how many examples there are in Macclesfield of strong women who took an active part in organising and financing the early chapels. These pious, strong-willed mothers and elder sisters often became the dominant spiritual influence in their households, sometimes vying directly with their husbands for the allegiance of a favourite son or sons — Elizabeth Clulow, Mary Stockdale Roe, and Martha Cooper, Adam Rushton's mother, are but three examples. Joshua Thorley tells how an older sister first led him to God, and Robert Roe looked on his cousin, Hester Ann Roe, as a spiritual guide.[78] Hannah Swindells, who became a leading figure at Sunderland Street Chapel, was raised in a virtual matriarchy. Her mother was a devout woman who 'possessed a vigorous understanding [and] . . . devoted a considerable portion of her time and attention to the intellectual and spiritual improvement of her daughter.' Young Hannah was converted by her mother at the age of thirteen in 1794 and in turn converted (the memoirist says 'subdued') her father, a man who had 'lived without God' and was a source of 'domestic uneasiness'.[79]

To an intelligent young woman of the middle class like Hester Ann Roe, Methodism offered a serious, purposeful alternative to a life of balls and flirtations and idle waiting for a suitable marriage.[80] She was converted to Methodism at the age of seventeen, and at the relatively advanced age of twenty-eight married James Rogers, one of the most renowned of Wesley's preachers. As a woman, Hester Rogers was unusual, though certainly not unique, in winning a wide audience for her religious writings and a high reputation in her own right within the Connexion. Such accomplishments would have been more difficult, or less likely, in the 1820s and 1830s as compared with the 1780s and 1790s.

As the Society moved towards full denominational status, the grip of the male clergy (and laity) on chapel affairs tightened. In the Macclesfield Wesleyan chapels there were almost no female Class Leaders, no female preachers, and few female Sunday school teachers, even in the early days.[81] By the mid-1820s there were more women teaching, but none served on the Sunday school committees or held any other chapel office.[82] Women's material contributions, however, continued to be welcome, and many a wealthy widow played this role. Widows like Mrs Palfreyman, who contributed £800 toward the building of the new Brunswick Chapel in 1824, may well have found ways to exercise indirect power through gift-giving — but in the financial realm, as in others, most women were in no position to compete effectively with men.

The increasing formalisation of chapel government and the development of a separate, paid Wesleyan clergy tended to drive women away from the centre of affairs and into such auxiliary activities as sick-visiting, assisting the poor, teaching young children, and distributing tracts. As in other spheres of life where women have been excluded from the direct exercise of power, Methodist women tended more and more to create a separate and parallel hierarchy of their own — a world of wives — wherein fine gradations of social status, with appropriate niceties of dress and manner, counted for much. Memoirist George Slater, a shrewd and frank commentator on Cheshire religious history, noticed how Miss Maclardie of Macclesfield was elevated by her distinguished marriage: 'Mrs. [Jabez] Bunting was regarded as the queen of Methodist society.' There was a rivalry between the leading minister's wives, who 'were all expected to observe religious propriety, especially in public, but they were nevertheless human, and some of them were very human indeed. Mrs. Bunting was a capital talker, and enjoyed great latitude. Her words sometimes tasted of a little pepper.'[83]

There was always an intimate connection between religion and social life in general. People came to chapel to find friends and sweethearts; and religious values, especially for the most devout, permeated all social intercourse. The courtship of Adam Rushton's parents stressed the religious motif. George Rushton, a farm labourer who loved nature study, drilling with his regiment of Cheshire Cavalry, and performing traditional ballads in tavern singing matches, chose as his sweetheart Martha Cooper, who came from a family of 'farmers, weavers, musicians, Methodists, and, to a considerable extent, readers and students of valuable books . . . . Misunderstandings would sometimes arise, and visits became few and far between, but Bible and hymn book, benedictions and prayers, always bridged over these chasms . . . . [Her] love letters were always full of references to psalmists, prophets, evangelists, and Wesley's hymns.'[84] When Adam himself reached marriageable age, he became fascinated by a pretty engraving of three angels which belonged to his mother. He went to chapel each Sunday hoping to find a young woman there who could match his favourite of the three in beauty and holiness of manner, and after some trial and error (with young ladies who proved too flighty) he succeeded.[85]

In spite of their aura of primness and Puritanism, the chapels played an important part in the town's general cultural life. If they condemned many popular pastimes — dancing, theatre-going, gambling, and rustic games — they offered their own alternatives. It is perhaps the very liveliness of chapel life, and not so much the dour disapproval of prudes and fundamentalists, that accounts for Macclesfield's lack of support for secularly-based music societies and commercial theatres (see chapter IV). Even the smallest chapels had their choirs, and at Sunderland Street, as at St Michael's, the singing was accompanied by an instrumental ensemble. The organ at Christ Church was a noble instrument, said to have belonged to Handel himself. Charity-sermon evenings always included a concert of vocal and instrumental selections, with Handel's sacred works as perennial favourites.[86]

David Simpson began a tradition of weekday evening lectures on subjects of general interest — popular science, ancient history, classics of Christian literature, and the like. Even his church sermons were as entertaining as they were instructive. His famous attack on the theatre, for instance, was (among other things) a short course in the history of the drama, with copious quotations, from the time of the Greeks. He was careful to underscore the pitfalls of the art, the temptations to impiety, immorality and unwholesome excitement it represented; but his hearers must have left feeling that they were recompensed in part for the secular delights they sacrificed.[87] In later years the Methodists went so far as to sponsor religious plays. Adam Rushton tells of an electrifying amateur performance of 'Daniel in the Lion's Den', featuring a 'crowd of princes, clad in eastern robes' and King Darius in scarlet robe and glittering crown. The loud cheers which greeted Daniel's deliverance were renewed as the evil princes and their wives and children were hurled into the den of lions. The play was received as a tremendous novelty and eagerly discussed in homes and workshops all over town; the most numerous faction thought the performance wonderful and educational, others found it dangerously frivolous, and a daring few even raised some skeptical questions about the facts of the story. These debates grew so heated that they had to be referred to the Sunday School authorities, who replied firmly that it was exceedingly sinful to doubt the Bible.[88]

The most outstanding contribution the Methodists made to community life outside the realm of religion was in the field of elementary education, where their Sunday schools filled what was very nearly a vacuum. Thomas Laqueur has suggested that the small, private, fee-paying schools of the eighteenth century may have functioned more effectively than scholars preoccupied with the rise of public education have allowed.[89] This was apparently not the case in Macclesfield; by the end of the century the urgent demand for popular education had far outstripped the supply. And day schools could not have satisfied the needs of families who depended upon the wages children could earn.

Apart from the Grammar School, 'a highly classical boarding institution' reserved for Anglicans, which admitted only a tiny élite, the town offered only a handful of more or less wretched dame schools and even fewer 'academies' and finishing schools for adolescent boys and girls.[90] Primary instruction was apparently so poor that even the privileged needed remedial help; the governors of the Grammar School complained in 1774 that 'children must go to other masters for writing and accounts which are not properly learned before they come to Grammar School.'[91]

Many children attended school only briefly or sporadically — and illiteracy rates, in so far as they can be guessed at, remained rather high. The evidence on literacy in Macclesfield before the rise of the Sunday schools is fragmentary and inconclusive in many respects, but there is a noticeable and continuing disparity between males and females. Corporation minutes for the second half of the eighteenth century indicate that 75 to 85 per cent of Corporation officers (mainly merchants, manufacturers, and professional men) could sign their names.[92] Both the Prestbury parish marriage registers and a sample of the depositions of Macclesfield witnesses at Quarter Sessions, representing a range of social levels, from farmers and artisans to substantial tradesmen and merchants, show a rise from *c.*55 per cent to *c.*70 per cent male literacy over the period, while female literacy rose from *c.*25 per cent to *c.*35 per cent.[93] By comparison, depositions of paupers show many fewer of both sexes able to sign. The depositions of 209 paupers in 1750 show 38 per cent of men and only 8 per cent of women signing; another 118 paupers' depositions, taken down between 1823 and 1826, show 62.8 per cent of men and 14.6 per cent of women signing.[94] The latter group were young adults of the very poorest class, most of them born and raised outside the town; many were recent immigrants from Ireland. The benefits of Sunday school training in writing, a source of so much bitter contention in evangelical circles, would seem to have fallen mainly on the male pupils.

The literacy figures for Macclesfield may be compared with Roger Schofield's national estimates (based on the marriage registers of 268 selected parishes) of about 60 per cent literacy for males and 40 per cent for females, with little change over the period. It would be particularly interesting to have more comprehensive data for Macclesfield in view of Schofield's observation of 'the superior literacy of market and county towns over the surrounding neighbourhood.' This finding he attributes to such towns' 'high proportion of occupations concerned with distribution and exchange, which required the ability to keep the records, . . .'[95]

Artisans' children seem to have been the most energetic in availing themselves of the full range of teaching offered by the Sunday schools. Adam Rushton left a vivid picture of his first school, which was the only one available in Hurdsfield in about 1825. He recalled

> a room full of children, some at play, some in mischief, and some repeating lessons in the broadest and roughest dialect of Cheshire. In the midst of this village babel was Nanny Clarke, a thin, gaunt, infirm old dame, with spectacles on nose, and birch-rod in hand. At frequent intervals the rod was heard going swish, swish all round the school.[96]

How different is Rushton's account of his beloved Macclesfield Sunday School, the non-denominational institution founded in 1796 by John Whitaker, a 24-year-old follower of David Simpson.[97] The school had originally been patterned after the early charity schools, and it opened its classes to 'poor Children of any description, except those who are afflicted with any contagious distemper, or, who are under five years of age, or, who go to some other school.'[98] All the teachers were volunteers, determined to 'lessen the sum of human wretchedness, by diffusing religious knowledge and useful learning among the lower classes of society.'[99] Whitaker started with about eighty children, and by Rushton's time (late 1820s) the school was serving more than two thousand.

Rushton tells of the varied and stimulating curriculum he encountered:

> In all the Bible classes of that time writing was taught . . . then came the glorious times of straight strokes, pothooks, and ladles . . . . Then, more exhilarating still, came forth words, sentences, and even my own name . . . . No engineer, architect, inventor, discoverer, or commander could have felt more exquisite pleasure.[100]

Memorising hymns stimulated a love of poetry, and a poem called 'The Pilgrim Fathers' brought forth an interest in history and adventure: 'I fell into a sort of enchanted dream of a free life in the

American backwoods.'[101] When he was put in charge of the School library he vowed to read straight through all its two hundred volumes, starting with the *Iliad*. (His delight in Homer came to the attention of the School authorities, who promptly removed the volume as an objectionable book.) Rushton's taste was exceptional; the most popular book in the library, he says, was Pollok's *The Course of Time*, a science-fiction-like theological work featuring crude and lurid descriptions of the torments of the damned.[102]

Rushton was something of a prodigy, but the Methodists catered for a wide range of needs. The same glow of pleasure in discovery and self-improvement is reflected in the brief story of farm labourer Edward White, who lived far out in the country, started work at the age of six and had no education in childhood. In his twenties he heard of a Methodist adult class, walked into town week after week, and proudly learned to read the Bible. Writing skill quickly followed and during his last illness, when he was twenty-seven, he struggled to compose his memoir, to leave a record of his life for his chapel-mates and his wife and four children.[103]

Clearly the chapel schools attracted some teachers of strong intellectual bent, who wished to impart secular subjects — from Pitman's shorthand to prosody. They encouraged bright working-class boys who felt cut off from workmates who cared nothing either for religion or learning. Rushton's closest friend at Sunday School was an older boy who discussed Shakespeare, Cowper, and Thomson, and spent Sunday morning reading through a borrowed encyclopedia with his young friend. But the standard Sunday school fare was limited. The schools seem to have devoted a great deal of their time to rote learning of religious texts and to discussion of cleanliness, punctuality, deportment, and morality.[104] Rushton soon ran through what the school library could impart, and was forced to turn to the library of the Useful Knowledge Society, to keen debates and discussions with the one or two rationalist autodidacts he encountered at work, and to visits with John Richards, the Chartist schoolmaster of Rainow, whose cottage home was his school, its white-washed walls decorated with 'plain, unframed prints of sages and reformers.'[105]

Long before Adam Rushton began these daring excursions there had developed a strong suspicion among conservative elements that too much secular learning was a dangerous thing for the mass of the population, and that institutions like the non-denominational Sunday School might prove subversive in their effect. It is ironic that this pre-eminently successful venture, which was almost immediately imitated by other local chapels and by the Anglicans, should have proven to be the rock upon which cordial, or at least co-operative, relations between Dissenters and the Establishment came crashing to pieces.

Violent controversy struck the Macclesfield School at a time when similar battles were taking place across the nation. The precipitating factor locally was the decision of the School Committee to launch a fund appeal for a large new school building in 1813.[106] The Anglicans, feeling that they had been pushed into the background by the Dissenting clergy and teachers who ran the School, published a list of complaints and threatened to establish their own National School, combining weekday and Sunday classes, under the direct supervision of the Bishop. They charged that Sunday School children were not brought to Anglican services, that writing was being taught during the hours of Divine service, and that the religious exercises conducted in the School were not according to the Anglican form.[107] The Committee declined to make any changes and in particular defended the teaching of writing. At this stage both sides became highly defensive, and political charges and countercharges were hurled. A correspondent signing himself 'Civis', insisted in the *Courier* that the Methodists were out to wreck the constitution, as 'in the days of Cromwell', that they were seducing 'the weak and less educated' away from the Church, and that they were every bit as alien to the English Establishment as the Papists.[108]

The Methodists indignantly replied that the Sunday School prided itself on teaching 'loyalty, honesty, and submission to employers', that they were only supplying the deficiencies of the Church — and doing it free of charge, that they could be counted 'amongst the most loyal subjects of the Empire', and, for good measure, that 'Civis' himself was behaving like a quasi-Papist.[109] There would be no need for Methodists, noted one sarcastic writer, if only the Church would do as much as they did to promote 'Industry, Sobriety, good order and moral decorum'; let the Church build new chapels with room for all who want to attend, let it offer the people the fervent preaching they desire.[110]

Realising that they could be pushed unwillingly into a break with the Church and an uncomfortably close alliance with more radical Dissenting groups, the moderate Wesleyans began to press for a compromise solution (suggesting that the Church and the Wesleyans share control of the School).[111] But it was too late. The Anglicans proceeded to open their National School, and the various factions of Wesleyans engaged in a destructive internecine wrangle over the School which dragged on for the next several years and ended with the moderates suing the radicals.[112]

The Sunday School became the focus of strains and rivalries which had been simmering for years. The open contest, however, made the religious atmosphere of the town more political than ever before. The Macclesfield Wesleyans were forced to make their position, in relation to competing bodies on their right and left, more explicit. The social gospel they chose to propagate was a conservative, loyalist one. In their Sunday School Report for 1825/6 they protested,

> [The School's] first and primary object, is not to make the children of the labouring classes discontented with their situation, to encourage a spirit of insubordination, and to raise them above their fellows in the same rank of life with themselves as has been too hastily asserted . . . it teaches humility, patience, and resignation and is calculated to fit its subjects to act a useful part in their allotted station in life.[113]

This, of course, was an official, leadership view; as Adam Rushton and others testify, the School continued to offer students a much wider and more exciting range of possibilities than the Report suggests. But such public declarations were signals that Methodism's 'heroic' period was coming to an end, and a new age of denominational consolidation and social quietism was beginning.

III

Noting that the Wesleyan Methodist movement in England grew twice as fast as the population in the years between 1800 and 1850, K.S. Inglis has tried to isolate particular factors contributing to this impressive organisational vitality. He found that Methodism was especially appealing to the middling ranks of society, and to the 'middling' sort of community:

> There was something about the social relations of a community neither agricultural nor urban that Methodism found congenial, and in the smaller industrial settlements working-class Methodists were often numerous. These places were unlike the traditional English village in that the inhabitants did not inherit feudal relationships, and unlike the large towns in that employers and employees lived fairly close to each other.[114]

He could have been writing about Macclesfield; add the peculiarly conservative, protectionist outlook of the silk industry, periodically drawing employers and workmen together in defence of the trade, and Macclesfield begins to look like the ideal Methodist recruiting ground. There are several respects in which Methodism seems to have been particularly well suited to an industrialising market town like Macclesfield.

It is easy enough to examine the chapels from a twentieth-century, or even a nineteenth-century, vantage-point and find them narrow and provincial, purveyors of a theology which preyed on fear and capitalised on disaster and exploitation. But from the vantage-point of a rural county like Cheshire in the eighteenth century, the expansive, optimistic, even cosmospolitan features of chapel life are visible as well.

During a period when the range of social and cultural services which could be expected from the modern secular community did not exist, the chapel filled many needs and created some useful transitional institutions — not least among them the evangelical Sunday school. Like other social bodies, it quickly learned how to dig its heels in and resist change, when challenged by new forces threatening to undermine its authority in one sphere or another. Still, the breadth of the appeal of Nonconformity in a community like Macclesfield before the 1830s is undeniable. Indeed, to compare the patchy and piecemeal influence of local radicals with the ongoing efforts of the Dissenting bodies would be rather like comparing a handful of commando raiders with an occupying army.

Ever since Elie Halévy first published his brief but penetrating remarks on the political role of Methodism, historians have been avidly debating the effect of Wesleyanism and its offshoots on radicalism and the emergence of class consciousness.[115] Halévy himself emphasised Methodism's mission to the middle classes: 'the hard-working and capable bourgeois had been imbued by the evangelical movement with a spirit from which the established order had nothing to fear.'[116] In England this stratum did not provide the sort of leadership which was so crucial to the Revolutionary movement in France. Later writers, notably Eric Hobsbawm and E.P. Thompson, have looked more closely at the working class. They have tended to use a rather mechanical model, wherein Methodism, seen as a discrete phenomenon alien to the context of working-class culture and community, operates as a more or less effective brake on a self-generating and self-propelling engine labelled 'working-class consciousness'. Hobsbawm is inclined to discount Methodist influence, arguing that 'the strength of Wesleyanism was probably not great enough, and not well enough distributed, to affect the political situation decisively.' And in any case, he finds plenty of Methodists who were also radicals.[117] Thompson, in his now-famous critique of Methodism, takes a much more uncompromising view of its pernicious influence. First the chapel authorities sought to strait-jacket the nascent self-liberating impulses of the workers, and then they rushed in to offer delusionary consolation. For Thompson revivalism, in essence, is the 'Chiliasm of despair'.[118] He has recently slightly modified his harshest strictures on Methodism as a cultural force, but even in his latest summation he continues to hold the view that, in the realm of politics, the chapel was the unalterable foe of working-class advancement.[119]

Thompson exaggerates in the picture he has drawn of autocratic rule by the Dissenting clergy, unilaterally imposing a counter-revolutionary and repressive ethical system on a largely working-class constituency of chapel-goers. As has been shown the position of the clergy was somewhat more precarious than he allows, both financially and in the 'politics' of chapel life. This was especially true in the early decades of Methodism, but there was always a good deal of give and take between the professional clergy and the leading elements of the laity in all Dissenting bodies at the local level, right up into the early Victorian period. Here the all-important 'middling' group, the newly-prosperous, ranging in status from artisans and shopkeepers to professional men and industrialists, played a key role. The values of this group increasingly dominated chapel life, as they dominated the economic, political, legal, and social institutions of the town.

Historians sympathetic to Methodism have tried to counter the charge that the Society was 'counter-revolutionary' by directing attention to the close ties between Methodism and the Victorian labour movement.[120] And Hobsbawm adds that there are important distinctions to be made between conservative Wesleyanism and the more radicalised breakaway groups which directed their message especially to the labouring classes. The evidence from Macclesfield clearly shows a relationship between chapel schisms and the class identity of congregations. But the time-scale of the emergence of class-based chapels suggests that the very formation of social classes, in the modern sense, and the introduction of class elements into religious affiliation were simultaneous and related processes.[121] To speak of Macclesfield Methodism in the 1750s as either middle class or working class in orientation would be misleading, because such clear-cut social categories are not identifiable in that period. The ambiguous social/political attitudes of local Methodism over the next seventy or eighty years accurately reflect a partially-formed and unevenly developed class consciousness among the town's population.

While it may be true that religion deflected and dampened energies that might otherwise have found political expression, the local Wesleyan clergy, far from taking an aggressive role in molding political attitudes, found it more appropriate to their evangelical purposes to stay out of politics as much as possible.[122] Consequently individual chapel-goers do not seem to have embraced the notion that Methodism and radicalism were mutually exclusive.[123]

Writing of the late nineteenth century, A. Ainsworth has put forth the thesis that 'socialism may perhaps be more correctly seen as *growing out of* and thus affording new relevance to religious themes.'[124] Applying his provocative and sensitive approach to a pre-Victorian context, one might suggest a roughly analogous interconnection between evangelical religion and class-conscious politics. The former, a many-sided psychological and cultural response to a transitional period in social and economic relations, was to some extent superceded by the latter from the 1830s onward.

Some recent writers have taken a non-condemnatory view of Methodism's relationship to the working classes. Alan D. Gilbert, for example, counters Thompson's dark and lurid picture by stressing that Nonconformity was particularly attractive to 'individuals and social groups whose economic and social positions were not only adequate but were actually improving.' He continues, 'Evangelical Nonconformity echoed the *aspirations* rather than the *despair* of the working classes.'[125] And Thomas Laqueur has argued that Methodist Sunday schools were to a large extent controlled and run by working-class parents and teachers, and were adapted by them to their own purposes.[126] But comparison of Macclesfield Sunday-school records with local directories suggests that teachers were generally drawn from a somewhat higher social level than their pupils (or were, like Adam Rushton, rapidly rising out of the working class). The most influential teachers tended to be those of higher social position, like Dr John Birchenall or Mayor Thomas Allen. Control of the Macclesfield schools was usually in the hands of a committee representing teachers, trustees, and other officers. When disputes arose it was almost always because of complaints from teachers, not parents. In smaller and poorer schools more control was exercised, not by parents, but by the clergy.

Perhaps the vexed question of whether Methodism controlled or was controlled by the working classes can never be answered. Perhaps it is the wrong question. For one thing it is simply not possible to correlate available figures for national, annual Methodist growth, *c.*1790 to 1850, in any convincing way with the advance of working-class consciousness, or with periods of radical political activity. The figures show an independent pattern of oscillation between strong increases and weaker slumps, a cycle of revivalism and decline which scholars have not yet been able to connect convincingly with patterns of demographic, economic, or political change.[127] We do not have the unbroken series of local statistics on membership which would be necessary if we are to relate chapel growth to phenomena such as Luddism or Chartism. And it is worth remembering that even the official annual statistics of membership reflect chapel growth, not popular religious enthusiasm.

The Dissenters themselves were sometimes prone to explain the expansion or stagnation of their congregations in fairly simple economic terms.[128] When trade was good and people had extra money in their hands chapels flourished. Despair or exaltation may have been the mainsprings of revivalism, but it was the weekly collection that enabled a chapel to grow and proselytise effectively. Such an explanation would seem to fit the data for Macclesfield as well as any other, and it would also allow in a loose way for the apparent alternation between radical and Methodist successes. It can be argued that economic hardship (sometimes) brought forth radical responses, while prosperity tended to foster Methodism, without having to accept that this was because one movement 'drove out' the other.[129] Hobsbawm makes a similar point: 'there was thus no revolution and Wesleyan Methodism was hostile to one; but it does not follow that the second fact was the cause of the first.'[130] Certainly there was hostility and open confrontation between the two social forces. But the whole issue is much clouded by the fact that both sides were so fond of making exaggerated claims about their impact upon each other. As we have seen, the Methodists were often prepared to state that they could pacify and discipline the lower classes, as a way of establishing a secure position for themselves under the wing of the Establishment. How seriously this sort of self-justification should be taken is another matter. If we were to read only the ultra-Tory pamphleteers of the period we might well conclude that the Methodists were dangerous firebrands, single-handedly responsible for the rebelliousness and insubordination of the lower orders.[131]

As far as Macclesfield was concerned the effect of Methodism was a far subtler and more complex matter. It was a town deeply resistant to change; there was much in its history and economic situation which contributed to making that so. Methodism, through its links with a national Connexion, its system of itineracy, and its re-creation of a sense of community — however artificial, limited, or temporary — offered (at least to those who could accept its doctrine and discipline) a reassuring structure and a secure base from which to confront and assimilate new developments.

VI

Conclusion

The preceding chapters have brought Macclesfield to the threshold of maturity as an industrial town. The next phase, a period of vigorous growth as the centre of national silk production, was brief, cut short abruptly by the Free Trade Treaty of 1860, as contemporaries so accurately foretold.

Local history, like biography, can be a reminder of the irreducible diversity that lies behind the generalisations of social theorists. In defence of the particular, G.W. Oxley has written, 'What matters is the precise details of the local situation, not an aggregate of such local details purporting to reflect the national scene and effectively cancelling out the local variations which were its most significant feature.'[1] Macclesfield is just the sort of place that is likely to be forgotten in national surveys. Yet Macclesfield is far from an isolated case; how many such places were there, occupying the middle ground, a buffer zone between rural and urban life, between the old regulated economy and the full rigour of *laissez-faire*, between the reassuring, perhaps monotonous comforts and trials of village existence and the temptations, exhilarations, and deprivations of the city?

The aims of this study have been, first, to describe how Macclesfield changed physically, and how its economic and social structure altered as a result of industrialisation; and second, to examine the political arrangements and cultural forms that reflected a social reality which was partly new, partly traditional, and significantly shaped by persuasive collective notions about moral relationships in former times. Some of these ideas were indiginous and venerable; others were brought as part of the cultural baggage of a flood of migrants; and some, like the passionately defended 'moral economy' of the handloom weavers, were hybrids — relatively recent, and always vulnerable, adaptations of traditional values to new conditions.

By the end of the period, as has been shown, the paternalism of farmer and labourer, master and apprentice, or the family workshop was being supplanted by more impersonal relations, conditioned by the requirements of the factory, the warehouse, and the bank. Among working people a new consciousness of class identity and class antagonism began to emerge, but any such consciousness, especially among skilled workers, was necessarily coloured and limited by prior loyalties to trade and craft.

The master silk-weavers' defensive strategy of attempting to preserve their price-lists and prerogatives while remaining indifferent to the situation of the factory weavers is one example of a crippling sectionalism. It could hardly be expected that a serious class-wide challenge to the employers' supremacy would be mounted when the élite of silk-workers went in fear of so many potential competitors, not only abroad but at home as well. The pretensions to superiority of skilled labour over less skilled, of weaver over spinner, of Briton over foreigner, of Protestant over Catholic, of native over newcomer, and of male adult over female or child labourer, were dearly bought distinctions. The cultural rigidity which enclosed women in a narrow sphere embracing kitchen, childcare, and chapel, while most men inhabited a segregated world of tavern, trade union and friendly society, reinforced the attitude that woman was a subordinate or an interloper in the workplace.

The cost of the sexual division of labour, not only in the direct exploitation of women, but in the fragmentation and weakening of the labour movement was, as it still is, appalling. No one, neither trade unionist nor political organiser, could properly claim to speak 'for the trade' when more than half the work-force stood apart, silent and not consulted. This was a problem that would remain. The proportion of females in the population of Macclesfield, averaging about 55 per cent from 1801 to 1841, rose considerably thereafter.[2] The silk industry in its long decline after 1860 relied more than ever on a female work-force. Ethnic and religious prejudice, too, persisted through the century; and evangelical religion, in its latter-day embrace of anti-Catholicism, anti-feminism, and the cult of respectability often encouraged these tendencies.

Peter Clark has pointed out that the hallmarks of developing towns in the eighteenth century are industrial growth based on increasing specialisation, including segmentation of the booming domestic market, combined with a continuing complex interrelationship between the economies of town and countryside.[3] Macclesfield, in its links with London, the Midlands silk-producing towns, and the East Cheshire region, fits the general model neatly. Along with the other provincial towns it enjoyed the benefits of improved transport and communication, and the sometimes mixed blessings of the expansion of professional and retail services. The town had its share of lawyers and editors, soon to be followed by politicians, policemen and administrators, to act as 'brokers or intermediaries' between town and nation.[4] Nevertheless, as a silk town Macclesfield was always something of a special case. The central acceptance of the proposition that English silk needed government protection, lent a distinctive conservative cast to the town's politics and outlook. Not only did this view restrain silk manufacturers from full acceptance of free trade principles, it also kept many working people from embracing any ideology based on class solidarity, class-wide organisation, or class power. Master weavers were very likely to see themselves as partners — junior partners to be sure — of large manufacturers in the common project of securing and defending the health of the trade. Predictably, mobilisation against a foreign enemy blunted class struggle at home. And this was a 'French war' in which there could be no armistice.

It was characteristic of Macclesfield that popular protest movements were based on a broad coalition of classes and interest-groups. The resistance to the New Poor Law of 1834, for example, gained wide allegiance and enjoyed remarkable success. Macclesfield employers hesitated to give a blanket endorsement to early capitalist ideology, yet they never shrank from the full and free exercise of the prerogatives of private wealth. The Ryles, the Brocklehursts, and other local magnates supervised community affairs in comfortable security, like doges in a little republic of property-holders. The Corporation was literally in their debt and figuratively in their hands. The banks were theirs, the press was theirs, and the magistracy, with ever fewer exceptions, followed their lead. The military, the penal code, and the moral authority of the Church were always in reserve, to be summoned up when disorder threatened. Political reform in Macclesfield overturned nothing. The municipal reform of 1835 slightly shifted and slightly narrowed the local franchise; it was the triumph of property qualification, sweeping away more ancient, less tidy definitions of freemanship. The chapels and Sunday Schools, too, in spite of some subversive implications of their early accomplishments, turned out not to be harbingers of the artisans' millennium. Rather they dedicated themselves to good works, good fellowship, self-improvement, and, for the most part, peaceable adjustment to the requirements of nineteenth-century life.

Familiar as they were with the uses of violence, in protest, in collective bargaining with intransigent superiors, and in intimidation, Macclesfield radicals also drew on common protectionist assumptions and projected a Utopian dream of harmony and plenty. This was the vision of Reuben Bullock, a radical silk-worker and long-time associate of John Doherty, the Manchester spinners' leader:

> If an act of parliament were obtained [to protect the trade] . . . things would go in great comfort, labour in our staple manufactories would gradually be getting its proper level, which would give a stimulus to all the rest; then this country would enjoy the sweets of plenty, with the blessings of peace; cheerfulness would adorn the face of the working man; the songs of poverty would leave our streets; the dissolute female, who perhaps, first bartered away her virtue for leave to toil, . . . might live by honest industry. The poor Irish would, . . . quickly mingle with those branches of business that would bring a due exchange of the comforts of life, without which their poverty must be stationery.[5]

And would this state of affairs injure the masters? 'No such thing; for what protects wages, protects profits, and profits advance before wages. The masters would, therefore, have an equal, and sometimes greater advantage than the work-people.'[6] Bullock was expressing the most generous impulses of a long and sporadic struggle for the dignity of labour and a decent standard of livelihood. If the remedy was doomed, the spirit survived.

By the 1820s and 1830s industrialisation was a pervasive physical presence, apparent everywhere in the factory chimneys looming up over close-packed streets of terraced houses. Behind the chimneys stood a cash economy, and for labouring people, as for the entrepreneur, money was an essential key to urban life. The tailor, the grocer, and the baker required it; self-improvement meant tool-rent and house-rent and rates to be paid, and club money and chapel money due every week. Money brought a kind of freedom, along with new dependencies and new insecurities. Overall, the gains, if not spectacular, were not negligible. The losses, so often intangible, are harder to assess. Residents of Macclesfield were more prosperous but more crowded; more oppressed by work discipline, but more mobile, more literate, and perhaps more independent-minded; longer-lived, but probably not freer from anxiety, discomfort, and infirmity than townspeople of a century earlier.

Certainly the cultural and political temper of Macclesfield changed significantly between 1750 and the mid-1830s. The town was bigger — filled with recent immigrants — and its industrial base sturdier. Manchester, Stockport, and Liverpool were much closer, and much more insistent influences than ever before. Macclesfield felt itself part of a larger world, a more sophisticated culture. Innovations in the organisation of community life may have been restrained or retarded by inertia and reverence for the past, but they could not be barred or blocked permanently. The course of future change was to be charted and guided, to a considerable extent, by a newly-emerging group — readers of Blue Books, social investigators, writers of local reports — the middlemen of social control. These were the sponsors of the new police force, the Union workhouse, public libraries and parks, a host of educational, medical, and sanitary schemes.

The civic improver, fired by an intense devotion to the idea of civic progress, was the 'new man' of the 1840s, 1850s, and 1860s, as the textile entrepreneur had been of the 1740s, 1750s, and 1760s. Such men usually came from middle-class families whose prosperity was a by-product of the textile boom, and who shared a common identity and self-confidence rooted in the experience and institutions of evangelical religion. Through determined effort, with wavering assistance from the national government, a new race of bureaucrats and committee-men helped to transform Macclesfield from a market centre to a municipality — more than merely an amalgam of private interests, but somehow less than the inward-looking, self-regulated community of pre-industrial times.

Notes for pages 1-5

I A Town built on Silk

1. John Burnett points out that in 1801 only 20% of the population of England and Wales were living in towns of more than 5000. Most people would never have seen a city, but would have experience of the local market town(s). Burnett, *A Social History of Housing* (Newton Abbot, 1978) p. 7.
2. Alan Armstrong, *Stability and Change in an English Country Town: a social study of York, 1801-1851* (London, 1974) p. 10.
3. Many of the town's streets changed name during this period. For convenience, the modern names will be used throughout the text.
4. For the structure of the Corporation, see Chapter IV, section I.
5. James Obelkevich, *Religion and Rural Society: South Lindsey, 1825-1875* (Oxford, 1976) p. 5.
6. For a survey of East Cheshire agricultural history, see C. Stella Davies, 'The Agricultural History of Cheshire, 1750-1850', *Remains, Historical and Literary . . . Published by the Chetham Society*, 3rd ser., vol. X (Manchester, 1960). For the relationship between surplus population and rural handicraft industry, Joan Thirsk, 'Industries in the Countryside', in F.J. Fisher (ed.), *Essays in the Economic and Social History of Tudor and Stuart England* (London, 1961) pp. 70-88.
7. Thomas Wedge, *General View of the Agriculture of the County Palatine of Chester . . .* (London, 1794) p. 26; Arthur Young, *A Six Months Tour in the North of England* (London, 1770); Henry Holland, *General View of the Agriculture of Cheshire* (London, 1808) pp. 86, 345, and *passim*.
8. Henry Holland, *Agriculture of Cheshire*, p. 296.
9. See C.L. Mellowes, 'The Geographical Basis of the West Pennine Silk Industry', *Journal of the Textile Institute*, XXV (1934) 376-88.
10. W. Harrison, 'The Development of the Turnpike System in Lancashire and Cheshire', *TLCAS*, IV (1886) 80-92.
11. [Francis Gastrell], 'Notitia Cestrensis, I.', *Remains, Historical and Literary . . . Published by the Chetham Society,* vol. VIII (Manchester, 1845) p. 289. We can assume that 'family' as used by Gastrell refers to all resident members of a household, including servants.
12. Peter Laslett, 'Mean Household Size in England since the Sixteenth Century', in P. Laslett and Richard Wall (eds), *Household and Family in Past Time* (London, 1972) pp. 125-58. The national average numbers of persons per family were 4.69 in 1801 and 4.74 in 1811; J. Burnett, *History of Housing*, p. 5.

Notes for pages 5-7.

13. For comparison, the census returns for 1811 gave the total population at 12,999 and the number of families as 2741, yielding an average family size of 4.49; the census of 1821 gave 17,746 population and 3662 families, yielding an average family size of 4.85.

    An earlier population estimate than Gastrell's which the bishop mentions without comment, speaks of 'at least 2,000 [families] in the town and precinct'. This figure must be exaggerated: CRO, EDA 6/1/2, 'An Enquiry made within the Deanery of Macclesfield of the Valuation of Livings . . . [for] the Governors of the Bounty of Queen Ann . . .' [1704?].
14. CRO, EDP 181/7. John Corry guesses 'about 5000' for the town and neighbourhood in 1763; *The History of Macclesfield* (London, 1817) p. 69.
15. Ibid., p. 120.
16. 'The returns were supposed to be very short of the real state of the population'. Daniel and Samuel Lysons, *Magna Britannia. . .* (London, 1810), vol. II, part 2, p. 736. So growth may have been somewhat faster than has been supposed in the 1780s and 1790s, and somewhat slower thereafter.
17. C. Stella Davies, *A History of Macclesfield* (Manchester, [1961]) p. 376.
18. For the best accounts of the post-1850 history of the town see C. Stella Davies, *History of Macclesfield* and J.N. Jackson, 'The Population and Industrial Structure of Macclesfield' (Manchester University Ph.D., 1960). On emigration from Macclesfield, R.D. Margrave, 'The Emigration of Silk Workers from England to the United States of America in the Nineteenth Century, . . .' (London University (LSE) Ph.D., 1981).
19. The disproportion continued; the figure for females in 1811 was 54.2% and for 1821, 52.5%.
20. See CCRO, Earwaker Collection, 63/2/34. 'A Table of the Population. . . of the Prestbury Division of the Hundred of Macclesfield.'
21. See scattered references to the place of origin of paupers and other migrants in Quarter Sessions depositions for the late eighteenth century, QJF and QJB series, CRO, and in a bundle of paupers' depositions taken down between *c.*1823 and 1825 in CRO, Clulow Papers, Box 10.
22. John Corry, *History*, p. 56.
23. CRO, EDV 7/1/96, 'Visitation: Articles of Inquiry, 1778' reports 'not more than six or seven papists and all of them poor'; CRO,

Notes for pages 7-10.

EDV 7/2/103 'Visitation: Articles of Inquiry, 1789' says there are about thirty in the parish 'of no rank.' By 1821 the report says, simply, 'chiefly Irish weavers'; CRO, EDV 7/6/308.

24. Other large groups came from Staffordshire, Ireland, Lancashire, Derbyshire, Yorkshire, and London, in that order. See J.N. Jackson, 'Population and Industrial Structure', Appendix, Table 2.4, 'Principal Birthplaces of Inhabitants, 1851', based on the census returns for that year.
25. Clulow Papers, MPL. As she was accused of practising deceits upon the local residents she was probably fortune-telling or begging under false pretences. The magistrates, John Ryle and Charles Wood, were leading textile manufacturers and brothers-in-law. See also the testimony of David Rowbotham, a migrant from Lancashire, in 'Report of the Select Committee on the Silk Trade', P.P., 1831-32, XIX, 819-20.
26. CRO, QJF 240/1.
27. CRO, Clulow Papers, Box 10.
28. For recent accounts of the French silk manufacture in the eighteenth century, see Maurice Garden, *Lyon et les lyonnais au XVIIIe siècle* (Paris, 1975); and Robert J. Bezucha, *The Lyon Uprising of 1834: social and political conflict in the Early July Monarchy* (Cambridge, Mass., 1974) Chap. 1.
29. The full story of the London trade is told in N.K.A. Rothstein, 'The Silk Industry in London, 1702-66' (London University M.A., 1961) and W.M. Jordan, 'The Silk Industry in London, 1760-1830' (London University M.A., 1931). Other essential surveys are Frank Warner, *The Silk Industry of the United Kingdom: its origin and development* (London, 1921); Gerald B. Hertz, 'The English Silk Industry in the Eighteenth Century', *English Historical Review,* XXIV (1909) 710-27; and Donald Coleman, *Courtaulds: an economic and social history* (Oxford, 1969) vol. I.
30. See W.H. Chaloner, 'Sir Thomas Lombe (1685-1739) and the British Silk Industry', *History Today*, 3 (1953) 778-85.
31. For a description of this mill, see J.H. Massey, 'The Silk Mills of Macclesfield' (Thesis, final exam. R.I.B.A., School of Architecture, Manchester University, 1959) pp. 4-5.
32. John Aiken, *A Description of the Country from Thirty to Forty Miles round Manchester* (London, 1795) p. 436.

For the existence of the button trade in Macclesfield as early as the sixteenth century see Corporation Accounts, 1574, cited in J.P. Earwaker, *East Cheshire: past and present* (London, 1880) vol. II, p. 485. See also letters on the early seventeenth-century trade in

Notes for pages 10-15.

THSLC, IV (1851-52) 196-7.

33. T. Worthington Barlow (ed.), *Cheshire and Lancashire Historical Collector*, vol. I (1853) 6, quoting a portion (now lost) of Samuel Finney's ms. 'Survey of the Parish of Wilmslow'.
34. See page from account book, now lost, reproduced following p. 12 in Mary Crozier, *An Old Silk Family* (Aberdeen, 1947).
35. John Corry, *History*, p. 56.
36. William Tunnicliff, *A Topographical Survey of the Counties of Stafford, Chester, and Lancaster . . .* (Nantwich, 1787) pp. 66-7; John Aiken, *Description of the Country*, p. 438.
37. [James Pigot], *Commercial Directory for 1816-17* (Manchester, 1816) p. 215.
38. John Corry, *History*, p. 57; D.K. Wharton-Street, 'The Silk Industry of Macclesfield', (Manchester University B.A., 1965) pp. 21-2.
39. From the Anglo Saxon 'thraw', to whirl or spin.
40. On hand-twisting in 1664, W.H. Clarke, 'On the Charters, Documents and Insignia relating to the Ancient Manor and Borough of Macclesfield', *TLCAS*, XXII (1904) 160; seven 'twisters' are listed as holding stalls in the market in 1732, Birkenhead Central Library, Macclesfield Collection, MA Box I II/12, 'Copy of Stallage Court Book for 1732'.
41. See, for example, Birkenhead CL, Macclesfield Coll., MA C/III/2 and MA I V/4.
42. On Brindley's Cheshire career, Samuel Smiles, *Lives of the Engineers,* vol. I (London, 1861), pp 307-33.
43. The definitive account of Roe's life and career is W.H. Chaloner, 'Charles Roe of Macclesfield (1715-81): an eighteenth-century industrialist', *TLCAS*, LXII (1951), 133-56; LXIII (1952), 52-86.
44. For detailed descriptions of this, and all the other major mill complexes of the eighteenth and early nineteenth centuries, see J.H. Massey, 'Silk Mills'. Massey had access to photographs taken during demolition of part of Roe's mill in 1951, and he examined the remaining portion of the fabric himself.
45. W.H. Chaloner, 'Charles Roe', *TLCAS*, LXII (1951) 138. Chaloner refers to the Royal Depot Mills Mss., now apparently lost.
46. The works are described vividly in J. Aiken, *Description of the Country*, pp. 438-9.
47. *House of Lords Journal*, XXXI (1766) 350.
48. W.H. Chaloner, quoting a letter of the Duke's, in 'Charles Roe', *TLCAS*, LXII (1951) 155.

Notes for pages 16-22.

49. See ibid., LXIII (1952), 83-5.
50. John Corry, *History*, p. 56.
51. J.H. Massey, 'Silk Mills', pp. 8, 8A, 10.
52. Ibid., p. 45.
53. Mary Crozier, *An Old Silk Family*, pp. 18-19.
54. [Emma Dent], *In Memory of John Brocklehurst, M.P.* (n.p., 1897) p. 3.
55. C.S. Davies, *History of Macclesfield*, p. 132.
56. [Emma Dent], *John Brocklehurst*, p. 4.
57. Daintry's background was similar to the Brocklehursts'; his family were landowners from Leek. L.S. Presnell, *Country Banking in the Industrial Revolution* (London, 1956) p. 29.
58. L.H. Grindon, *Manchester Banks and Bankers* (Manchester, 1878) p. 113.
59. Boulton and Watt Collection, Birmingham Public Library, 'Record of Drawings of Engines at the Firm of Boulton and Watt compiled by Harry Hazleton . . .,' Microfilm copy, Manchester University Library, M16.
60. P.P., 1831-2, XIX, 785-6. Brocklehurst added that the owner of this mill went bankrupt and the mill sold in 1827 for £1700 plus £200 for the machinery.
61. Guildhall Library, MS 11,937A, Sun Fire Office: Register of Country Losses, Henry Barlow and Co., 1824.
62. Quoted in *Macclesfield Times and Courier*, 3 March 1953.
63. Henry Holland, *Agriculture of Cheshire*, p. 15.
64. J.H. Clapham, 'The Spitalfields Acts: 1773-1824', *Economic Journal*, XXVI (1916) 459-71.
65. John Corry, *History*, p. 68.
66. 'Report of the Select Committee on the Silk Trade'. P.P., 1831-2, XIX, 808, testimony of John Prout, weaver.
67. D.K. Wharton-Street, 'Silk Industry', p. 45.
68. 'Report on Silkweavers' Petitions'. P.P., 1818, IX, 98. Apparently wives are not counted here, so the '313 married' weavers would represent 313 male weavers plus wives.
69. John Wootton, 'Macclesfield Past', or 'The History of Macclesfield', a prize essay written in 1866 and published in instalments in *MCH* in 1880. The clippings are collected in a scrapbook in MPL. The information given here appears on page 9 of the scrapbook.
70. P.P., 1831-2, XIX, 775-6. Brocklehurst went on to say that, owing to trade depression, the number of spindles had dropped to 117,192 and workers to 3622 in 1832.

Notes for pages 22-26.

71. J.H. Massey, 'Silk Mills', p. 12.
72. P.P., 1818, IX, 67, 87. Employer John Ryle estimated about 2*s* 6*d* per week; the workmen said 3*s*.
The processes of preparing the thread and setting up the loom — ill-paid work usually done by women — are described in detail in Laura S. Strumingher, *Women and the Making of the Working Class: Lyon 1830-1870* (St Alban's, Vermont, 1979) Chap. 2.
73. P.P., 1818, IX, 67. John Ryle said 3*s* per 'cut' of seven yards of bandannas in 1818.
74. Ibid., pp. 67 and *passim*.
75. John Wootton, 'Macclesfield Past', MPL scrapbook, pp. 7-8.
76. *House of Commons Journals* (hereafter HCJ), XXX, 1765, 216-18.
77. *HCJ*, XXXI, 1766, 726-7.
78. Robert Head, *Congleton Past and Present* (Congleton, 1887) pp. 147-8.
79. *HCJ*, XXX, 1765, 212-13.
80. J. Corry, *History*, p. 107.
81. Mary Crozier, *An Old Silk Family*, p. 20.
82. *A Walk through the Public Institutions of Macclesfield* (Macclesfield, 1888) p. 11.
83. D.K. Wharton-Street, 'Silk Industry', p. 41.
84. The first cotton firm mentioned is 'Cockshott and Co.' in Peter Broster, *The Chester Guide* . . . (Chester, [1781]); this firm is not mentioned by John Corry in his brief sketch of the history of the trade.
85. John Wootton, 'Macclesfield Past', MPL scrapbook, p. 6.
86. For a vivid description of the trades of Macclesfield in about 1810 see D. and S. Lysons, *Magna Britannia*, vol. II, 735-6.
87. On the growth of retailing in this period see S.I. Mitchell, 'Urban Markets and Retail Distribution 1730-1815, with Particular Reference to Macclesfield, Stockport, and Chester' (Oxford University, D.Phil., 1974).
88. P.M. Giles, 'The Felt-Hatting Industry *c.*1500-1850, with Special Reference to Lancashire and Cheshire', *TLCAS*, LXIX (1959) 104-32.
89. J.N. Jackson, 'Population and Industrial Structure', p. 23.
90. Macclesfield Town Hall, Corporation Minute Books, vol. I (1769-1824), entry for 21 March 1800.
91. On the enclosures see C. Stella Davies, 'Agricultural History', pp. 65-7; and D.K. Wharton-Street, 'Silk Industry', p. 37.

Notes for pages 29-35.

II Masters and Servants

1. James Roe, *Sermons on Several Subjects and Occasions* (York, 1766) p. 8.
2. Sidney and Beatrice Webb, *The History of Trade Unionism* (London, 1926 ed.) pp. 45-6.
3. For a discussion of the transition from the society of rank and order to that of distinct classes 'ranged against one another', as the development of factory industry substituted Carlyle's 'cash nexus' for Southey's 'bonds of attachment', see Asa Briggs, 'The Language of "Class" in Early Nineteenth-century England', in A. Briggs and John Saville (eds), *Essays in Labour History, in Memory of G.D.H. Cole* (London, 1960) pp. 43-73.
4. E.P. Thompson, 'Patrician Society, Plebeian Culture', *Journal of Social History*, VII (1973-4) 396-7.
5. Ibid. and Thompson, 'Eighteenth-century English Society: class struggle without class?', *Social History,* III, no. 2 (1978) 133-65. Thompson finds the 'critical clue[s] to this structural equilibrium of gentry-crowd relations' in the weakness of the central state, 'the particular inheritance of Law', and a grudging but necessary tolerance, on occasion, for the 'licence of the crowd', p. 145.
6. D.C. Coleman, *The Economy of England, 1450-1750* (London, 1977) p. 159.
7. Among the silk-workers mentioned there was only one weaver, and he was from Derbyshire.
8. Samuel Smiles, *Lives of the Engineers*, vol. I (London, 1861) 314-15.
9. W.M. Jordan, 'The Silk Industry in London, 1760-1830' (London University M.A., 1931) p. 12.
10. See, for example, (2nd) Report of the Select Committee on Silk Ribbon Weavers' Petitions, P.P. 1818, IX, 88, testimony of John Foster, weaver, who had worked in Dublin for about thirteen years, migrated to Macclesfield, and became a leader of the organised weavers.

    The London silk-weavers had a long and violent history of defence of their trade regulations; for the eighteenth-century struggles which culminated in the passage of the Spitalfields Act in 1773, giving virtually a 'fresh lease of life to the old Tudor protective legislation', see George Rudé, *The Crowd in History: a study of popular disturbances in France and England, 1730-1848* (New York, 1964). Also, M. Dorothy George, *London Life in the Eighteenth Century* (Harmondsworth, 1966) pp. 179-96; and

Notes for pages 35-36.

W.M. Jordan, 'The Silk Industry in London', pp. 86-91.

11. Eric Hobsbawm, 'Custom, Wages and Work-load in Nineteenth Century Industry', in Briggs and Saville (eds), *Essays in Labour History*, pp. 115 ff. This essay surveys the relationship of status and wage expectations, the criteria for determining a 'fair day's work', and the prevalence of customary over market calculations in setting wage levels — all legacies from eighteenth-century practice. See also, John Rule, *The Experience of Labour in Eighteenth-Century English Industry* (New York, 1981) Chap. 2.
12. See Mayor Thomas Allen's Notebook, entry for 22 July 1824; in this case of an absconding apprentice who was said to have bound himself, the magistrate ordered the boy back to work, noting, 'An infant can bind himself'.

    On the history of apprenticeship regulations, their modification in the eighteenth century, and employers' efforts to repeal them, see J. Rule, *Experience of Labour*, Chap. 4.
13. See, for example, the case of Joseph Bentley, aged fifteen, bound to a weaver for six years, in C. Stella Davies (ed.), *A History of Macclesfield* (Manchester, [1961]), p. 130; a sixteen-year-old bound to Brocklehurst's for five years, in Mary Crozier, *An Old Silk Family* (Aberdeen, 1947), p. 30; and a girl bound to a weaver for four years, indenture in CRO, Clulow Papers, Box 15.
14. Or fewer, depending on the number of his own children he employed, see P.P., 1818, IX, 90-2. Also, John Wootton, 'Macclesfield Past', MPL scrapbook, p. 6.
15. At the other end of the scale, a cobbler recalled, 'If a shoemaker took an apprentice, and boarded him entirely and washed his clothes, it was usual to get £5 or more: but if the lad spent Sundays at his home, and the washing were done there, no money was paid'. Reminiscence of A. Whittaker in Alfred Fryer, *Wilmslow Graves and Grave Thoughts from Wilmslow* (Stockport, 1886) p. 97.
16. For a typical weaver's indenture under the live-in system in 1813 see P.P., 1818, IX, 93-4. For a premium of £50 paid to learn all of the silk business, *MC*, 22 September 1822; this was for three years only, the father to pay maintenance.
17. See the case of Benjamin Oldfield, bound as a pattern-drawer to Daintry and Wood, cotton manufacturers, in 1805; he was to be paid a weekly wage, rising in yearly increments from 5*s* to 11*s*, CRO, Clulow Papers, Box 15; and indenture of David Birchenough, bound to Robert Goddard, weaver, in 1805 at half pay, mother to find clothes and lodging, Clulow Papers, Box 14.
18. P.P., 1818, IX, 98-9 (John Foster, weaver).

Notes for pages 36-38.

19. MPL, Thomas Allen's Notebook, *passim*; and CRO, QJF 204/4/46, Knutsford Sessions, 8 October 1776, case of apprentice joining the Army to escape his master.
20. A. Fryer, *Wilmslow Graves*, pp. 92-3. After this experience Earnshaw was glad to escape to a small cotton factory where she earned 2*s* a week, of which one went for lodging and 'a shilling for my porridge'.
21. P.P., 1818, IX, 88. (John Foster, weaver).
22. J. Wootton, 'Macclesfield Past', MPL scrapbook, p. 6.
23. See the testimony of John Foster, weaver, who said he had to let his two half-pay apprentices go in 1818 for lack of work; of these only one had been regularly indentured, and both had been with other masters before him. P.P., 1818, IX, 88.
24. On stratification in the early nineteenth-century working class, E.P. Thompson, *The Making of the English Working Class* (London, 1963) pp. 234 ff.
25. This is in contrast to the view of Frances Collier, who says that, 'the most important social effect of the factory system was the increase it made possible in the earning power of the family.' 'The Family Economy of the Working Classes in the Cotton Industry, 1784-1833', *Remains, Historical and Literary . . . published by the Chetham Society*, vol. XII, 3rd series (Manchester, 1965) p. 16.
26. Arthur Young, *A Six Months Tour in the North of England* (London, 1770) p. 300.
27. John Corry, *The History of Macclesfield* (London, 1817) pp. 66-7. Traveller John Byng, who visited the Macclesfield Copper Works in 1796, thought the best workmen there were but meanly paid at 14*s* a week. J. Byng, *The Torrington Diaries . . . between the Years 1781 and 1794,* vol. III, (ed.) C. Bruyn Andrews (London, 1930) p. 122.
28. Macclesfield Corporation Records (now lost for these years?), quoted in J.N. Jackson, 'The Population and Industrial Structure of Macclesfield' (Manchester University Ph.D., 1960) p. 8.
29. For praise of the silk trade as a means of employing the poor, inmates of workhouses, soldiers' and sailors' widows, etc., see W.M. Jordan, 'The Silk Industry in London', pp. 19-20.
30. The employment of local pauper children seems to have been a regular practice in cotton mills from the 1790s onward; see entries of wages paid by Daintry and Wood from 1802 in Chetham's Library, Manchester, Sutton Accounts: Poor House Accounts, 1797-1818. Also monthly lists of children's wages from 1798, ibid. The pauper children worked at winding and cotton-spinning for

Notes for pages 34-41.

wages varying (probably by age) from 3*d* a day to 3*s* 11½*d* a week. The wages were paid directly to the Overseers of the Poor. Only a few children's names — about half a dozen on average — are listed for each month.

31. William Bray, 'Sketch of a Tour into Derbyshire and Yorkshire' (written in 1777), in John Pinkerton (ed.), *A General Collection of the Best and Most Interesting Voyages and Travels in all Parts of the World,* vol. II (London, 1808) p. 371.

    One local historian, extolling the benefits of hand-spinning, admired the 'vigour and agility . . . the clear florid countenances, the fine streight persons, strength, activity, and free open (let me say) graceful air and carriage of the young people brought up in it, far beyond the preceding generation.' Samuel Finney's ms. 'Survey of the Parish of Wilmslow' [written in the 1780s?], quoted in T. Worthington Barlow (ed.), *Cheshire and Lancashire Historical Collector*, I (1853) 8.
32. PRO, PCI/33/A87, Part 1, Return of the Mayor [Michael Daintry] to the Duke of Portland's Circular Letter, 26 March 1796.
33. J. Corry, *History of Macclesfield,* p. 58.
34. P.P., 1818, IX, 76 (Henry Critchley, silk mfr).
35. Overseers sometimes did apprentice their charges formally, with indentures, but most 'pauper apprentices' were just factory workers — their service sometimes gained them a settlement in the town and sometimes not. See advertisement of John Rowbotham, silk throwster, for 30 girls aged 9 to 12 'as apprentices'. *MC*, 4 January 1823.
36. Allen kept a ms. notebook in which he briefly described every case he heard in the local magistrates' court. Because the pages have been rebound out of order, dating is uncertain, but the volume appears to cover March 1823 to October 1824. The employers in these cases were both millowners and small masters, but Allen's sketchy notes do not allow the distinguishing of master/journeyman cases from factory disputes.
37. The *Macclesfield Courier* (23 September 1826) said it was to the credit of the female sex 'that they never combine against their employers, in order to obtain higher wages, or to impose regulations of any kind.'

    When they did appear in court, women were by no means exempt from stiff sentences; see the case of Charlotte Seal, sentenced to three months' hard labour for leaving her employer, a silk manufacturer, in 1810: CRO, Clulow Papers, Box 14.
38. MPL, Thomas Allen's Notebook, 27 October 1823.

Notes for pages 41-42.

39. See, for example, evidence in the case of William Smale's silk-stealing ring, n.d.: CRO, Clulow Papers, Box 4. For mention of the 'Turkey merchants', *MC*, 30 October 1824. Certain innkeepers and lodging-house keepers made a business of receiving stolen silk; *MC*, 14 July 1827. Also statement of Mary Pickford, 31 October 1816: CRO, Clulow Papers, Box 10.
40. On attempts to control embezzlement through legislation, J. Rule, *Experience of Labour*, pp. 130-1; Rule, Chap. 5, also discusses the workers' persistent counter-charges that employers resorted to late or non-payment of wages, payment in kind, improper fines and rents, and other exploitative measures, especially when trade was poor.

    For examples of some heavy sentences: 1812, six months' hard labour for stealing 10 lb. raw silk, CRO, Clulow Papers, Box 14; *c.*1814, fine of £20 for buying 1 lb. skein silk, ibid., Box 4; three women sentenced to death for silk stealing, Chester Assizes, 30 August 1817 and 29 April 1818, account in *Macclesfield Express*, 4 January 1968; John Clarke (possibly a previous offender) sentenced to 14 years' transportation for stealing 3 lb. 1 oz. of silk, *MC*, 19 April 1828.
41. See search warrants in CRO, Clulow Papers, Box 10.
42. Thomas Hollinshead testified that he was induced to organise a gang of thieves when 'in want of employment'. His story and others suggest that there were a number of marginal throwsters and manufacturers in town who depended on cheap (i.e., stolen) silk in order to stay in business. Notes on the case in CRO: Clulow Papers, Box 4. See *MC*, 19 April 1828 for a case of stolen silk worth 14*s* a lb. sold for 9*s* a lb.
43. Adam Rushton, *My Life, as Farmer's Boy, Factory Lad, Teacher and Preacher, 1821-1909* (Manchester, 1909) p. 29.
44. Ibid., pp. 29-34.
45. Testimony in *Hutchinson* v. *Collier* [1801]: CRO, Clulow Papers, Box 4.

    For fatal accidents to children in silk mills, see CRO, QJF 225/1/69, 10 January 1797; T. Allen's Notebook, 5 May 1823; ibid., 18 December 1823, Ralph Boothby 'an infant of five years old, who was caught in the straps of the Machinery'; ibid., 22 October 1824, William Downes, 'a boy of eight years old, who was caught by the machinery and hanged by the strings of his pinafore'; and case of Susannah Warburton, aged 7, in CRO, Clulow Papers, Box 15.
46. Sidney Pollard, *The Genesis of Modern Management* (London,

Notes for pages 42-47.

1965) pp. 162-3.

47. P.P., 1818, IX, 77, 86.
48. Ibid., p. 166.
48. A. Fryer, *Wilmslow Graves*, p. 97. Whittaker compared his family's situation with that of some who were even worse off: ' "I knew a farm servant, and all that he gate besides his mate and lodging were 2*s* a week." [Fryer], "How did he find his clothes?" "Well, he were very poorly clad." '
50. Chetham's Library, Sutton Accounts — Surveyors of Highways, 1764-1814 (A.7.13/31985); P.P., 1818, IX, 95-6; and 'Report of the Select Committee on the Silk Trade', P.P., 1831-2, XIX, 781-3, 811.
51. There was apparently a tendency to under-report occupational data for workers other than the head of household; see P.M. Tillott, 'Sources of Inaccuracy in the 1851 and 1861 Censuses', in E.A. Wrigley (ed.), *Nineteenth-Century Society: essays in the use of quantitative methods for the study of social data* (Cambridge, 1972) pp. 121-7.

    John Prout gives an example of the sex- and age-structure of the work-force of a Macclesfield silk-spinning mill, with average weekly wages:

1 maker-up	20*s*
3 stewards	16*s*
7 millmen	10*s* 6*d*
1 watchman	10*s* 6*d*
2 porters	9*s*
14 spinning mill boys	5*s*
60 women and children	3*s* 6*d*

A Practical View of the Silk Trade (Macclesfield, 1829) p. 53.

52. P.P., 1832, XIX, 775, 811, 813. See also, P.P., 1818, IX, 87, 97, 103.
53. P.P., 1818, IX, 85 (Henry Critchley, silk manufacturer, speaking of the years before 1815, when the price-list was still in effect). A solicitor representing the striking Macclesfield hatters in 1806 suggested that it was commonly held that the Combination Acts had to be passed because juries were so well known for letting men off on conspiracy charges. Summary of Mr Cross's defence, *King* v. *Davenport* [1806]: CRO, Clulow Papers, Box 25.
54. In their final form the Acts provided for trial before two magistrates (not being masters in the trade concerned). Prosecution was only for offences 'wilfully and maliciously' committed. Penalties were up to three months' imprisonment, and theoretically

Notes for pages 47-50.

masters and men were equally liable (in practice, masters were rarely prosecuted under these laws). On the Combination Acts, see Sidney and Beatrice Webb, *History of Trade Unionism*, Chap. 2; M.D. George, 'The Combination Laws reconsidered', *Economic Journal Supplement* (May 1927) 214-28; and ibid., 'The Combination Laws', *Economic History Review*, VI (1936) 172-8.

Industrial strife actually intensified after 1800, but 'employers continued to rely mainly on the older legal controls.' A.E. Musson, *British Trade Unions, 1800-1875* (London, 1972) p. 24.

55. Notes on the case: CRO, Clulow Papers, Box 16.
56. Among the account entries are 7*s* 6*d* for writing petitions, 2*s* for ruling 24 signature sheets, and 'paid Charles Hooley Warning Trade for ffield [*sic*] meeting — 2.6', ibid.
57. Testimony of employers Henry Lowe and Matthew Wheelton in *King* v. *Davenport* [1806]: CRO, Clulow Papers, Box 25.
58. See CRO QJB/29a, Knutsford Session, 8 October 1805, and QJF 233/4. The accused were Matthew Mellor (aged 36), Francis Powdrell (30), Thomas Goodwin (22), Thomas Birchenough (15), and John Walker.
59. Testimony of S. Taylor, from draft brief for the prosecution (now lost?), Knutsford Session, October 1805, quoted in David Bethell, ' "The sin" of demanding higher wages', *MC,* 14 November 1968.
60. Ibid.
61. Except where noted all information on the strike comes from notes on *King* v. *Davenport et al.*, in CRO, Clulow Papers, Box 25. On the history of hatters' combinations, J. Rule, *Experience of Labour*, pp. 156-8.
62. Two of these lists are preserved among the documents in ibid.
63. CRO, QJF 234/3 and QJB/29a, Knutsford Session, 15 July 1806. The men were committed for trial at Quarter Sessions by two Macclesfield magistrates, Thomas Brocklehurst and William Ayton, silk manufacturers.
64. CRO, Clulow Papers, Box 25. Allen fell foul of the strikers again when his wife divulged some strike business to the employer Henry Lowe.

    Lowe stated that at first about twenty or thirty men left work, and three or four later returned. Matthew Wheelton said he employed ten men in town 'and as many out of it' — of these about ten struck and one returned.
65. Ibid., but see also the testimony of John Smith, who said he accepted work and refused to give it up. There is no mention of any reprisals against him.

Notes for pages 51-55.

66. Ibid., solicitor Cross's defence statement (notes by John Clulow, who appeared for the plaintiffs).
67. Testimony of Lowe and Wheelton, ibid.
68. CRO, QJB/29a, Knutsford Session, 15 July 1806.
69. Agreement reproduced in P.P., 1818, IX, 90-2.
70. *MC,* 16 April 1812.
71. P.P., 1818, IX, 97 (John Foster, weaver).
72. Ibid., p. 67 (John Ryle, silk manufacturer). Ryle added the traditional argument of the employers that people employed in the factories might be on relief if they were not given this work to do; ibid., p. 68.
73. Ibid., p. 97 (John Foster, weaver).
74. Henry Critchley testified that weavers in his mill were hired as servants, and that this was the usual practice. P.P., 1818, IX, 77. See also an account of a turn-out of factory weavers in a dispute with their employers over loom-rent. During the dispute the men cut and destroyed work in the looms, although this was now a felony punishable by transportation under a new act of Robert Peel's. S. Higginbotham is mentioned as a solicitor in the case for the 'Silk Association', that is, the masters' association. *MC*, 26 January 1828.
75. P.P., 1818, IX, 97 (John Foster, weaver).
76. Ibid., p. 64 (John Ryle, silk mfr.). For typical examples of each side of the story, see William Hale, 'An Appeal to the Public in Defence of the Spitalfields Act' (1822) and 'A Reply to Mr. Hale's Appeal . . . ' in *The Spitalfields Acts, Seven Pamphlets, 1818-1828* (New York, 1972).
77. P.P., 1818, IX, 92 (John Foster, weaver).
78. Ibid., p. 79.
79. Quoted in 'A Reply to Mr. Hale's Appeal', in *Spitalfields Acts*, p. 90.
80. P.P., 1818, IX, 82. See the men's charges of intimidation, ibid., p. 105 (John Smith, weaver).
81. Ibid., p. 88, and letter of Henry Hobhouse (on behalf of Home Secretary Robert Peel) to Mayor of Macclesfield, 29 March 1823, in MPL, Clulow Papers.
82. P.P., 1818, IX, 63. The evidence tends to show that, except in periods of severe crisis in the cotton trade, wages were somewhat higher in Manchester than in the country districts. See, for example, F. Collier, 'The Family Economy of the Working Classes', chap. 3. On the other hand, Manchester employers *had* instituted a wage reduction in 1812, so the Macclesfield masters

Notes for pages 55-58.

could claim to be adjusting to Manchester rates. Ibid., pp. 63, 152.

83. Ibid., pp. 63-4, 76-8, 87-8, 105. The very low rate was paid by Benjamin Kelley, formerly an employee of H. Critchley, who had set himself up in business with about fourteen looms in his shop and as many out. He soon went bankrupt.
84. In 1818 John Ryle employed about 600 people, less than half of them in his factory, and Henry Critchley '150 or 160' looms, only fifty of them in his factory. Ibid., pp. 65, 76.
85. See also C. Stella Davies, *History of Macclesfield,* pp. 192-3, and W. Hale, 'An Appeal to the Public'. One small master in London said that the end of regulation would leave 'but two classes, the great capitalists and the labourers.' W.M. Jordan, 'The Silk Industry in London', p. 180.

    Clive Behagg, 'Custom, Class and Change: the trade societies of Birmingham', *Social History*, IV (1979) 472-3.
86. Account of the meeting in J. Corry, *History*, pp. 11-12.
87. *MC*, 15 March 1817. The mayor and Corporation were not so favourably disposed; the Macclesfield Squadron under Captains Daintry and Hall, both silk manufacturers, were called out, and constables patrolled inns and lodging-houses. Five were arrested.
88. J. Corry, *History*, p. 109.
89. On the Club see *MC*, 5 April and 7 June 1817.
90. See, e.g., P.P., 1818, IX, 68-9 (John Ryle, silk mfr).
91. On Moore's efforts, J.L. and Barbara Hammond, *The Skilled Labourer, 1760-1832* (London, 1920) p. 215.
92. For example, an advertisement offered 40*s* to 50*s* a week for an 'expert silk dyer', *MC*, 31 May 1823. The town was experiencing a building boom at this time, and a turn-out of brick-setters revived old complaints about workmen idling away 'St. Monday'; see *MC*, 7 June 1823. The men asked for, and got, an extra 6*d* a day, raising their wage to 4*s* a day.
93. See table of average grain prices for 1815 to 1821, showing 1817 as the high point and a steady decline to 1821, *Manchester Guardian*, 24 November 1821.

    Migrants also came from Spitalfields, where trade was very bad at this time. See deposition of William Bates, a migrant from London in 1822: CRO, Clulow Papers, Box 10.
94. P.P., 1832, XIX, 775, 790. Brocklehurst went on to say that earnings had further worsened after 1826, until in 1832 weavers were averaging only 6*s* a week, and mill-workers only 2*s* 10½*d* for a 'short-time' week of 44 hours.
95. Details of the provisions of the act are in G.R. Porter, *Progress of*

Notes for pages 58-59.

the Nation . . . , vol. I (London, 1836) 255-8; and F. Collier, 'Family Economy of the Working Classes', pp. 11-12. For Macclesfield reaction, *MC*, 27 February and 27 March 1824, 5 and 29 October 1825.

96. William Huskisson, *Speeches*, vol. II (London, 1831) p. 249. A full statement of the case against free trade in silk can be found in J. Prout, *A Practical View of the Silk Trade.*

97. Accounts of the riot are in MPL, Thomas Allen's Notebook, 5 April 1824; *MC*, 10, 17, 24 April 1824; and J. Wootton 'Macclesfield Past', p. 8, which, however, contains some inaccuracies. The *Courier* attacked the London *Morning Chronicle* and the *Chester Guardian*, which criticised the Yeomanry and supported the workmen. See also, J. and B. Hammond, *The Town Labourer, 1760-1832* (New York, 1967) pp. 22-3.

 The usual hours of work in the mills were 6 a.m. to 6 p.m., with an hour off for dinner at noon and short breaks for breakfast and tea. On Saturday the workday was ten hours and forty minutes. Many worked two additional hours overtime daily. P.P., 1832, XIX, 775. So the men were protesting, not so much against the long workday, as against the idea that it should be mandatory.

98. The story of the campaign for repeal is told in J. and B. Hammond, *The Skilled Labourer,* pp. 216-20. For primary materials, *The Spitalfields Acts, Seven Pamphlets*. For Huskisson's arguments against the Acts, *Speeches*, vol. II, 187-91.

99. The *Macclesfield Courier* reported, for 1825 alone:

19 Feb:	partial turn-out of silk-workers; won wage increase
5 Mar.:	weavers' demand to reinstate old price-list
12 Mar.:	Congleton silk-workers' strike for same wages paid at Macclesfield; masters refuse
23 Apr.:	brickmakers turn-out for an extra 6*d* per 1000
23 Apr.:	colliers at Poynton turn-out — reportedly asking for 5*s* per day
11 June:	turn-out of journeyman tailors
18 June:	bricklayers' turn-out; succeed in getting an extra 6*d* and a quart of ale a day
2 and 9 July	sawyers' dispute; saws and frames belonging to men who refused to join 'the union' broken or carried away; two strangers hired as blacklegs met by turn-outs and 'liberally supplied with bread and cheese, and seven shillings in silver' and escorted out of town. *MC*, says the sawyers

Notes for pages 59-62.

well paid, earning 30*s* to 50*s* a week; masters threaten to build a new saw mill, since men so refractory

The well-known advertisement in the *Courier*, 26 March 1826 (quoted by Huskisson in Parliament and by several historians since), beginning 'Wanted Immediately: From 4 to 5 thousand persons from 7 to 20 years of age, to be employed in the Throwing and Manufacture of Silk . . .' was, according to the workmen, merely a crude attempt by the masters to intimidate their workpeople.

100. For the causes of the slump from late 1824 to early 1826, Thomas Tooke, *A History of Prices and of the State of the Circulation from 1793 to 1837*, vol. II (London, 1838) pp. 144-57. On 7 January 1826 the *Macclesfield Courier* reported 7000 to 8000 out of work, many mills stopped, and others open only 3½ days. See also *MC*, 11 February 1826.
101. Entry for 23 November 1826, in *The Journal of Sir Walter Scott, 1825-32*, vol. I, (London: n.d.) 322.
102. Earlier attempts by the master weavers to speak for the trade as a whole had met rebuffs, as in 1817, when they drew up a very deferentially-worded address to the manufacturers, calling for 'a living price', and got no satisfaction. For this address, see P.P., 1818, IX, 88-90.
103. 'Rules and Orders to Be Observed by the Silk Weavers of Macclesfield' (Macclesfield, 1826) pp. 1-2. Cf. London rules discussed in Samuel Sholl, 'A Short Historical Account of the Silk Industry' (London, 1811) and Lujo Brentano, *On the History and Development of Gilds and the Origin of Trade-Unions* (London, 1870) pp. 125-7.
104. *MC*, 4 February 1826. There were 1300 present and many hundreds could not get into the hall. The petition was approved unanimously, but women and children were excluded from signing.
105. Letter and account of riot in *MC*, 4 March 1826. The letter was signed by fourteen members of the Committee, all but two of them master weavers.
106. *MC*, 11 March 1826, and letter on Corn Laws, *MC*, 1 April 1826. For further evidence of the split between the radicals and the union leadership see the account of an angry exchange between William Adam and John Prout *et al.* at a weavers' meeting, *MC*, 14 April 1827.
107. *MC*, 29 September 1827.
108. The following account of the dispute is from *MC*, 4 and 11

Notes for pages 62-71.

November 1926.
109. *MC*, 10, 17, 24 November 1827.
110. *MC*, 8 December 1827. For opposing views of the effectiveness of the tactic, John Foster, *Class Struggle and the Industrial Revolution* (London, 1974) pp. 53-5; and D.S. Gadian, 'Class Consciousness in Oldham and Other North-West Industrial Towns 1830-1850', *Historical Journal*, XXI (1978) 162.
111. *MC*, 22 December 1827.
112. *MC*, 6 January 1827 — text not given.
113. *MC*, 24 May 1828.
114. P.P., 1832, XIX, 819 (Thomas Cope, weaver).
115. J. Wootton, 'Macclesfield Past', MPL scrapbook, p. 9.
116. Ibid., p. 10. The issues in the 1832 dispute are vividly set forth in three broadsides, 21 and 22 November 1832 and n.d., in the Working Class Movement Library, Old Trafford, Manchester.
117. See P.P., 1832, XIX, 775-81, 790-2, 801.
118. Ibid., p. 792.
119. Ibid., p. 814.
120. Ibid., p. 820.
121. Adapted from tables in ibid., p. 821.
122. Compare the similar responses of French silk-weavers to crisis conditions in the 1850s and 1860s: George J. Sheridan, Jr, 'Household and Craft in an Industrialising Economy: the case of the silk weavers of Lyon', in John M. Merriman (ed.), *Consciousness and Class Experience in Nineteenth-Century Europe* (New York, 1979) pp. 111 ff.
123. J. Wootton, 'Macclesfield Past', MPL scrapbook, p. 10.
124. Hammonds, *Skilled Labourer*, pp. 10-11.
125. *MC*, 29 July 1826.
126. E.P. Thompson, 'Patrician Society', pp. 382-3.
127. Mary Howitt, *An Autobiography*, vol. II, (ed.) Margaret Howitt (London, 1889) p. 106, letter of 21 May 1854.
128. C. Behagg, 'Custom, Class and Change', p. 480.
129. Gareth Stedman Jones, 'Class Struggle and the Industrial Revolution', *New Left Review*, no. 90 (Mar.-Apr. 1975) p. 51.
130. *MC*, 27 March 1880.

III Standard of Living

1. For a survey which takes a largely 'catastrophic' approach to the history of nineteenth-century health and health care, see

Notes for pages 72-73.

F.B. Smith, *The People's Health, 1830-1910* (London, 1979).

2. John Foster, *Class Struggle and the Industrial Revolution: early industrial capitalism in three English towns* (London, 1974) p. 91.
3. See, for example, E.J. Hobsbawm, 'The British Standard of Living, 1790-1850', *Economic History Review*, 2nd ser. X (1957); R.M. Hartwell, 'The Rising Standard of Living in England, 1800-1850', *EHR,* 2nd ser. XIII (1961); the discussion between Hartwell and Hobsbawm in *EHR*, 2nd ser. XVI (1963); and J.E. Williams, 'The British Standard of Living, 1750-1850', *EHR*, 2nd ser. XIX (1966).

   T.S. Willan rightly warns of the difficulty of constructing commodity price-series from eighteenth-century data. He also underscores the vagueness of occupational descriptions in early directories; Abraham Dent of Kirkby Stephen, usually listed as a grocer, was clearly (from his own records) also a stationer, bookseller, mercer, and dealer in bills. Willan, *An Eighteenth-Century Shopkeeper: Abraham Dent of Kirkby Stephen* (Manchester, 1970) pp. 12 ff.
4. J. Foster, *Class Struggle*, pp. 91-2 and *passim.*
5. This estimate must be a generous one, as it refers only to primary poverty and assumes full employment of all occupied family members; the situation would obviously be far worse during hard times. Foster further notes that in towns like Oldham 'poverty was not so much the special experience of a particular group within the labour force as a regular feature of the life of almost *all* working families at certain stages in their development, especially in old age or before young children could start earning,' ibid., pp. 96 and 258.
6. Ibid., p. 96. For the pitfalls of this kind of calculation, see Michael Anderson, *Family Structure in Nineteenth Century Lancashire* (London, 1971) p. 30. But Anderson's own calculations, for Preston in 1851, yield a similar 20% of families below the poverty line. Anderson's figures are distorted in that he excluded handloom weavers, women's part-time employment, and lodger income as factors too uncertain to be added into his wages estimates. Like Foster, he found sharp fluctuations according to the life-cycle stages of families; see Anderson, pp. 31 and 202.

   For a brief critique of both Foster and Anderson, J.H. Treble, *Urban Poverty in Britain, 1830-1914* (London, 1979) pp. 18-19.

   The plight of handloom weavers in the face of mechanisation is illustrated by a recent estimate that half of all weavers in Scotland in 1834 fell below the primary poverty line; see N. Murray, 'A Social History of the Scottish Handloom Weavers, 1790-1850'

Notes for pages 73-77.

(Strathclyde University Ph.D., 1976), cited in Treble, *Urban Poverty*, p. 18.

7. CRO, QJF 196/1/72, 171, 7 and 8 November 1767.
8. Angus Bethune Reach, *Manchester and the Textile Districts in 1849*, (ed.) C. Aspin (Helmshore, 1972, reprint ed.) p. 93. Reach, a London journalist, wrote a series of sketches of northern towns which were published in the *Morning Chronicle* in 1849/50 as part of the series 'Labour and the Poor', to which Henry Mayhew contributed the London portions.
9. Mrs Edward Heritage ordered a sofa for £2 10*s* in 1838, and her shoemaker husband paid the debt with 'three pare of Boots with Cloth tops and got up of good Materials.' 'Weekly Payments Ledger', entry for 29 October 1838, in Thomas Challinor Papers, in the possession of Mr and Mrs J.R.C. Callender, Macclesfield.
10. Friedrich Engels, *The Condition of the Working Class in England* (Oxford, 1958) p. 102. See also, James Winter, 'Widowed Mothers and Mutual Aid in Early Victorian Britain', *Journal of Social History*, XVII (1983) 113-23.
11. John Corry, *The History of Macclesfield* (London, 1817) p. 66. Cf. Arthur Young's figures for Knutsford in 1770: barley bread — no price given, cheese 2½*d* lb, beef 2½*d* lb, potatoes 1*s* 2*d* bushel, candles 7*d* lb, soap 6*d* lb, labourer's house rent 30*s*-£3 a year, heat 20*s* a year. *A Six Months Tour in the North of England* (London, 1770) p. 299.
12. J. Corry, *History*, p. 68.
13. CRO, QJB/21a, 10 January 1758; see also QJF 186/1/47, 48; and similar data in Alan Booth, 'Food Riots in the North-west of England, 1790-1801', *Past and Present*, no. 77 (1977) 84-107. S.I. Mitchell in 'Food Shortages and Public Order in Cheshire, 1757-1812', *TLCAS*, LXXXI (1982) 42-66, argues that eighteenth-century Cheshire riots were relatively infrequent, small in scale. They were almost always aimed at setting price maximums and were 'linked to a perceived failure of the authorities to . . . regulate the market.'
14. CRO, QJF 190/3/92, 12 July 1762; for details of the riot see also, QJB/22a, 13 July 1762; QJF 190/3/34, 35, 38, 89.
15. PRO, PCI/33/A87, 'Privy Council Unbound Papers'; and text of broadsheet, 19 September 1800, reproduced in *MCH*, 3 October 1874.
16. T.L. Richardson, 'The Agricultural Labourer's Standard of Living in Kent, 1790-1840', in Derek Oddy and Derek Miller (eds), *The Making of the Modern British Diet* (London, 1976) p. 106 and 106,

Notes for pages 77-78.

n. 34. Richardson found that in the same period the index of real wages for labourers in his district fell by 14%.

17. Alfred Fryer, *Wilmslow Graves and Grave Thoughts from Wilmslow* (Stockport, 1886), reminiscence of Andrew Whittaker, p. 97. Whittaker was mistaken in suggesting that eating barley bread was seen as a hardship; rye and barley breads, and oatcakes, were the ordinary fare of the working classes during this period. In 1801 local farm acreage planted in grain was divided, 45% in wheat, 45% in oats, and 5% each in barley and potatoes; wheat gained steadily in popularity from the mid-eighteenth century; figures from S.I. Mitchell, 'Urban Markets and Retail Distribution, 1730-1815, with Special Reference to Macclesfield, Stockport, and Chester' (Oxford University D.Phil., 1974) pp. 63 and 80, based on PRO, HO 67/6, 'Acreage Returns, 1801: Diocese of Chester'.
18. A. Fryer, *Wilmslow Graves*, reminiscence of Ellen Mottram, weaver, p. 93. She added, 'We did not think the simple food a hardship so long as we had a sufficiency', and others interviewed by Fryer echoed this point.
19. See *MC*, 20 July 1825.
20. T.L. Richardson, 'Standard of Living in Kent', p. 106, n. 38.
21. Testimony from 'Report of the Select Committee on Handloom Weavers', 1835, p. XIII, cited in J.H. Treble, *Urban Poverty*, p. 25.
22. 'Report of the Select Committee on the Silk Trade', Great Britain, P.P., 1831-2, XIX, 775 (John Brocklehurst).
23. A.B. Reach, *Textile Districts in 1849*, p. 88.
24. Adam Rushton, *My Life, as Farmer's Boy, Factory Lad, Teacher and Preacher, 1821-1909* (Manchester, 1909) pp. 21-2, 29. The Rushtons charged 6*d* for 20 lb of potatoes — less than half the market price. Adam Rushton also remembered the incursions of the town against his father's attempts to preserve a semblance of rural existence, 'Rough lads broke down fences in the fields, and stole fruit from the garden', p. 29.
25. For the development of retailing in Macclesfield, see S.I. Mitchell, 'Urban Markets'. T.H. Worrall, *Reminiscences of Early Life spent in My Native Town of Macclesfield* (Macclesfield, [1897]) gives details of various shops and merchants.
26. J. Corry, *History*, p. 50. Such wholesale transactions generally took place at inns; on inns as depots of retail trade, with innkeepers acting as rudimentary bankers, see Mitchell, 'Urban Markets', pp. 53-4. For the debate on new trade practices, ibid., pp. 161-2, 178.

Notes for pages 79-81.

27. Ibid., pp. 167-8. Mitchell shows that markets and fairs continued to flourish, and that the total of market tolls collected rose steadily from £90 in 1777 to £340 in 1834.

    The five annual fairs in the early nineteenth century were held on 6 May, 22 June, 11 July, 4 October, and 11 November, 'principally for cloth, cutlery, toys, and pedlars wares' and serving a wide area beyond the town. Birkenhead Central Library, Macclesfield Collection, MAI VI/6.

    As they gained in strength and influence the retailers began to take over the regulatory functions of the Corporation. A society for the protection of the retail trade (against unlicensed auctioneers, hawkers, etc.) met for the first time in 1823; *MC*, 4 February 1823.
28. [J. Plant and T. Gregory], *The History and Directory of Macclesfield* (Manchester, 1825) pp. 159-60, 162.
29. S.I. Mitchell, 'Urban Markets', p. 175. *English Reports* (London, 1910) CX, 504-7 for King's Bench: *Mayor, Aldermen and Burgesses of Macclesfield* v. *Pedley*, 1833; and *Burgesses of Macclesfield* v. *Chapman*, 1843. On the Shambles, John Earles, *Streets and Houses of Old Macclesfield* (Macclesfield, 1915) pp. 97-8.
30. See detailed list of bakers' charges on broadsheet, 23 May 1836, in CCRO, CR 63/2/341.
31. See *MC*, 10 March 1827, an account of two absconding contractors who fled owing both back wages and tradesmen's bills for their tommy shop. One Macclesfield butcher alone was owed £37.
32. G.B. Wilson, *Alcohol and the Nation: a contribution to the study of the liquor problem in the United Kingdom from 1800 to 1935* (London, 1940) p. 335.

    By 1841 there were about 200 licensed premises and more than 60 beershops in the town, serving a population of about 24,000; C. Stella Davies, *A History of Macclesfield* (Manchester, [1961]) p. 167.
33. A.E. Dingle, 'Drink and Working-Class Living Standards in Britain, 1870-1914', in D. Oddy and D. Miller (eds), *Modern British Diet*, p. 123.
34. Especially if we assume a cheap, high-carbohydrate diet; see ibid., pp. 122-4.
35. *MCH*, 19 September 1874 (a description apparently referring to the eighteenth century).
36. Quoted in *MCH*, 5 December 1870, local history column.
37. CRO, QJF 193/4/83, 13 September 1765.
38. See broadside, 16 October 1789, outlining the rules laid down at

Notes for pages 81-83.

Borough Sessions.

39. MPL, Thomas Allen's Notebook, *passim*.
40. Ibid., entries for 19 April and 12 June 1823.
41. For an account of the early days of the Macclesfield temperance movement see A. Rushton, *My Life*, Chap. 7.
42. On the physical and psychological/cultural inducements to drink in the 1820s, Brian Harrison, *Drink and the Victorians: the temperance question in England, 1815-1872* (London, 1971) pp. 37-44.
43. For Swanwick's career, 1760-1832, S.I. Mitchell, 'Urban Markets', pp. 354-62, an account based on the extensive collection of Swanwick papers in the possession of Mrs Marie Moss, Prestbury, Cheshire. On fashions of the eighteenth century, T.W. Barlow (ed.), *Historical Collector*, I, p. 6.
44. T.H. Worrall, *Reminiscences*, pp. 14-15.
45. *MC*, 16 July 1825.
46. CRO, QAP 3/18, 8 November 1806. Another convict transported at the same time had a sparser wardrobe, including two bedgowns, one of which she wore, as she had no gown or cloak.
47. A. Fryer, *Wilmslow Graves*, p. 92.
48. For thefts of clothes see, e.g., the case of several items stolen from a widow by her female lodger: CRO, QJF 222/4/101, 3 August 1794; testimony of cotton-spinner Edward Brickhill, whose new shoes were stolen at a pub and later found at a pawnbroker's: CRO, QJF 220/4/133, 14 August 1792; in another case one Thomas Mason is described first as a pawnbroker and later as a 'dealer in second-hand Cloathes': CRO, QJF 221/4/139, 1 August 1793. On fencing of stolen clothes see also CRO, QJF 193/4/83, 12 September 1765; and QJF 184/4/235, 19 July 1756.
49. S.I. Mitchell, 'Urban Markets', p. 204.
50. Industrial proprietors often leased land at 2*d* or 4*d* a square yard to builders who would construct whole streets of dwellings. No evidence has been found of building being financed by artisan clubs as happened among the silk-weavers of Middleton from the 1790s and in Nottingham in the 1820s. S.D. Chapman, 'Working-class Housing in Nottingham during the Industrial Revolution', in Chapman (ed.), *The History of Working-class Housing: a symposium* (Newton Abbot, 1971) pp. 147 and 269. Chapman reports the cost of building a worker's house in Nottingham in this period as £70-£90.
51. *MC*, 12 February 1823, report of sale of property of N. Higginbotham, bankrupt. Included are two pubs renting for £40

Notes for pages 83-85.

and £50 a year respectively.

52. J. Smith, *Report*, pp. 18 and 41; and Challinor mss., 'Weekly Payments' ledger. Challinor also rented a house and shop for £10 a year and a clergyman's house at the same price.

    For comparison, three-storey houses (with workroom above the living quarters) rented for 2*s* 6*d* in Nottingham in 1825, while two-storey houses went for 1*s* 6*d*: S. Chapman, 'Working-class Housing in Nottingham', pp. 150 and 155. Chapman estimates that rents rose during the population and trade boom of the period 1790 to 1820 and remained stable between *c.*1825 and 1850.

53. J. Wootton, 'Macclesfield Past', in *MCH*, 7 August 1880.
54. Letter signed 'Amicus' in *MC*, 10 July 1824. The same correspondent judged that there had been more building between 1821 and 1824 than in the thirteen years preceding, *MC*, 26 June 1824. For a detailed street-by-street listing of new houses built, *MC*, 10 July 1824. The areas of heaviest building were Hurdsfield (289), Sutton (351, 168 of these on John Ryle's land), and the Chester Road vicinity (107).
55. Built in 1728 by the Glovers, silk merchants, and purchased by John Brocklehurst for £1000 in 1782; see J. Earles, *Streets and Houses*, p. 134.
56. See ibid., pp. 114-15. One Park Green house was successively occupied by the Daintry, Wood, and Ryle families, all closely connected by marriage.
57. Ibid., pp. 95-6.
58. There were a few back-to-backs, especially in the crowded area near the Brocklehursts' mills; see 'Borough of Macclesfield: Housing and Town Planning Act. Inspection of District Report Book, No. 1, 1911-29', entry for 19 December 1919, in MPL.
59. J. Corry, *History*, p. 75.
60. See, e.g., accounts of R. Hine, grocer, Mr Watts, linen-draper, and Mr Braithwaite, surgeon, in 'Day Book', 1834-35, Challinor mss. Also lists of household goods of John Norbury, grocer, in *MC*, 25 June 1825; and of George Bradshaw, hatter, who lived in an elaborately furnished four-bedroomed house adjoining his hat factory: *MC*, 20 August 1825.
61. Challinor also allowed established customers to act as surety for new customers they introduced. Jos. Boothby promised that John Hooley's bill would be paid at 3*s* a week, every Saturday night, and Challinor noted next to the ledger entry, 'Huly lives in Warterloo Street. Boothby opposite Hurdsfield Church'. 'Weekly Payments' ledger, Challinor mss.

Notes for pages 86-90.

62. Ibid. Other entries show £9 12*s* worth of furniture paid off at 5*s* a week for 109 weeks, and £7 18*s* paid off at 5*s* for 95 weeks. Challinor seems to have been buying up property from families who had to leave town or move into lodgings; one house contained two looms, value 42*s*. Cf. the will of Thomas Robinson of Rainow, labourer, who left his wife £1 and 6 chairs, 2 tables, an oak screen, bed and bedding, a clock, and 2 chests. To his eldest son two cottages, to his second son 5*s*, and to his grandson his watch: his clothes to be divided between his sons. Will, 2 May 1838, copy in MPL, Marks and Spencer Deeds.
63. A.B. Reach, *Textile Districts in 1849*, p. 93. See also Bamford, *Early Days*, 98-9.
64. My measurements; in 1975 these houses stood empty, awaiting demolition.
65. A. Fryer, *Wilmslow Graves*, p. 92.
66. Isaac A. Finney, *Macklesfelde in Ye Olden time . . .* (Macclesfield, 1873) p. 117. 'It was pleasant to see the floor nicely cleaned, and the red or white sand scattered, or so disposed as to form stars, or hearts, and flowers and true love knots'.
67. The water reached a height of five feet in some streets, and several lives were lost; J. Earles, *Streets and Houses*, pp. 132-3. On dampness in houses see also, James Smith, *Report to the General Board of Health on a Preliminary Inquiry into . . . the Borough of Macclesfield* (London, 1850) p. 19.
68. CRO, QJF 220/1/115, 11 November 1791.
69. CRO, QJF 219/2/139, 2 May 1791.
70. For a description of such lodging-houses in Liverpool see J.H. Treble, 'Liverpool Working-class Housing, 1801-1851', in Chapman (ed.), *Working-class Housing*, pp. 182-4. The Liverpool houses charged 2*d* or 3*d* a night in the 1840s; often three or four persons slept in a bed, or mixed-sex groups lay on straw on the floor. For vagrants' lodging-houses in Macclesfield in the 1840s see annual reports of the Macclesfield Local Board of Health for 1857 and 1858, both in MPL.
71. Examples from 'First Annual Report, Macclesfield Local Board of Health', 1853, ms. copy in minute book of Local Board of Health and Improvement Committee, 1852-60, Macclesfield Town Hall, pp. 81-2. The new code required one privy for two houses.
72. John Frissell, grown-up son of a poor family, shared his bed with Thomas Brown and his son, lodgers, *MC*, 11 September 1824; see also, Alexander Strachan, *The Voice of God in the Storm* (pamphlet on the 1839 flood) (London, 1839) p. 11.

Notes for pages 90-92.

73. *MC*, 28 July, 18 September 1827.
74. *MC*, 24 May 1828.
75. John Burnett, *A Social History of Housing, 1815-1970* (Newton Abbot, 1978) p. 6.
76. J. Wootton, 'Macclesfield Past', *MCH*, 7 August 1880. A similar state of municipal inertia prevailed in much larger urban centres during this period. The situation in Liverpool is vividly described in François Vigier, *Change and Apathy: Liverpool and Manchester during the Industrial Revolution* (Cambridge, Mass., 1970) pp. 53-61; for Nottingham, see Roy A. Church, *Economic and Social Change in a Midland Town: Victorian Nottingham, 1815-1900* (London, 1966) pp. 10-11. In Manchester, however, there was a considerable extension of amenities after 1800, under a reformed and energetic body of Commissioners of Police; Vigier, *Change and Apathy*, pp. 120-7.
77. J. Wootton, 'Macclesfield Past', *MCH*, 7 August 1880. See also J. Corry, *History*, p. 106, and J. Smith, *Report*, p. 16.
78. I. Finney, *Macklesfelde*, pp. 84-5. Until the mid-nineteenth century a town watchman patrolled the streets with a lantern and warning rattle, calling the hours.
79. C.S. Davies, *History of Macclesfield*, p. 174. For complaints about the inactivity of commissioners see *MC*, 25 December 1824.
80. Davies, p. 174. Hundreds of summonses were issued for non-payment of police rates, many to people 'of the poorest class' who were allowed to pay by instalments; *MC*, 12 May, 13 October 1827.
81. Broadsheet, 1769, in CCRO, CR 63/2/341. For text of a 1781 agreement to replace old lead municipal water pipes with new piping of alder wood, laid in tempered clay, *MCH,* 19 June 1875.
82. On ancient wells still in use in the mid-nineteenth century, J. Earles, *Streets and Houses*, p. 125. On the filthiness of the Bollin and other streams, J. Smith, *Report,* p. 27. See also F. Williamson, 'George Sorrocold of Derby: a pioneer of water supply,' *Journal of the Derbyshire Archaeological and Natural History Society*, no. 57 (1936) 85.
83. J. Wootton, 'Macclesfield Past', *MCH*, 7 August 1880.
84. Little was accomplished until the 1840s; C.S. Davies, *History of Macclesfield*, pp. 176-7.
85. Ibid., pp. 170 and 252. There were hardly any water closets in Macclesfield until the end of the nineteenth century.
86. J. Smith, *Report*, p. 33.
87. Mortality during these epidemics was so high as to raise the death rate for those years by *c.*25% and 50% respectively over the

Notes for pages 92-95.

average for the decade 1767-77. *History of Cheshire*, vol. II, (Chester, 1778) p. 889.

88. A. Reach, *Textile Districts in 1849*, p. 89.
89. J. Earles, *Streets and Houses*, pp. 135-6.
90. T.H. Worrall, *Reminiscences*, p. 26. Birchinall lived as a gentleman and does not seem to have practiced extensively; he increasingly devoted his time to religious activities. Fashionable doctors felt some obligation to attend to the poor, on a charitable basis; see, e.g. memorial in St Michael's Church to William Norton, M.D. (1732?-93). Norton, an Oxford graduate, is described as 'Physician of the Poor [and] Zealous Supporter of the Establishment of his Country'. Reproduced in J.P. Earwaker, *East Cheshire: past and present*, vol. II (London, 1880) p. 499.
91. CRO, P. 84/a, Christ Church Register. Cockson's son, James, followed his father's career and called himself simply 'surgeon' in *Pigot and Dean's Directory for Manchester, Salford, etc. for 1824-25* . . . (Manchester, [1824]) p. 372.
92. See the case of a little girl who died after being treated by Hadfield for worms with 'an infusion of tobacco boiled in water, as a glister.' Her father said that she had often been treated by H. before for the same ailment; *MC*, 18 January 1823. By the end of his career Hadfield's annual profits reached £500; *MC*, 7 July 1827.
93. *MC*, 24 May 1823 and MPL, Thomas Allen's Notebook, 20 May 1823. Neild claimed to be able to make gold with a 'Philosopher's Stone', and sold some to a gullible peddler. For another case of a quack doctor see Allen's Notebook, 24 December 1824. On popular medicine and 'amateur doctoring', see also T.C. Barker and J.R. Harris, *A Merseyside Town in the Industrial Revolution: St. Helens, 1750-1900* (London, 1959) pp. 140-1.
94. A. Reach, *Textile Districts in 1849*, p. 88.
95. T.H. Worrall, *Reminiscences*, p. 5.
96. Ibid., p. 25.
97. For a case in which Dr Francis Newbold ordered a strait-jacket for a suicidal patient see *MC*, 11 November 1826. There were four pauper lunatics from Macclesfield in the county asylum in 1836, maintained by the Overseers of the Poor at a cost of 4*s* 6*d* each a week; letter of J. Fawkner to Poor Law Commissioners, 26 August 1836, in PRO, MH 12/968. Five pupils from Macclesfield attended the Manchester Deaf and Dumb Asylum from its opening in 1825 to March 1836, at a cost to the Overseers of £100 per student for a five-year stay; letter from Joshua Lingard, hon. sec. of the Asylum, to Macclesfield Overseers of the Poor, 2 March 1836, in

Notes for pages 95-98.

ibid.

98. *Pigot and Dean's Directory . . . 1824-25*, pp. 371-6.
99. Isaac A. Finney, *Notes on the Antiquities of Macclesfield* (4th ed., Macclesfield, 1871) p. 52.
100. A. Fryer, *Wilmslow Graves*, p. 94; this would have been in the early nineteenth century.
101. *MC*, 30 October 1824; the *Courier* ridiculed the popular view that doctors might have had something to do with the crime. The body was later found, with a note of apology attached, in a Manchester churchyard.
102. The presence of George Pearson as president, John Ryle and Charles Wood as vice-presidents, and J.S. Daintry as treasurer of the institution would seem to support Stella Davies' contention that the new concern for public health was essentially an employers' initiative; C.S. Davies, *History of Macclesfield*, p. 254.
103. *MC*, 18 October 1823. Slack left £2000 to the Dispensary in his will.
104. *MC*, 16 and 23 August 1828.
105. J. Corry, *History*, p. 107.
106. J. Smith, *Report*, pp. 14-15. The conditions in which the Irish poor had to live gave weight to such fears. In one court Smith found several Irish families living in a two-room house; in this group alone there were 24 persons suffering from fever. Ibid., p. 20.
107. T.H. Worrall, *Reminiscences*, p. 43.
108. J. Corry, *History*, pp. 276-7; Corry incorrectly gives Simpson's age at death as fifty-four. Cf. the similar pattern of early deaths in the family of Alderman Jasper Hulley (d. 1806); notes in CCRO, CR63/1/69, 122.
109. *MC*, 7 January 1826.
110. Accounts of Dr Samuel Stone, Swanwick Papers. As was usual with genteel clients, the doctor allowed long credit. When Stone died in 1796 the Swanwicks were several years in arrears.
111. Smith, *Report*, p. 14.
112. Ibid., p. 6. On early attempts to improve sanitation see pp. 1-7. A death rate above 23 per 1000 was considered unhealthy enough to require an inspection and report to the General Board of Health, under the Public Health Act, 11 & 12 Victoria, cap. 63.
113. Ibid., p. 14. Cf. figures for burials in St Michael's Churchyard, showing 50.4% aged five or under in 1813, 48% in 1823, and 39.5% in 1833. CRO, P 85/5/1, St Michael's Register. These figures may under-represent the lower classes, but they seem to indicate a trend towards improved infant survival.
114. Smith, *Report*, pp. 9, 11.

Notes for pages 98-102.

115. CRO, QAP 3/18/25, 'Reports and Returns of Convicts Transported'.
116. Of eleven burials in 1776/7 where location is indicated, however, six are in the 'Common Ground' reserved for the poor. Buried in the 'poor's ground' were wives or children of a silk-winder, a husbandman, two brass melters, and one illegitimate child; among those in purchased plots were relatives of a surgeon, a breeches-maker, a silk throwster, and a Methodist preacher: CRO, P 84/1, Christ Church Register.
117. On health problems arising from inadequate burial grounds see Smith, *Report*, pp. 31-2.
118. G.W. Oxley discusses pensions as the standard form of relief in the eighteenth century in *Poor Relief in England and Wales, 1601-1834* (Newton Abbot, 1974) pp. 62-5.
119. See Chetham's Library, Sutton Poor House Accounts, Overseers' Payments to Pensioners, 1791-9.
120. I. Finney, *Macklesfelde*, unnumbered appendix, 'Benefactions to the Churches'. This meagre amount would have been supplemented by part of the regular weekly collection and by donations for special purposes. In addition there were a few charitable bequests administered by the Corporation.
121. On the jubilee festivities see Birkenhead Central Library, Macclesfield Collection, MAI III/5. A similar pattern of development in poor relief, from the normal eighteenth-century forms of assistance (mainly out-relief) to the crisis solutions of the early nineteenth century has been described for the smaller towns of S.W. Lancashire; see G.W. Oxley, 'The Permanent Poor in South-west Lancashire under the Old Poor Law', in J.R. Harris (ed.), *Liverpool and Merseyside: essays in the economic and social history of the port and its hinterland* (London, 1969) pp. 16-49; also T. Barker and J. Harris, *St. Helens*, pp. 137-9.
122. CRO, QJF 193/1/89, 8 December 1764.
123. CRO, QJF 206/2/106, 18 February 1778.
124. See MPL, Thomas Allen's Notebook for references to gypsy fortune-tellers, a French street singer, Jewish peddlers, and other vagrants.
125. See, e.g., *MC*, 2 December 1826 and 4 April 1828.
126. J. Wootton, 'Macclesfield Past', MPL scrapbook, p. 14.
127. J. Byng, *The Torrington Diaries . . . between the Years 1781 and 1794* (ed.) C. Bruyn Andrews (London, 1930) vol. II, p. 122. For a list of early Macclesfield clubs, with dates of origin, CRO, QDS, 'Friendly Societies, deposited rules, etc.', 1855.

Notes for pages 103-108.

128. (2nd) Report of the Select Committee on Silk Ribbon Weavers' Petitions, P.P., 1818, IX, 102. For a list of the benefit clubs' assets in the Macclesfield Savings Bank for each year from 1827 to 1835 see J. Wootton, 'Macclesfield Past', MPL scrapbook, p. 14.
129. Ibid.
130. For these complaints see P.P., 1818, IX, 95-6.
131. *MC*, 1 April and 20 May 1826.
132. P.P., 1831-2, XIX, 781. These figures must refer to a larger district than the Borough alone, as the total population of the Borough was only about 20,000 at this time.
133. *MC*, 27 May 1826.
134. P.P., 1831-2, XIX, 811 (John Prout, weaver).
135. 'Municipal Corporations in England and Wales: reports upon certain boroughs drawn by T.J. Hogg, Esq.' P.P., 1837-8, XXXV, 820-1.
136. Protests from all these groups are preserved in PRO, MH 12/968, Correspondence, 1834-42.

IV Social Order and Social Tension

1. See J.S. Morrill, *Cheshire 1630-1660: County Government and Society during the English Revolution* (London, 1974). Morrill's book, the only full-length study of any aspect of modern Cheshire political history, concludes with the suggestion that the particular configurations of each local community continued to predominate over national issues in county politics long after the Restoration (p. 333).
2. Accounts in John Corry, *The History of Macclesfield* (London, 1817) and copy of a letter from John Stafford, town clerk, in Birkenhead Central Library, Macclesfield Collection, MAI V/6. Stafford commented, 'Tho' they let the debtors out of Goal [*sic*] at large soon after they came into Town and many thousands of Country people came in on Munday They did not Raise a Man Except one Single Goal Bird.'
3. See, e.g., Isaac F. Finney, *Notes on the Antiquities of Macclesfield*, 4th ed. (Macclesfield, 1871) pp. 55-8; and Alfred Fryer, *Wilmslow Graves and Grave Thoughts from Wilmslow* (Stockport, 1886) p. 94. Cumberland's victorious forces were greeted with frenzied relief, and the Duke himself was an honoured guest at John Stafford's mansion.
4. Romney Sedgwick, *The History of Parliament, 1715-54* (Oxford,

Notes for pages 108-111.

1970) pp. 202-3; and Lewis Namier and John Brooke, *The History of Parliament, 1754-1790* (Oxford, 1964) p. 221; also biographical entries for individual M.P.'s in each volume. The Cheshire county electorate in the eighteenth century numbered only about 5000.

5. In this election Macclesfield voters favoured the Tories by a small margin — 66 to 58 votes. 'List of the Voters of Cheshire at the Election for Two Members for the County', 1727, in CCRO, Earwaker Collection, CR63/2/14.
6. Records of attendance and notations of new freemen elected are in Macclesfield Town Hall, Corporation Minute Books, I, 1769-1824.
7. A complete list of mayors for these years is in J.P. Earwaker, *East Cheshire: past and present,* vol. II (London, 1880), 466-7.
8. Macclesfield Town Hall, Mayor's Accounts, 1709-1809.
9. Corporation Minute Books, I, 1769-1824, entries for 1801; and Mayor's Accounts, 1709-1809, entries for 1808 and 1809.
10. See, e.g., Corporation Minute Books, I, 1769-1824, entries for 1780, 1794 and 1809, on George and Benjamin Oldfield, Joseph and Peter Fowler, and Thomas and Peter Wright (town clerks).
11. List of Recorders, in J.P. Earwaker, *East Cheshire,* vol. II, 467-8. The office was contested eight times from 1750 to 1833 and was abolished by municipal referendum in the 1830s.
12. James Abercrombie, son of Sir Ralph Abercrombie, eventually sat in Parliament and served as Speaker of the House; he became Viscount Dunfermline.
13. On John Roe's character see the letters of Ann Wroe, a pious widow and distant relative of the Roes; she commented, 'I hope he will come out a *New Character after Marriage* — I have been very faithful to him in telling all that People disapprove in his conduct.' A.W. to Hannah Nicholson, 12 March 1804, in Manchester Central Library, Nicholson Family Papers.
14. '[Charles Roe] might not have been dead more than a year from the respect shown his family'; ibid.
15. Joseph Nightingale, 'The Election: a satirical drama' (Stockport, 1804), copy in MPL.
16. J. Corry, *History*, pp. 84-92 for voting list. See also J.P. Earwaker, *East Cheshire*, vol. II, p. 468.
17. A list of town clerks is in ibid.
18. Their collected papers, Clulow's at the Cheshire County Record Office and Wright's at the Birkenhead Central Library, are the only two surviving archives of legal and political manuscripts from the town for this period.
19. Grimsditch, 'a jolly rollicking man' with 'rich dark brown eyes',

Notes for pages 111-116.

who 'took well with the ladies', eventually went far in Macclesfield politics; he was later elected M.P. for the Borough several times. T.H. Worrall, *Reminiscences of Early Life spent in My Native Town of Macclesfield* (Macclesfield, [1897]) p. 12. On Parrott, Earwaker, *East Cheshire*, vol. II, p. 468.

20. *MC*, 23 April 1814.
21. J. Corry, *History*, p. 80. The latter may have been John Bacon, cutler, listed in William Cowdroy's *Directory and Guide for the City and County of Chester . . .* (Chester, 1789).
22. J. Corry, *History*, p. 80.
23. *MC*, 6 September 1823.
24. Text of petition and details in J. Corry, *History*, pp. 113-15.
25. Testimony on 1819 riots in CRO, Clulow Papers, Box 25, *John Clulow* v. *Thomas Hall and Thomas Robinson*, Chester Spring Assizes, 1820.
26. On Swindells, *MC*, 14 February 1824; on Swann, *Stockport Advertiser*, 21 May and 20 June 1824; *Poor Man's Guardian*, 12 November 1831; E.P. Thompson, *The Making of the English Working Class* (London, 1963) pp. 731-2.
27. John Earles called West 'a lord of language'; *Streets and Houses of Old Macclesfield* (Macclesfield, 1915), p. 117.
28. A memorial reminiscence of John West by G.J. Harney appeared in the *Macclesfield Advertiser*, 4 March 1887. For further details of West's career see biographical entry by Naomi Reid in J.M. Bellamy and J. Saville (eds), *Dictionary of Labour Biography*, vol. VII (London, 1984) pp. 245-50.
29. J. Earles, *Old Macclesfield*, p. 118.
30. Petition quoted in John Wootton's essay, 'Macclesfield Past', in *MCH*, 7 August 1880.
31. A broadsheet voters list of 1835 in CCRO, CR63/2/341, shows 578 Macclesfield property-owners qualified for the county franchise.
32. John Adshead to John Cruttenden Lea, 1875, quoted in J. Earles, *Old Macclesfield*, pp. 50-1; see also p. 113. A vivid account of election rioting in 1733 is in CCRO, CR63/2/341. On later abuses, Howard F. Hughes, 'The Macclesfield Election of 1880, and its Consequences' (Leeds University, B.A. dissertation, Special Studies, 1962).
33. T.C. Worrall, *Reminiscences*, p. 13. During his long career in Parliament Brocklehurst spoke only on matters directly related to the silk trade.
34. Patrick Joyce, *Work, Society, and Politics: the culture of the factory in later Victorian England* (Brighton, 1980); see especially

Notes for pages 116-120.

chapters 3 and 4. Joyce argues that the factory communities of Lancashire and Yorkshire internalised a paternalistic ethos, and that the group interests and values of dependents, while distinct from those of the large employers, were more often than not expressed through a political system based on deference to employer leadership and the preservation of social stability.

35. C.S. Davies, *History of Macclesfield*, p. 175.
36. Macclesfield Town Hall, Corporation Minute Books, vol. II, 1835-54.
37. 'Macclesfield Past', *MCH*, 7 August 1880. Those whose landlords compounded for their rates were not admitted until the Small Tenement Act of 1859.
38. A similar number were qualified to be police commissioners under the Macclesfield Police & Improvement Act of 1825.
39. C.S. Davies, *History of Macclesfield*, p. 196. On the new generation of reform-minded civil servants who became active after 1840 — under constant prodding from the indefatigable John May, the Edwin Chadwick of Macclesfield — see ibid., pp. 176-9.
40. D.C. Moore, 'Concession or Cure: the social premises of the first Reform Act', *Historical Journal*, IX (1966) 56.
41. Ibid.; D.C. Moore expands on the idea of the 'deference community' as the characteristic unit of political activity in *The Politics of Deference* (Hassocks, 1976).
42. D.C. Moore, 'Concession or Cure', p. 56.
43. Peter Searby, 'Chartists and Freemen in Coventry, 1838-1860', *Social History*, no. 6 (October 1977) 761-84.
44. J.J. Tobias, *Crime and Industrial Society in the Nineteenth Century* (London, 1967) p. 11.
45. Ibid., p. 17.
46. See, e.g., J. Corry, *History*, p. 68.
47. Ibid., p. 71.
48. R. Quinault, 'The Warwickshire Magistracy and Public Order, *c.*1830-1870', in J. Stevenson and R. Quinault (eds), *Popular Protest and Public Order* (London, 1974) pp. 181-3, 211-12.

    On the ambivalence of magistrates, torn between official pressures towards strict enforcement and traditional/local/personal considerations, Douglas Hay, 'Property, Authority and the Criminal Law', in Hay *et al.* (eds), *Albion's Fatal Tree: crime and society in eighteenth-century England* (London, 1975) pp. 35-49.
49. T.C. Curtis, 'Quarter Sessions Appearances and Their Background: a seventeenth-century regional study', in J.S.

Notes for pages 120-122.

Cockburn (ed.), *Crime in England, 1500-1800* (Princeton, 1977) pp. 135-54. J.M. Beattie's work on crime in mid-eighteenth-century Surrey also indicates that neighbourly suspicion or approval could be an important factor, even in metropolitan trials. J.M. Beattie, 'Crime and the Courts in Surrey, 1736-1753', in ibid., pp. 173-4.

50. T.C. Curtis, 'Quarter Sessions Appearances', p. 154.
51. See MPL, Thomas Allen's Notebook. In many cases the exact nature of the charge or dispute is unclear.
52. T.C. Curtis, 'Quarter Sessions Appearances', p. 147.
53. See CRO, EDP 181/7, Churchwardens' Presentments — Macclesfield, 1754. On the lack of popular respect for Church courts, see G.R. Elton, 'Introduction: Crime and the Historian', in J.S. Cockburn (ed.), *Crime in England*, p. 3.
54. The unfortunate James Tatton was driven through the streets in this way. His ordeal began in an altercation with a neighbour. Tatton testified in court: 'I then said "You'd better houd your jaw", but he then began a *cossing* me — oh dear me! how he did *coss*! He called me a thief, and said I was forsworn, and all for nothing! He then put his hand (we will not describe *where*) and asked me to kiss it'; *MC*, 28 October 1826.

    On riding the stang, *Macclesfield Express*, 24 March 1973, local history column by 'The Stroller' [Clifford Rathbone].

    There were other popular tactics for warning and retribution; for examples of anonymous letters, see MPL, Clulow Papers; for barn-burning in 1832, *Macclesfield Express*, 1 November 1968.
55. For a brief review of the debate, see Victor Bailey, 'Crime, Criminal Justice and Authority in England', in *Bulletin of the Society for the Study of Labour History*, no. 40 (Spring 1980) 38.
56. See comments in CRO, QAP/3, 'Reports and Returns of Convicts Transported . . . ,' entries for 1810s and 1820s; and *MC*, September 1824, *passim*, citing cases such as that of seventeen-year-old Samuel Heathcote, horse-thief, who was transported in 1820, as his father and grandfather had been before him; CRO, QAP/3/132.
57. For an excellent survey of the legal definition of 'riot' — a flexible one in the early nineteenth century — and the consequent difficulties faced by the historian studying the phenomenon, see D. Philips, 'Riots and Public Order in the Black Country, 1835-1860', in Stevenson and Quinault (eds), *Popular Protest*, pp. 144-7. Philips considers that 'whether a gathering became a disturbance or "riot" was often decided by how the authorities labelled that gathering, or what action they took or did not take, to disperse it,'

Notes for pages 122-126.

p. 144. This would apply to many of the disturbances which occurred in Macclesfield between 1812 and the 1830s.

58. *MC*, 6 December 1828; also *MC*, 1 March and 25 September 1828.
59. *MC*, 2 December 1826.
60. *MC*, 1 and 8 July, 5 August, and 11 November 1826. The *Courier* pointed out that some of these children were Irish; some were unemployed or runaway apprentices, 'almost naked, filthy in the extreme, and associated with a horde of young thieves'; *MC*, 11 November 1826.
61. See *MC*, 30 September 1826, on the Sutton sisters; and Thomas Allen's Notebook, on the Bloor family, and Phoebe and Sarah Boothby. Allen tried eight women and four men as keepers of disorderly houses in 1823 to 1825.
62. Boothby's frequent court appearances — six in 1823 alone — include charges of assault and drunkenness. She was imprisoned several times for keeping disorderly premises, but managed to set up in business again promptly. On Sarah Boothby, see also *MC*, 23 July 1825.
63. Both Thomas Hewson, prime curate of St Michael's Church in the 1770s, and Town Clerk John Clulow seem to have been heavy drinkers and were involved in cases of assault, but their social position shielded them from the full legal consequences of their behaviour; CRO, QJB/24a, 23 April and 16 July 1776.
64. *MC*, 29 November and 6 December 1828.
65. J.M. Beattie, 'The Criminality of Women in Eighteenth-Century England', *Journal of Social History*, VIII (1975) 89.
66. *MC*, 14 July 1827, and MPL, Thomas Allen's Notebook, *passim*.
67. *MC*, 30 August and 18 October 1828. The problem of inconsistency in sentencing standards persisted through the century; see L. Radzinowicz and R. Hood, 'Judicial Discretion and Sentencing Standards: Victorian attempts to solve a perennial problem', *University of Pennsylvania Law Review*, 127 (1979) 1288-1349.
68. See, e.g., *MC*, 18 March 1826, a case of wife-abuse; 15 December 1827, an account in dialect of a wife's complaint of assault by her husband; 28 January 1826, a dispute about non-payment of rent; and 25 March 1826, a 'humorous' account of a brawl between an Irishwoman and an Englishwoman. The effect in all these cases is to make the Irish seem ridiculous.
69. *MC*, 16 July 1825.
70. *MC*, 4 November 1826.
71. *MC*, 20 May 1826.
72. *Macclesfield Guardian*, 19 September 1874, 'Local Notes and

Notes for pages 126-128.

Queries'. The premises are here described (*c.*1745) as a rambling complex of small buildings, including stables, sheds and a garden; evidently the jail was a converted farmstead.

73. See transcript of testimony concerning the jail in 1758 in CCRO, CR63/2/341. The Corporation apparently paid the lessee by the prisoner, and Lankford, a silk-throwster, may have used prison labour in his business. By 1780 the property was worth an initial payment of £100 plus 16*s* 6*d* rent per year; see lease by Earl Cholmondeley to James Poole, 25 March 1780, quoted in *Macclesfield Guardian*, 19 September 1874.
74. The House of Correction was sold by the Corporation in 1784 to a silk dealer; *Macclesfield Guardian*, 24 July 1875 (clipping in CCRO, CR63/1/28).
75. CRO, QAP/5/64. Of this group four were transported and one acquitted. Another Macclesfield man, in the same year, was held for 216 days, then tried and transported for life.
76. C.S. Davies, *History of Macclesfield*, p. 180.
77. Their 18*s* a week was paid from the rates and from fines collected in the local courts — a system which led to many abuses. For a list of the first Watch Committee and extracts from its minutes, see [W.G. Symmons], *A Short History of the Macclesfield Borough Police* (n.p., [1947]) pp.6-7. Oddly enough a very rough comparison of frequency of arrest shows little difference in performance under the new police system. For a single year in the early 1820s Mayor Thomas Allen recorded about 337 prosecutions for drunkenness and assault, a ratio (to the population of 1821) of 1:52.65. The first official statistics of convictions, compiled by Chief Constable Harper for 1845, report 464 such offences in that year, a ratio (to the population of 1841) of 1:52.01: MPL, Thomas Allen's Notebook; and [W.G. Symmons], *Macclesfield Borough Police*, p. 11. Of course, without knowing the difference in the actual rates of commission of these crimes (as opposed to the rates of arrests or convictions) it is not possible to draw any conclusion as to the relative efficiency of the new force.
78. On hostility to the new police forces, R.D. Storch, 'The Plague of Blue Locusts: police reform and popular resistance in Northern England, 1840-1857', *International Review of Social History*, XX (1975) 61-90.
79. Hulley paid for most of the equipment for his own troop, which often drilled in the Churchyard. For lists of supporters of the troop, with their donations see broadsides dated 1794 and 1798 in CCRO, CR63/2/341.

Notes for pages 128-130.

80. An account of a review by the Prince of Gloucester in 1803 is in J. Earles, *Old Macclesfield*, pp. 174-5.
81. Quoted in C.S. Davies, *History of Macclesfield*, p. 180.
82. PRO, HO 40/2/1, Lt. Col. G. Nettlethorpe to General Acland, 14 May 1812 and 2 June 1812. Nettlethorpe was on the spot and reported his own observations. The more wild-eyed reports were usually second-hand; for example, Capt. Francis Rushton wrote of armed meetings on the moors near Macclesfield, and expressed his suspicion that the citizens' patrols were in league with the radicals. Rushton had also heard of a plot to attack the barracks. HO 40/2/1, Capt. F. Rushton to Lt. Col. Ruppell, 11 and 12 May 1812.
83. F.O. Darvall, *Popular Disturbances and Public Order in Regency England* (London, 1969 ed.), especially chapters VIII, X, and XV. George Rudé, *The Crowd in History: a study of Popular Disturbances in France and England, 1730-1848* (New York, 1964) chap. V. E.J. Hobsbawm, 'The Machine Breakers', in *Labouring Men* (Garden City, N.Y., 1967) pp. 7-26.

    E.P. Thompson's view of Luddism as a politically motivated, ideologically unified and consciously subversive movement applies better to the larger textile towns of Lancashire and the East Midlands and to parts of the West Riding of Yorkshire.
84. For detailed description and participants' testimony on the 1812 riots see CRO, Clulow Papers, Box 5, Testimony in *King* v. *Stubbs*, May 1812; and *Aston's Manchester Commercial Advertiser*, 21 April 1812.

    On the transition, *c.*1790-1820, from older forms of mass violence such as food riots to newer forms, like strikes, machine-breaking and 'collective bargaining by riot' (in Hobsbawm's phrase), see J. Stevenson, 'Food Riots in England, 1792-1818', in Stevenson and Quinault (eds) *Popular Protest*, pp. 62-3. Stevenson sees a general shift of violent incidents away from rural locales to manufacturing centres, paralleling the shift of protesters' demands from prices to wages.
85. *MC*, 4 March and 6 May 1826.
86. J. Wootton, 'Macclesfield Past', MPL scrapbook.
87. See CRO, MG 11, Enrolment List — 1st Regiment Militia (Cheshire), 1803; CRO, MG 22/12, Militia Records, 1813.
88. Exempted categories were: those who were poor and had at least two children, apprentices and articled clerks, the infirm and those under 5′2″, and those who had been balloted within the past six years. CRO, MG 6/20, Militia Returns, 1812.
89. CRO, MG 24/2, [Home Office] to Earl of Stamford and

Notes for pages 130-133.

Warrington, 28 April 1812.

90. *MC*, 18 February 1828.
91. Bounties varied from £15 to more than £40 from town to town; see CRO, MG 8, Militia Bounty Payments, undated.
92. See A. Fryer, *Wilmslow Graves*, p. 96.
93. CRO, QAM 2, Militia Book, 1760-1763; the weekly allowance was 2*s* for the wife, plus 1*s* per child.
94. [Frederick Leary], *The Earl of Chester's Yeoman Cavalry: its formation and services, 1797 to 1897* (Edinburgh, 1898) p. 82.
95. Rowdiness: *MC*, 18 November 1826; camp followers: *MC*, 5 August and 16 September 1826; homosexuality: *MC*, 29 April 1826, the case of William Jackson, a factory worker with a record of homosexual associations. Jackson was blackmailed by T.H. Wood, who denied the charge unconvincingly, 'I merely went to Jackson and said, I understood he had been with a soldier, and then I recommended him to clear up the matter, That was all.'
96. *MC*, 26 June 1824, on an Oddfellows parade, sermon, and dinner; *MC*, 11 October 1828, Wakes parade.
97. The ceremony is described in Robert Brown, *Combermere Lodge of Union, No. 295, Macclesfield: a hundred year's history* (Macclesfield, 1893) p. 22.
98. On the participation of the 'better classes' in old rural sports and games, T.E. Gibson, 'Some Old Country Sports — from the Crosby Records', *THSLC,* XXXIII (1881) 1-22.
99. 'History of the Regulations Governing the Licensing of Ale-houses', broadside dated October 1789, in the collection of Mrs Marie Moss, Prestbury; see also 'Abstract of Various Laws for the Better Ordering of Society', broadside *c.*1790, in CCRO, CR63/2/341. There seem to have been few prosecutions under these regulations, but they may have induced publicans to keep a warier eye on their patrons.
100. Douglas A. Reid notes this 'centrifugal movement' of disreputable traditional pastimes in his study of Birmingham Wakes; Reid, 'Interpreting the Festival Calendar: Wakes and Fairs as Carnivals', in R. Storch (ed.), *Popular Culture and Custom in Nineteenth-Century England* (London: 1982) pp. 133-4.
101. A. Fryer, *Wilmslow Graves*, p. 98.
102. Alex Helm, 'The Cheshire Soul-caking Play', in *Journal of the English Folk Dance and Song Society*, VI (1950) 50. Souling was 'almost obsolete' by the 1850s, I. Finney, *Macklesfelde*, pp. 119-20.
103. *MC*, 30 April 1825.
104. *MC*, 13 December 1828.

Notes for pages 133-136.

105. J. Earles, *Old Macclesfield*, pp. 55-6.
106. See a list of sharpsters arrested at the 1805 Wakes — including the Barton family, a father and two teenaged daughters from Wigan, who specialised in crooked dice and a game called 'Pricking in the Belt'; CRO, QJF 233/3, printed broadside, 1805. Also, *MC*, 12 May 1827.
107. *Cheshire Sheaf*, Series 1, vol. 2 (1882) 353.
108. Two playbills, dated 1813 and 1815, in J. Earles, *Old Macclesfield*, pp. 60-1. More details of theatrical programmes in *MC*, 3 and 10 April 1824. These programmes were clearly not aimed at working-class audiences; ticket prices ranged from 3*s* (boxes) to 1*s* (gallery).
109. *MC*, 15 February 1817.
110. *MC*, 11 November 1826, on both groups.
111. D. Reid, 'Interpreting the Festival Calendar', in R. Storch (ed.), *Popular Culture*, pp. 125-53.
112. Hugh Cunningham, *Leisure and the Industrial Revolution, c.1780-c.1880* (London, 1980) p. 22. Also Peter Bailey, *Leisure and Class in Victorian England: rational recreation and the contest for control, 1830-1885* (London, 1978). The general history of the transition from pre-industrial to more modern, 'rational' forms of recreation can be found in R.W. Malcolmson, *Popular Recreations in English Society, 1700-1850* (Cambridge, 1973).
113. Copy of Rules and questions is in CCRO, CR63/2/341; see Wilmslow Historical Society, *Cotton Town: Bollington and the Swindells Family in the nineteenth century* (Wilmslow, 1973) p. 14 for a description of a similar society at Stockport.
114. John Armstrong, *History of Freemasonry in Cheshire* (London, 1901) pp. 17, 56; [Henry Kelly], *History of Freemasonry in Macclesfield from the Year 1717* (Macclesfield, n.d.) pp. 4, 5; and Robert Brown, *Combermere Lodge of Union*, pp. 14-17.
115. CRO, Quarter Sessions Papers, Freemasonry Returns, 1799. These lists of members, which had to be filed annually if lodges were to be exempt under the Unlawful Societies Act of 1799, are notoriously incomplete. Publicans, almost as a matter of course, tended to be Masons. The majority of members of all lodges were small masters and artisans, with a scattering of farmers and professional men of the lower echelons (schoolmasters, excise officials, lesser clergymen).
116. J. Earles, *Old Macclesfield*, p. 48.
117. For the background to the founding of the Society, see R.C. Wilson, 'The Objectives and Achievements of the Chester Mechanics' Institution and the Macclesfield Society for acquiring

Notes for pages 136-145.

Useful Knowledge' (Manchester University M.Ed., 1968) Chap. 3.

118. Ibid., pp. 111, 165; and *MC*, 30 November 1833. An address summarising the history of the Society by its president, John Brocklehurst, is in *MC*, 30 September 1837.
119. See a letter signed 'A Friend to Knowledge' in *MC*, 28 March 1835.
120. A privately-owned subscription library had existed in town since about 1770, but the annual cost was prohibitive — first one and later as much as three guineas. There was also a substantial entrance fee on first joining; *MC*, 2 March 1811.
121. R.C. Wilson, 'Objectives and Achievements', p. 158.
122. J. Corry, *History*, p. 101.
123. For prosecutions, see CRO, QJF 204/12/74.
124. Wilmslow Historical Society, *Cotton Town*, p. 18.

V The Evangelical Revolution

1. R.B. Walker, 'Religious Changes in Cheshire, 1750-1850', *Journal of Ecclesiastical History*, XVII (1977) 77-94.
2. George Slater, *Chronicles of Lives and Religion in Cheshire and Elsewhere* (London, 1891) pp. 8-9.
3. Biographical sketches of 18th and 19th century incumbents of St Michael's are in J.P. Earwaker, *East Cheshire: past and present* vol. II, (London, 1880) 506-8; some of Earwaker's ms. notes for this section are in CCRO, CR63/1/30. See also Birkenhead Central Library, MA C/V/1, 'Extracts of Several Nominations to the Living of Macclesfield — from the [Diocesan] Registry, 1775-1778'.
4. Raised, in several increments, to £214 in 1834.
5. A list of pew-holders and sketch plan of the church are in Samuel Stone Papers, CCRO, CR3/1/42.
6. On the general history of early British Methodism, see William J. Townsend *et al., A New History of Methodism*, vol. I (London, 1909); and Rupert Davies and Gordon Rupp (eds), *A History of the Methodist Church in Great Britain*, 2 vols (London, 1965; 1978).
7. E.A. Rose, 'Methodism in Cheshire to 1800', *TLCAS*, LXVIII (1975) 22-37. Rose stresses that small revivalist societies were well established in East Cheshire years before Wesley's first visit. Bennet himself had been influenced by non-Wesleyan itinerants. He became a Methodist in 1743, built up his own 'round', quarrelled with Wesley in 1752, and died a Dissenting minister in 1759.

   The only comprehensive history of Macclesfield Methodism is

Notes for pages 145-147.

Benjamin Smith, *Methodism in Macclesfield* (London, 1875). This work is naively sectarian and awkwardly constructed, but it is the most detailed account and has been heavily used by all later writers on the subject.

8. Theophilus Lessey, 'Memoir of George Pearson of Macclesfield', *Methodist Magazine*, XXI (1808) 273-6. Pearson was still leading two classes at his death in 1807 at the age of eighty-eight. He died calmly and confidently, remarking to his brother, '[I] shall be in heaven before 12 o'clock.' See also, Melville Horne, *A Sermon on the Death of Mr. G. Pearson Senr. of Macclesfield . . .* (Macclesfield, 1807).
9. Wesley's *Journal*, quoted in B. Smith, *Methodism in Macclesfield*, pp. 51-2. See also an account of a love feast and a sermon by Wesley in Macclesfield (1777) in Alexander Strachan, *Recollections of the Life and Times of the Late Reverend George Lowe* (London, 1848) pp. 63-5.
10. C.S. Davies, *History of Macclesfield*, p. 330.
11. For details of negotiations concerning the building of this meeting-house, see Robert Pilter to James Everett, 4 April 1827, in Methodist Archives, John Rylands Library; also B. Smith, *Methodism in Macclesfield*, pp. 74-7.
12. See, e.g., list in CRO, EMS 6/18/1, 'Sunderland Street Chapel, Accounts and Trustees' Minutes'.
13. Wesley's *Journal*, 31 March 1787, quoted in E.A. Rose, 'Methodism in Cheshire', p. 29.
14. Robert Jackson, 'A Memoir of Mr. Joshua Thorley of Macclesfield', *Wesleyan Methodist Magazine*, 4th ser., IV (1848) 481-92. See also notes by and about Thorley in CRO, EMC 1/13/1, 'Memorial Book', a collection of autobiographical fragments and friends' recollections apparently used in preparing funeral sermons; and B. Smith, *Methodism in Macclesfield*, pp. 242-9.
15. CRO, EMS 6/18/1, 'Sunderland Street Chapel, Accounts and Trustees' Minutes'; and B. Smith, *Methodism in Macclesfield*, pp. 232-2; 251.
16. C.S. Davies, *History of Macclesfield*, p. 329.
17. Accounts of Simpson's life (1745-1799) are in J. Johnson, *Memoir of Simpson*; John Gaulter, 'Memoir of the Rev. David Simpson', in D. Simpson, *A Plea for Religion and the Sacred Writings, addressed to the Disciples of Thomas Paine* (Liverpool, 1812); and A.L. Hunt, *David Simpson and the Evangelical Revival* (London, 1927). There is a collection of Simpson's manuscript sermons and published writings at St John's College, Cambridge.

Notes for pages 148-150.

18. See Berridge's strong letter of advice to Simpson, then facing bitter opposition in Macclesfield, 8 August 1775, quoted in J. Johnson, *Memoir of Simpson*, pp. 15-16.
19. The first complaints were made in 1774, the substance of the charges being that Simpson was a Methodist; for further charges, see Thomas Hewson to Bishop of Chester, 19 November 1775, Birkenhead Central Library, MA C/N/20.
20. Wesley's *Journal*, 9 April 1777, quoted in D. Knapp, 'The Ancient Town of Macclesfield and its Methodism', *Methodist Recorder*, September 1904, p. 9.

    Sketches of incumbents of Christ Church are in J.P. Earwaker, *East Cheshire*, vol. II, 509-10. The church was opened for divine service by Simpson on Christmas Day 1775, but not consecrated until 1779, after a private Act of Parliament was passed, vesting the right of appointment in Charles Roe and his heirs. The living was worth £100 per year, twice the value of St Michael's.
21. E.A. Rose, 'Methodism in Cheshire', p. 31.
22. D. Simpson, 'Strictures on Religious Opinion', in bound volume of Simpson's sermons and tracts, Dr Williams' Library, mss. Lindsey P.P.6, p. 173. The reference to Price is on p. 36.
23. 'On Benificence', in ibid., pp. 180-3, 194 ff.
24. J. Gaulter, 'Memoir', pp. 11-12. The only source or evidence cited is an appendix Simpson added to the second (1798) edition of his 'Plea for Religion', in which he seems to suggest that he is planning to embrace Methodism.
25. Petition of inhabitants of Macclesfield to Bishop of Chester, 1774, in Birkenhead Central Library, MA C/LV/10.
26. CRO, EDV 7/1/96, 'Visitation: Articles of Inquiry, 1778'.
27. CRO, EDV 7/2/103, 'Visitation: Articles of Inquiry, 1789'. These figures are obviously rough, but reasonable, guesses. The Methodists themselves enrolled 290 members in Macclesfield in 1788 and 501 members in 1794; Duke University Library, George Story Collection, Macclesfield Circuit membership list, 1788, and CRO EMC 1/4, 'List of Members, etc., Macclesfield Circuit, Wesleyan Methodists, 1793-95'.
28. P. Stigant makes this point, also noting that chapel membership was a highly unstable quantity. There was a continual influx of new members, counterbalanced by the loss of old ones. See his 'Wesleyan Methodism and Working-Class Radicalism in the North, 1792-1821', *Northern History*, VI (1971) 99.
29. For the 1821 figures, see CRO, EDV 7/6/308, 'Visitation: Articles of Inquiry'.

Notes for pages 151-154.

30. See, e.g., Thomas Hewson to Bishop of Chester, 19 November 1775, Birkenhead Central Library, MA C/N/20.
31. W.R. Ward, *Religion and Society in England, 1790-1850* (London, 1972) pp. 126-7.
32. Thomas Wood, *Observations on Orthodox Christianity and Socinian Error; Occasioned by the Change of Sentiment in the Religious Creed of the Rev. Joseph N-T-N-LE* (London, 1813). Also JN to John Clulow, 10 April 1809, John Rylands Library, Methodist Archives.
33. CRO, EMC 1/13/1. 'Memorial Book'. Also William Thompson, *Letters of William Thompson, lately deceased . . .* 2nd ed. (Preston, 1818). Thompson, a cotton-worker and autodidact, converted to Quakerism after a period as a devout Methodist. Cf. R.B. Walker, 'Religious Changes', pp. 84-5.
34. CRO, EDP 181/17, Churchwardens' Presentments, 1754.
35. *Methodist Magazine*, XLVII (1824) 475. On this occasion Bunting held three services, each of which attracted at least 1500 people.
36. On the authorities' disapproval of Dow, Richard Carwardine, *Transatlantic Revivalism: Popular Evangelicalism in Britain and America, 1790-1865* (Greenwich, 1978) pp. 104-6. On revivalism, John Baxter, 'The Great Yorkshire Revival of 1792-96: a study of mass revival among the Methodists', *Sociological Yearbook of Religion in Britain*, no. 7 (1974) 46-76. Baxter links this wave of revivals, which reached as far as Macclesfield, to famine, natural disasters, and the economic dislocations of war. He also suggests, tentatively, a cyclical pattern of revivals which may reflect a need to renew faith and commitment in each new generation of members.
37. B. Smith, *Methodism in Macclesfield*, pp. 308-10; George Slater, *Chronicles of Lives and Religion in Cheshire and Elsewhere* (London, 1891) pp. 32-3; and *Cheshire Village Memories*, vol. II (Tilston Court, 1961) p. 107. See also James Obelkevich's chapter on popular religion and superstition in *Religion and Rural Society: South Lindsey, 1825-1875* (Oxford, 1976) pp. 259-312. Obelkevich concludes that 'popular Protestantism worked paradoxically to bring about the demystification of Christianity — particularly of the sacraments — while leaving nature still saturated with magical forces', p. 302. The power of paganism was diluted in a more urban context such as that of Macclesfield, but many vestiges remained.
38. See William Thompson to Joseph Benson, 20 January 1798, quoted in *Proceedings of the Wesley Historical Society,* VIII (1912) 198. For chapel membership: incomplete register of christenings and burials, CRO, EMS 5/1/1&2; and a list of donors to the fund for

Notes for pages 154-156.

the new chapel in CRO, EMC 5/1/14, 'Minutes of Leaders' Meetings: Methodist New Connexion Circuit, 1824-1851'.

39. See CRO, EMS 11/2, 'Fence (New Connexion) Sunday School, Register of Admissions'.
40. CRO, EMS 11/3. 'Fence (New Connexion) Sunday School, Memorandum Book, *c.*1824-1853', especially entries for 1831 and 1832.
41. CRO, EMC 1/14, 'Methodist New Connexion, Minutes of Quarterly Meetings, 1824-1851'. The problem of single versus married clergy also plagued the Wesleyans. Wesley himself favoured the former, for both doctrinal and practical reasons, but by the 1820s and 1830s the trend was strongly towards the latter, and was contributing to the decline of itineracy.
42. Ibid.
43. Ann Brownsword's Journal, *PMM*, 1821, p. 19. On Hugh Bourne's meetings at Macclesfield, *PMM*, 1820, pp. 230, 231, 234; and 1821, p. 19. The Wesleyans, more staid in public, sometimes indulged in similar outpourings in private; see Adam Rushton's account of a Sunday night prayer meeting, *c.*1830, in Adam Rushton, *My Life, as Farmer's Boy, Factory Lad, Teacher and Preacher, 1821-1909* (Manchester, 1909) p. 18.
44. *PMM*, 1835, pp. 63-4.
45. In a group of 44 male members from Macclesfield whose occupations are given in the baptismal register between 1823 and 1835 there are 10 silk weavers, 12 other textile workers, 8 labourers, 2 sawyers, 2 joiners, 1 turner, 1 miller, 1 iron drawer, 1 slater, 1 whitesmith, 1 brick setter, 1 basket-maker, 1 tailor, 1 dealer in earthenware, and 1 shopkeeper. Also listed are several cotton-workers from Bollington and colliers from Poynton. CRO, EMC 1/18/20, 'Register of Christenings, 1823-1845'.
46. John Garner's Journal, *PMM*, 1819, p. 231.
47. *PMM*, 1836, pp. 280-1.
48. See Ann Brownsword's Journal, *PMM*, 1820, p. 233; Ann Stanna's Journal, ibid., p. 234; and Ann Brownsword's Journal, *PMM*, 1821, p. 19.
49. *PMM*, 1821, p. 15. See also Hugh Bourne's funeral sermon on Catherine Worrall, a 20-year-old silk-worker, *PMM*, 1821, p. 61; and obituary of Ann Rigby, 24-year-old factory worker, *PMM*, 1845, pp. 470-1.
50. For the history of Independency in Macclesfield, [W. Urwicke (ed.)], *Historical Sketch of Nonconformity in the County Palatine of Chester by Various Ministers and Laymen in the County*

Notes for pages 156-162.

(London, 1864) pp. 235 ff.; Frederick James Powicke, *A History of the Cheshire County Union of Congregational Churches* (Manchester, 1907) pp. 206 ff.; and 'Congregationalism in Macclesfield', [*MCH*?], 3 November 1877, clipping in CCRO, CR63/1/27.

51. [Urwicke], *Sketch*, p. 235. On Palmer, see H. Lismer Short, 'Macclesfield's First Unitarian Minister', *Transactions of the Unitarian Historical Society*, X, no. 3 (1953) 142-7.
52. Townley Street Chapel, 'Church-book', quoted in [Urwicke], *Sketch*, pp. 236-7.
53. 'Congregationalism in Macclesfield', see footnote 50.
54. Enrolment figures from *Congregational Magazine*, 1821, quoted in [Urwicke], *Sketch*, pp. 242-3.
55. Charity-sermon circular, 1804, quoted, ibid.
56. CRO, EFC 10/1/2, 'Minutes of Macclesfield Preparative Meeting', mostly eighteenth century. The congregation dwindled until the meeting-house had to be closed, in 1877.
57. W.T. Whitley, *Baptists of North-west England, 1649-1913* (London, 1913) pp. 333-40.
58. A. Rushton, *My Life*, p. 47.
59. CRO, EDV 7/2/103. 'Visitation: Articles of Inquiry, 1789'. This estimate is probably low; see CRO, EDA 6/5, 'Listing of Papists in the Diocese of Chester', which gives 38 for Macclesfield in 1767.
60. CRO, EDV 7/6/308, 'Visitation: Articles of Inquiry 1821', and obituary of Father Hall, *MCH*, clipping, *c.*1876, in CCRO, CR63/1/27.
61. There is a list of such premises and some newly built chapels, 1780-1833, in CRO, QDR, *Miscellaneous Documents relating to Nonconformists* (three unnumbered boxes), 'Register of Dissenting Chapels', and 'Return of Nonconformist Places of Worship'.
62. J. Obelkevich, *Religion and Rural Society*, pp. 216 ff.
63. A. Rushton, *My Life*, p. 60.
64. CRO, EMS 6/2/1, 'Minutes of Leaders' Meeting: Sunderland Street Chapel, 1814-1894'.
65. CRO, EMC 1/9/1&2, 'Wesleyan Methodists: Minutes of Local Preachers' Meetings, 1820-1857', entry for 2 January 1832.
66. 'A Short Account of the Experience of Mr. John Boothby', *Arminian Magazine*, XVI (1793) 479-84. The quotation from Isaiah that Boothby refers to reads in the authorised version: 'Moreover the light of the moon shall be as the light of the sun, and the light of the sun shall be sevenfold . . .'. See also R. Jackson, 'Memoir of J. Thorley', p. 483; Thorley was converted just after he finished his

Notes for pages 162-167.

apprenticeship to a particularly strict master.

67. A.J. French, *The Life of John Birchenall* (London, [1881?] pp. 15-16.
68. Ibid., pp. 17-18.
69. Details of the lives of these and the other Roe children are in W.H. Chaloner, 'Charles Roe of Macclesfield (1715-81): an eighteenth-century industrialist', *TLCAS,* LXIII (1952) 83-5.
70. For Robert Roe (1754-82), see 'The Experience of Mr. Robert Roe', *Arminian Magazine* (later *Methodist Magazine*) May 1783, pp. 521-4, 580-2, 638-41; and 1794, pp. 19-22, 76-81, 132-7, 186-9, 344-8 and *passim*. Many extracts from his journal are also reproduced in Charles Beswick, 'Notes on the History of Macclesfield', a scrapbook of his columns from the *Macclesfield Times and East Cheshire Observer*, 1924-30, in MPL; the quotations here are from cols. 207 and 209.
71. James Johnson, *Memoir of the Rev. David Simpson, M.A.* (Macclesfield, 1878) p. 24.
72. CRO EMC 1/4, Membership List, Macclesfield (Wesleyan) Society, 1794 is a census of society membership. It shows 501 members, of whom 56% are women. Cf. J. Baxter, 'Great Yorkshire Revival', p. 74, n. 68, showing the heavy preponderance of female members in Sheffield and Leeds Methodist Societies in the 1790s.
73. John Ryles [*sic*], 'A Memoir of Rachel Bower, of Macclesfield', *Methodist Magazine,* XXX (1807) 323-6.
74. A. Rushton, *My Life*, pp. 55-60.
75. See the list of questions in 'Rules of the Band-Societies, drawn up December 25, 1738', quoted in R. Davies and G. Rupp, eds, *Methodist Church*, vol. I, 191. Among the questions are these: 'Consider! Do you desire we should tell you whatsoever we think, whatsoever we hear, concerning you? . . . Do you desire that . . . we should cut to the quick, and search your heart to the bottom?' On the history and relationship of classes and bands, see also Frank Baker, 'The People called Methodists, 3. Polity', in ibid., pp. 218-25.
76. See also Rushton's highly emotional account of his mother's death-bed, in *My Life*, pp. 136-8.
77. B. Smith, *Methodism in Macclesfield*, pp. 125-7, 322-5.
78. R. Jackson, 'Memoir of J. Thorley', pp. 463.
79. A.S., 'Memoir of Mrs. [Hannah] Swindells of Macclesfield', *Methodist Magazine*, LXV (1842) 191-2.
80. On Hester Ann (Roe) Rogers (1756-94), see *The Experience and*

Notes for pages 167-170.

Letters Spiritual of Mrs. Hester Ann Rogers (Halifax, 1841, ed.).

81. See e.g., CRO, EMS 6/4/1&2, 'Sunderland Street Chapel Accounts', with lists of class leaders, *c.*1806-42.
82. See e.g., CRO, EMS 13/4/1, 'Mill Street Wesleyan School, Minutes of Teachers' Meeting, 1814-1851.
83. G. Slater, *Chronicle of Lives and Religion*, p. 23.
84. A. Rushton, *My Life,* pp. 13-14.
85. Ibid., pp. 96-8.
86. See three programmes, 1809, 1810, and 1812, reproduced in Ernest A. Orme, *A Brief History of the Hurdsfield Sunday School* (Macclesfield, 1908) pp. 12, 13, and 15. For a detailed account of the musical ensemble at St Michael's see Raymond Richards, *Old Cheshire Churches* (London, 1947) p. 396.
87. David Simpson, *A Discourse on Stage Entertainments* (Birmingham, 1787).
88. A. Rushton, *My Life,* pp. 33-4.
89. Thomas Laqueur, 'Working-Class Demand and the Growth of English Elementary Education, 1750-1850', in Lawrence Stone (ed.), *Schooling and Society: studies in the history of education* (Baltimore, 1976) pp. 192-205.
90. On the Grammar School, see G.E. Wilson, 'A History of Macclesfield Grammar School in the County of Cheshire from *c.*1503-*c.*1890' (Leeds University M.Ed., 1952), especially Chap. 7; and *The Reports of the Commissioners appointed in Pursuance of Various Acts of Parliament to enquire concerning Charities . . . relating to the County of Chester, 1819-1837* (London: Henry Gray, [*c.*1837] pp. 518 ff. On elementary education in general, B.F. Chadwick, 'Educational Provision in the Macclesfield Hundred of Cheshire during the Nineteenth Century' (Manchester University M.Ed., 1965).
91. Governors' petition to Parliament, 1774, quoted in G.E. Wilson, 'Macclesfield Grammar School', p. 141.
92. Macclesfield Town Hall, Corporation Minute Book, I, 1769-1824.
93. The CRO QJF Series (Quarter Sessions Files), which includes signed depositions by defendants, plaintiffs, and witnesses, ends in 1800. CRO Mf 40, Reels 5-9 (Prestbury Marriage Registers) have been examined for several years in the 1750s and at 10-year intervals from 1780 to 1820. For the 1750s, figures are for the whole parish; thereafter figures used are for Macclesfield only. Literacy rates of *c.*70% (male) and *c.*35% (female) remained stable between 1800 and 1820).
94. CRO, QJF/178/1-4 (1750) and Clulow Papers, Box 10, bundle of

Notes for pages 170-172.

examinations re: pauper settlements, 1823 to 1826. The 1750 data are for all of Cheshire, the 1823 to 1826 depositions for Macclesfield alone.

95. R.S. Schofield, 'Dimensions of Illiteracy, 1750-1850', *Explorations in Economic History*, X (1973) 442-5, 453.
96. A. Rushton, *My Life*, p. 17. But a much brighter picture is painted by John Birchenall; he attended a similar but very well-regulated school, and then an 'academy' run by a Presbyterian minister who was a fine Greek scholar. Birchenall's father, a well-to-do cotton manufacturer, could afford the best schools available, and eventually sent his son away, aged fifteen, to 'a respectable classical and commercial school in Chester'; see A.J. French, *Life of Birchenall*, pp. 11-12.
97. For the history of the school, see Robert Mellor, *A Short History of Macclesfield Sunday School, 1796-1946* (Macclesfield, 1947); and *Macclesfield Sunday School — Centennial Celebrations* (Macclesfield, 1896). On John Whitaker, R.S. McAll, *The Efficacy of the Grace of God: a sermon preached in the Macclesfield Sunday School, November 12, 1820, on occasion of the death of John Whitaker, Esq., the founder and superintendent of that Institution* (Macclesfield, 1820). A recent comprehensive study of the Sunday school movement nationally is Thomas Walter Laqueur, *Religion and Respectability: Sunday schools and working class culture, 1780-1850* (New Haven, 1976); see especially Chap. 3, parts ii, iii, iv, and vi.
98. 'Plan for the Management of the Sunday-School, Macclesfield, 1 May 1796' (Macclesfield, 1798) p. 3.
99. See Whitaker's First Report, quoted in R. Mellor, *Short History*, p. [1].
100. A. Rushton, *My Life*, p. 24; on the curriculum see pp. 45 ff.
101. Ibid., p. 26.
102. There is no catalogue for the school, but a library-list from the much smaller Fence (New Connexion) School includes, in addition to standard devotional works, Cowper's poems, Locke's essays, *Paradise Lost*, ancient and modern histories, and a geography book. CRO, EMS 11/3, 'Fence Sunday School, Memorandum Book'.
103. J. Wright, *A Record of Happy Deaths, No. 3*, (Macclesfield, 1846) pp. 34-6. See also [J. Wright], *A Memoir of Sarah Wayte . . .* (Macclesfield, 1822). Wright was the superintendent of the Macclesfield Sunday School.
104. On Methodism in general and Sunday schools in particular as

Notes for pages 172-175.

agents of social control, indoctrinating the working class with values and patterns of behaviour appropriate to the needs of a capitalist economy see, E.P. Thompson, 'Time, Work-Discipline and Industrial Capitalism', *Past and Present*, no. 38 (1967) 56-97. Thompson elaborates on what he sees as the very sharp, head-on collision between the new values of the chapel and older pre-industrial culture in *The Making of the English Working Class* (London, 1963) Chap. XI. A brief essay critical of Thompson, and making some telling points in regard to his analysis of Methodism, is R. Currie and R.M. Hartwell, 'The Making of the English Working Class?', *Economic History Review* 2nd ser., XVIII (1965) 633-43. Thompson's reply to Currie and Hartwell, in which he modifies his view of Methodism very little, can be found in the appendix to a new edition of his book (Harmondsworth, 1968) pp. 916-22.

105. A. Rushton, *My Life*, p. 65.
106. The history of the controversy is given, from the Methodist point of view, in 'Phileleutherus', *A Defence of the British Constitution against the Attacks of Civis . . .* (London, 1813).
107. See *MC*, 11 February 1813, statement by the Rev. Lawrence Heapy and the Rev. William C. Cruttenden.
108. *MC*, 27 February 1813. 'Civis' was a Tory lawyer, Mr Cooke.
109. *MC*, 3 April 1813.
110. John Hughes, *A Plea for Religious Liberty . . .* (Macclesfield, 1813).
111. 'Address to the Members of the Methodist Society . . . relative to the Correspondence [with] the Managers of the Sunday School' (Macclesfield: Edward Bayley, 1814).
112. *Report of the Proceedings in the Matter of the Macclesfield Sunday School, heard in the Court of Exchequer, 19 November 1818* (Manchester, 1819).
113. 'Twenty-ninth Report of the Macclesfield Sunday School . . .' (n.p., [1826]), in John Rylands Library, Methodist Archives, Box L.H.
114. K.S. Inglis, *Churches and the Working Classes in Victorian England* (London, 1963) p. 10.
115. See, in addition to works cited below, Bernard Semmel, *The Methodist Revolution* (New York, 1973); Michael Hill, *A Sociology of Religion* (London, 1973); V.G. Kiernan, 'Evangelicalism and the French Revolution', *Past and Present*, no. 1 (1952) 44-56; and Paul T. Phillips, 'Methodism, Political Order and Revolution', *Studies in Religion*, V (1975-6) 186-90.

Notes for pages 176-177.

116. Elie Halévy, *A History of the English People in the Nineteenth Century*, vol. I: *England in 1815* (New York, 1949 ed.), part III, p. 425. See also Michael Hill's comment, 'The Halévy thesis . . . is not primarily a statement about working-class religiosity (a concept largely disclaimed by Halévy) but about the social and religious linkage and mobility that Methodism made possible.' *Sociology of Religion*, p. 202.
117. Eric Hobsbawm, 'Methodism and the Threat of Revolution', in *Labouring Men* (London, 1964) pp. 23-33. Hobsbawm relies almost exclusively on the Religious Census of 1851 as a measure of denominational strength, a practice which is open to criticism.
118. E.P. Thompson, *The Making of the English Working Class*, p. 388.
119. See Thompson's review article, 'On History, Sociology and Historical Relevance', *British Journal of Sociology*, XXVII (1976) 387-402.
120. For example, R.F. Wearmouth, *Methodism and the Common People of England* (London, 1945); and ibid., *Methodism and the Working-Class Movements of England, 1800-1850* (London, 1937).
121. Alan D. Gilbert's survey of the occupational make-up of various Nonconformist groups (nationally), *c.*1800-1837, shows considerably less variation between groups than has generally been assumed. But the variations he does find are the expected ones, e.g., the Primitives have more miners and the Wesleyans more merchants. See Gilbert, *Religion and Society in Industrial England* (London, 1976) Table 3:1, p. 63. Some of his occupational categories are so broad as to obscure possibly significant economic and status differences.
122. On the avoidance of politics by the Wesleyan leadership, and the essentially defensive nature of their protestations of loyalty, see Anthony Armstrong, *The Church of England, the Methodists and Society, 1700-1850* (Totowa, N.J., 1973) pp. 192-3.
123. See Rushton's description of his growing sympathy for Chartism and his rejection of his mother's political quietism, *My Life*, pp. 63 ff.
124. A.J. Ainsworth, 'Religion in the Working Class Community, and the Evolution of Socialism in Late Nineteenth Century Lancashire: a case of working class consciousness', *Histoire sociale/Social History* X (1977) 355. See also his conclusion, arguing that 'religious sentiment was by no means absent among the main body of the working class . . . Religion offered hope, coherence and self-respect in a hostile world'; p. 380.

Notes for pages 178-183.

125. A.D. Gilbert, *Religion and Society*, p. 83.
126. See Thomas W. Laqueur, *Religion and Respectability,* especially Chap. 6.
127. Annual growth rates of Methodism (nationally) are summarised in R. Carwardine, *Transatlantic Revivalism*, Table 6, pp. 46-7. He compares British rates with those for America, which follow a markedly different pattern. The British figures, culled from Minutes of Annual Conferences, are also discussed in Robert Currie, Alan D. Gilbert, and Lee Horsley, *Churches and Churchgoers: patterns of Church growth in the British Isles since 1700* (Oxford, 1977) pp. 40-2.
128. See, for example, letter from the Rev. James Jackson of Macclesfield, *Methodist Magazine*, 1843, p. 596; and CRO, EM 1/13/2-8, 'Names of the Wesleyan Methodist Ministers . . . ,' a broadside giving Macclesfield circuit membership figures annually, 1772-1862. Also, W.R. Ward, 'Church and Society in the First Half of the Nineteenth Century', in R. Davies and G. Rupp (eds), *A History of the Methodist Church*, vol. II, 45.
129. W.R. Ward, however, is inclined to give great importance to the Peterloo crisis, which, he says, 'forever severed official Methodism from urban revivalism.' *Religion and Society in England*, p. 93.
130. E. Hobsbawm, 'Methodism and the Threat of Revolution', p. 24.
131. E. Halévy, *England in 1815*, p. 426.

VI Conclusion

1. G.W. Oxley, *Poor Relief in England and Wales, 1601-1834* (Newton Abbot, 1974) p. 59.
2. C. Stella Davies, *A History of Macclesfield* (Manchester, [1961]) p. 230.
3. An enlightening survey of the issues affecting the growth of eighteenth-century provincial towns can be found in Peter Clarke (ed.), *Country Towns in Pre-Industrial England* (Leicester, 1981) pp. 15-31.
4. See ibid., p. 23.
5. Reuben Bullock, *On Mending the Times* (Macclesfield, 1833) p. 16; on Bullock's activity as a radical, see, A.E. Musson and R.G. Kirby, *The Voice of the People: John Doherty, 1798-1854: Trade Unionist, Radical and Factory Reformer* (Manchester, 1975) pp. 165, 258, 397, and 406.
6. R. Bullock, *On Mending the Times*, pp. 8-9.

Bibliography

1. Manuscript sources

Birkenhead:
- Birkenhead Central Library, Macclesfield Collection

Chester:
- Cheshire County Record Office,
  - Clulow Papers
  - Diocesan Records
    - Administration
    - Bishop's Transcripts
    - Visitation
  - Ecclesiastical Parish Records, Macclesfield
  - Finney of Fulshaw Papers
  - Methodist Records, Macclesfield Circuit
  - Microfilm
    - Census Returns for 1841 (originals in PRO)
    - Ecclesiastical Census of 1851 (originals in PRO)
    - Nonconformist Registers, 1648-1837 (originals in PRO)
  - Militia Records
  - Probate Records (series WS and WI), with printed and typescript indexes
  - Quarter Sessions Records
    - Sessions Books
    - Sessions Files
    - Elections
    - Enclosure Awards
    - Freemasons
    - Friendly and Benefit Building Societies
    - Militia
    - Nonconformists
    - Papists
  - Society of Friends Records, Macclesfield Preparative Meeting

Durham (North Carolina):
- Perkins Library, Duke University, George Story Collection

London:
- Dr Williams' Library
  - Lindsey P.P.6
- Guildhall Library,
  - Royal Exchange Assurance Mss.
  - Sun Insurance Office Mss.
- Public Record Office,
  - Home Office Papers (HO 40 and 67)
  - Ministry of Health, Poor Law Union Papers (MH 12/968-9)
  - Privy Council Unbound Papers (PC1/-)

Macclesfield:
- Macclesfield Public Library, Miscellaneous Mss. in Local History Collection
- Private collection of Mr and Mrs J.R.C. Callander,
  - Thomas Challinor Papers

Macclesfield Town Hall
Corporation Minutes, 2 vols.
Minute Book, Local Board of Health

Manchester:
Chethams' Library, Sutton Workhouse Accounts
Manchester Central Library, Nicholson Papers
John Rylands Library,
Methodist Archives
Wedgwood Correspondence (English MS. 1101, 1102)

Prestbury (Cheshire):
Private Collection of Mrs Marie Moss, John Swanwick Papers

2. Official sources

Great Britain. General Board of Health. *Report to the General Board of Health on a Preliminary Inquiry into . . . the Borough of Macclesfield by James Smith, with Plans* (London: HMSO, 1850).

Great Britain. Parliament. *An Act for Better Lighting, Watching, and Improving the Borough and Township of Macclesfield . . .* (London: HMSO, 1825).

_______ *House of Commons Journal.*

_______ *House of Lords Journal.*

_______ *Report of the Committee of the House of Commons on the Silk Trade in the Year 1766* (Coventry: M. Merridew, 1831).

_______ *Report of the Select Committee on the Silk Trade,* 1831-32, XIX.

_______ *Municipal Corporations in England and Wales: Reports upon Certain Boroughs drawn by T.J. Hogg, Esq.*, 1837-38, XXXV. (Macclesfield, pp. 799-822).

_______ *(Second) Report of Select Committee on Silk Ribbon Weavers' Petitions*, 1818, IX.

_______ *Select Committee Report on Children employed in the Manufactories of the United Kingdom*, 1816, III.

3. Theses and Dissertations

Chadwick, B.F., 'Educational Provision in the Macclesfield Hundred of Cheshire during the Nineteenth Century' (Manchester University M.Ed., 1965).

Hughes, H.F., 'The Macclesfield Election of 1880, and its Consequences' (Leeds University B.A. dissertation, Special Studies, 1962).

Jackson, J.N., 'The Population and Industrial Structure of Macclesfield' [*c.* 1851-1951] (Manchester University Ph.D., 1960).

Jordan, W.M., 'The Silk Industry in London, 1760-1830' (London University M.A., 1931).

Kirk, R., 'Class and Fragmentation: some aspects of working-class life in north-east Cheshire and south-east Lancashire, 1850-1870' (Pittsburgh University Ph.D., 1974).

Malmgreen, G., 'Economy and Culture in an Industrializing Town: Macclesfield, Cheshire, 1750-1835' (Indiana University Ph.D., 1981).

Margrave, R.D., 'The Emigration of Silk Workers from England to the United States of America in the Nineteenth Century, with Special Reference to Coventry, Macclesfield, Paterson, New Jersey and South Manchester, Connecticut' (London University (LSE) Ph.D., 1981).

Massey, J.H., 'The Silk Mills of Macclesfield' (Manchester University, School of

Architecture R.I.B.A. thesis, 1959).

Mitchell, S.I., 'Urban Markets and Retail Distribution, 1730-1815, with Particular Reference to Macclesfield, Stockport, and Chester' (Oxford University D.Phil., 1974).

Moss, R., 'The Origins and Influence of Methodism in the North Staffordshire Potteries before 1820' (London University M.A., 1949).

Rothstein, N.K.A., 'The Silk Industry in London, 1702-66' (London University M.A., 1961).

Wharton-Street, D.K., 'The Silk Industry of Macclesfield' (Manchester University, Department of Geography, B.A., 1965).

Wilson, G.E., 'A History of Macclesfield Grammar School in the County of Cheshire, 1503-*c.*1890' (Leeds University M.Ed., 1952).

Wilson, R.C., 'The Objectives and Achievements of the Chester Mechanics' Institution and the Macclesfield Society for acquiring Useful Knowledge' (Manchester University M.Ed., 1968).

4. Contemporary Newspapers and Periodicals

Adam's Weekly Courant (later *Chester Courant*)
Arminian Magazine (later *Methodist Magazine, Wesleyan Methodist Magazine*)
Cheshire and Lancashire Historical Collector
Edinburgh Review
Exchange Herald; Aston's Manchester Commercial Advertiser
Gentleman's Magazine
Macclesfield Courier (later *Macclesfield Courier and Herald,* etc.)
Macclesfield, Stockport and Congleton Chronicle
Manchester Weekly Times
Manchester Mercury
Non-descript
Political Repository; or, Weekly Magazine
Poor Man's Guardian
Primitive Methodist Magazine
Quarterly Review
Stockport Advertiser
Westminster Review

5. Contemporary Printed Sources (before 1860)

Address to the Members of the Methodist Society and the Friends of Methodism Relative to the Correspondence which has lately taken place between the Managers of the Sunday School and the Methodists in Macclesfield (Macclesfield: J. Wilson, 1814).

Aiken, John, *A Description of the Country from Thirty to Forty Miles round Manchester* (London: John Stockdale, 1795; reprint ed. Newton Abbot: David and Charles, 1968).

An Account of the Celebration of the Jubilee of the Macclesfield Sunday School (Macclesfield: M. Burgess, printer, 1846).

The Antidote: wherein are shewn the character and object of the 'Protestant Associations', . . . by a Protestant Dissenter (Macclesfield: M. Burgess, printer, [1839?]).

Badnall, Richard, *A View of the Silk Trade* (London: John Miller, 1828).

Bagshaw, Samuel, *History, Gazetteer, and Directory of the County of Chester. . .* (Sheffield: author, 1850).

Baines, Thomas, *Lancashire and Cheshire: past and present*, 2 vols (London: William Mackenzie, 1868, 1869).

Ballance, John, *Remarks on some of the Important Errors contained in Mr. Badnall's Pamphlet entitled 'A View of the Silk Trade'*, (London: J.M. Richardson, 1829).

Bamford, Samuel, *Early Days* (London: Simpkin, Marshall, 1849; reprint ed. New York: Augustus Kelley, 1967).

________ *Passages in the Life of a Radical* (London: Simpkin, Marshall, 1844; reprint ed. London: MacGibbon and Kee, 1967).

Bowring, John, 'Report from Select Committee on the Silk Trade . . . 1832', in *Westminster Review*, XVIII (Jan 1833) 1-31.

Brand, John, *Observations on Popular Antiquities*, 3 vols, revised and edited by Sir Henry Ellis (London: Charles Knight, 1841-2).

Bray, William, 'Sketch of a Tour into Derbyshire and Yorkshire' (1777), in John Pinkerton, ed., *A General Collection of the Best and Most Interesting Voyages and Travels in All Parts of the World*, vol. II (London: Longman, Hurst, Rees, and Orme, 1808).

Bullock, Reuben, *On Mending the Times* (Macclesfield: J. Swinnerton, 1833).

Buxton, Thomas F., *Memoirs of Sir Thomas Fowell Buxton* (ed.) Charles Buxton (London: John Murray, 1852).

Carlisle, Nicholas, *A Concise Description of the Endowed Grammar Schools in England and Wales . . .* , 2 vols (London: Baldwin, Cradock, and Joy, 1818).

A Collection of the Miscellaneous Pieces to be performed at Christ-Church, Macclesfield on Saturday, June 23, 1781 (Macclesfield: T. Bayley, [1781]).

Corry, John, *The History of Macclesfield* (London: author, 1817).

Cowdroy, William, *The Directory and Guide for the City and County of Chester . . .* (Chester: author, 1789).

Dodd, G., *The Textile Manufactures of Great Britain* (London: Charles Knight, 1844).

Engels, Friedrich, *The Condition of the Working Class in England* (Leipzig, 1845; trans. and edited by W.O. Henderson and W.H. Chaloner, Oxford: Basil Blackwell, 1958).

[Gastrell, Francis], 'Notitia Cestrensis, I.' *Remains, Historical and Literary . . . published by the Chetham Society*, vol. VIII (Manchester: Chetham Society, 1845).

Gower, Foote, *Sketch of the Materials for a . . . History of Cheshire . . .* (1771; 3rd ed., London: John Nichols, printer, 1800).

Hanshall, J.H., *History of the County Palatine of Chester* (1817; Chester: [author], 1823).

Head, George, *A Home Tour of the Manufacturing Districts of England in the Summer of 1835* (1836; reprint ed., London: Frank Cass, 1968).

The History of Cheshire, 2 vols (Chester: John Poole, 1778).

Holden, William, *Holden's Annual Directory. Class the Fifth. Combining the Calico, Cotton, Silk, Woollen & . . . Other Connected Manufacturers & Tradesmen . . .* (London: author, 1814).

Holland, Henry, *General View of the Agriculture of Cheshire . . .* (London: Printed for Richard Phillips by T. Gillet, 1808).

Horne, Melville, *An Address delivered . . . at a Public Meeting of the Macclesfield Auxiliary Bible Society . . . 30th of August 1820* (Macclesfield: E. Bayley, 1820).

________ *Anti-Curr, or the Protestant Address to the Public* (Manchester: J. Pratt, [1821]).

Horne, Melville, *A Sermon on the Death of Mr. G. Pearson Senr. of Macclesfield. . .* (Macclesfield: J. Wilson, 1807).

——— *A Sermon preached to the Loyal Macclesfield Foresters* (2 November 1803), 2nd ed. (London: W. Button and Son, and J. Hatchard, 1804).

Hughes, John, *A Plea for Religious Liberty; or a Vindication of the Methodists: to which is subjoined the Controversy between the Author and Civis in the Macclesfield Courier* (Macclesfield: E. Bayley, 1813).

Huskisson, William, *Speeches*, vol. II (London: John Murray, 1831).

Jackson, Robert, 'A Memoir of Mr. Joshua Thorley of Macclesfield'. *Wesleyan Methodist Magazine*, 4th ser., IV (1848) 481-92.

Lysons, Daniel, and Samuel Lysons, *Magna Britannia* . . . vol. II, part 2, *Cheshire* (London: T. Cadell and W. Davies, 1810).

McAll, Robert Stephens, *The Efficacy of the Grace of God: a sermon preached in the Macclesfield Sunday School, November 12, 1820, on occasion of the death of John Whitaker, Esq., the founder and superintendent of that Institution* (Macclesfield: E. Bayley, 1820).

McCulloch, J.R., *A Dictionary of Commerce and Commercial Navigation*, vol. II (London: Longman, Rees, Orme, Brown, Green, and Longman, 1837).

Macclesfield Sunday School, Committee, *Twenty-ninth Report of the Macclesfield Sunday School* (1825-26) (Macclesfield: E. Bayley, n.d.).

A Memoir of Sarah Wayte . . . (Macclesfield: J. Wright, 1822).

Moreau, César, *Rise and Progress of the Silk Trade in England from the Earliest Period to the Present Time: founded on official documents* (London: Sold by Treuttel and Würtz, 1826).

Nightingale, Joseph, *The Election: a satirical drama.* (Stockport: J. Clarke, 1804).

——— *Elegiac Thoughts occasioned by the Death of the Rev. D. Simpson, M.A.* . . . (Manchester: W. Shelmerdine, 1799).

Oldfield, T.H.B., *The Representative History of Great Britain*, vol. III (London: Baldwin, Cradock, and Joy, 1816).

'Phileleutherus', *A Defence of the British Constitution against the Attacks of Civis, upon the Methodists and Dissenters and the Conductors and Teachers of the Macclesfield Sunday School* . . . (London: William Heseltine, printer, 1813).

[Pigot, J.], *The Commercial Directory for 1816-17* (Manchester: Wardle and Pratt, and J. Pigot, 1816).

——— *Directory of Cheshire* ([Manchester?]: Pigot and Co., 1834).

——— *Directory of Manchester and Salford* (Manchester: J. Pigot and Son, 1838; Pigot and Slater, 1841).

——— and W. Dean, *Directory for Manchester, Salford, etc. for 1824-5* (Manchester: Dean and Pigot, 1824).

A Plan for the Management of the Sunday-School, Macclesfield . . . 1 May 1796 (Macclesfield: E. Bayley, 1798).

[Plant, J., and T. Gregory.], *The History and Directory of Macclesfield and its Vicinity* (Manchester: W.D. Varey, 1825).

Porter, G.R., *Progress of the Nation* . . . vol. I (London: Charles Knight and Co., 1836).

——— *A Treatise on the Origin, Progressive Improvement, and Present State of the Silk Manufacture* (London: Longman, Rees, Orme, Brown, and Green, 1831).

Prout, John, *A Practical View of the Silk Trade, embracing a Faithful Account of the Result of the Measures enacted in 1824, for the Encouragement of that Manufacture* (Macclesfield: J. Swinnerton, 1829).

Ramsay, Richard, *Poems on Various Subjects* (Macclesfield: J. Wilson, 1816).

Report of the Proceedings in the Matter of the Macclesfield Sunday School, heard in the Court of Exchequer (Manchester: R. and W. Dean, printers, 1819).

Roe, James, *Sermons on Several Subjects and Occasions* (York: A. Ward, printer, 1766).

Rogers, Hester Ann, *The Experience and Letters Spiritual of Mrs. Hester Ann Rogers*

(1793; Halifax: William Milner, 1841).
Rules and Orders to be observed by the Silk Weavers of Macclesfield (Macclesfield: E. Bayley, 1826).
[Scott, Walter], *The Journal of Sir Walter Scott, 1825-32*, vol. I (London: Thomas Nelson, n.d.).
Sholl, Samuel, *A Short Historical Account of the Silk Manufacture in England . . .* (London: author, 1811).
Simpson, David, Bound volume of miscellaneous printed sermons and tracts. In Dr. Williams' Library, Lindsey P.P. 6.
________ *A Plea for Religion and the Sacred Writings: addressed to the disciples of Thomas Paine . . . with a memoir . . . by the Rev. John Gaulter* (Liverpool: Nuttall, Fisher, and Dixon, [1812]).
________ *Sermons on Useful and Important Topics* (Macclesfield: author, 1774).
Strachan, Alexander, *The Voice of God in the Storm . . .* (London: John Mason, [1839]).
________ *Recollections of the Life and Times of the Late Reverend George Lowe* (London: John Mason, 1848).
Thompson, William, *Letters of William Thompson, lately deceased . . . ,* 2nd ed. (Preston: I. Wilcockson, 1818).
Tooke, Thomas, *A History of Prices and of the State of the Circulation from 1793 to 1837*, 6 vols (London: Longman, Orme, Brown, Green, and Longmans, 1838-1857).
Tunnicliff, William, *A Topographical Survey of the Counties of Stafford, Chester, and Lancashire . . .* (Nantwich: E. Snelson, printer, 1787).
Wedge, Thomas, *General View of the Agriculture of the County Palatine of Chester . . .* (London: C. MacRae, 1794).
Wilkes, John and Peter Barfoot, *The Universal British Directory of Trade and Commerce . . .* vol. III (London: Barfoot and Wilkes, [1794?]).
Wood, Thomas, *Observations on Orthodox Christianity and Socinian Error: occasioned by the change of sentiment in the religious creed of the Rev. Joseph N-T-N-G-LE* (London: W. Baynes, 1813).
Worrall, T.H., *Reminiscences of Early Life spent in my Native Town of Macclesfield* (Macclesfield: George Hine, [1897]).
Wright, J., (ed.), *A Record of Happy Deaths of Teachers Scholars and Others in connection with the Macclesfield Sunday School for 1846,* no. 3 (Macclesfield: M. Burgess, printer, [1846]).
Young, Arthur, *Tour through the North of England* vol. III (London: W. Strachan, W. Nicoll, *et al.*, 1770).

6. **Secondary Sources** (after 1860):

Ainsworth, A.J., 'Religion in the Working Class Community, and the Evolution of Socialism in Late Nineteenth Century Lancashire: a case of working class consciousness, *Histoire sociale/Social History*, X (1977) 354-80.
Alcock, Joan Pilsbury, *Methodism in Congleton: a history of the Wagg Street and the Kinsey Street Circuits in Congleton and the surrounding area* (n.p., [1967?]).
Anderson, Michael, *Family Structure in Nineteenth Century Lancashire,* (London: Cambridge University Press, 1974).
________ 'Sociological History and the Working-Class Family: Smelser revisited', *Social History,* no. 3 (October 1976) 317-34.
Andrews, Stuart, *Methodism and Society* (London: Longman, 1970).

Armstrong, Alan, *Stability and Change in an English County Town: a social study of York, 1801-1851* (London: Cambridge University Press, 1974).

Armstrong, Anthony, *The Church of England, the Methodists, and Society, 1700-1850* (London: University of London Press, 1973).

Armstrong, John, *A History of Freemasonry in Cheshire* (London: George Kenning, 1901).

Aston, Walter, 'Notes on Antiquarian Discoveries in Macclesfield', *TLCAS,* XXII (1904) 164-9.

Axon, W.E.A., *Cheshire Gleanings* (Manchester: Tubbs, Brook, and Chrystal, 1884).

_______ 'Sunday in Lancashire and Cheshire', *THSLC*, XXXIII (1881) 42-84.

Bailey, Peter, *Leisure and Class in Victorian England: rational recreation and the contest for control, 1830-1885* (London: Routledge and Kegan Paul, 1978).

Bailey, Victor, 'Crime, Criminal Justice and Authority in England', *Bulletin of the Society for the Study of Labour History*, no. 40 (Spring 1980) 36-46.

Barker, T.C. and J.R. Harris, *A Merseyside Town in the Industrial Revolution: St. Helens, 1750-1900* (London: Frank Cass, 1959).

Beattie, J.M., 'The Criminality of Women in Eighteenth-Century England', *Journal of Social History,* VIII (1975) 80-116.

_______ 'The Pattern of Crime in England, 1660-1800', *Past and Present*, no. 62 (1974) 47-95.

Beauquis, A., *Histoire économique de la soie* (Grenoble: Academie des Sciences morales et politiques, 1910).

Bellamy, J.M. and J. Saville (eds), *Dictionary of Labour Biography* vol. VII (London: Macmillan, 1984) [for entry on John West by N. Reid, pp. 245-50].

Behagg, Clive, 'Custom, Class and Change: the trade societies of Birmingham', *Social History*, IV, no. 3 (1979) 455-80.

Being a Short History of the Congregation worshipping at Park Green Congregational Church and of Townley Street Sunday School . . . (n.p., [1901?]).

B[ennett], J.H.E., 'Roe Family of Macclesfield and Liverpool', *Cheshire Sheaf*, ser. III, XXX (1935) 72, 74, 82, 83, 89, 91, 99.

_______ and J.C. Dewhurst (eds), *Quarter Sessions Records . . . for the County Palatine of Cheshire, 1559-1760 . . .* (Manchester: Record Society of Lancashire and Cheshire, 1940).

Beswick, Charles, 'Notes on the History of Macclesfield specially compiled for the *Macclesfield Times*' (1928-29?), with articles from the *Macclesfield Advertiser*, 1934. Clippings in Macclesfield Public Library, Local History Collection, Walter Smith's Scrapbooks, vol. I.

Bezucha, Robert J., *The Lyon Uprising of 1834: social and political conflict in the Early July Monarchy* (Cambridge, Mass.: Harvard University Press, 1974).

Booth, Alan, 'Food Riots in the North-west of England, 1790-1801', *Past and Present,* no. 77 (1977) 84-107.

Boyd, A.W., 'The Great Budworth Churchwardens' Accounts in the Eighteenth Century', *TLCAS*, XLIX (1933) 12-74.

Brentano, Lujo, *On the History and Development of Gilds and the Origin of Trade-Unions* (London: Trübner and Co., 1870).

Briggs, Asa and John Saville (eds), *Essays in Labour History: in memory of G.D.H. Cole* (London: Macmillan, 1960).

Brocklehurst, J.T. and Sons, *A Short Account of the History and Manufacture of Silk* (Macclesfield: Brocklehurst and Sons, 1912).

Bohstedt, John, *Riots and Community Politics in England and Wales, 1790-1810* (Cambridge, Mass.: Harvard University Press, 1983).

Brown, R[obert], *Combermere Lodge of Union, No. 295, Macclesfield: a hundred years' history* (Macclesfield: Claye, Brown, and Claye, 1893).

Brown, W. Henry, *The Silken Glow of Macclesfield; with the Jubilee History of the Macclesfield Silk Manufacturing Society, Ltd* (Manchester: Co-operative Printing Society, Ltd., [1938]).

Burgess, W.H., 'Dean Row Chapel Registers', *Transactions of the Unitarian History Society,* VI (1937) 167-8.

_______ *The Story of Dean Row Chapel, Wilmslow, Cheshire* (Hull: privately printed, 1924).

Burnett, John, *Plenty and Want: a social history of diet in England from 1815 to the present day* (Harmondsworth: Penguin Books, 1968).

_______ *A Social History of Housing, 1815-1970* (Newton Abbot: David and Charles, 1978).

Byng, John, *The Torrington Diaries . . . between the years 1781 and 1794,* edited by C. Bryn Andrews, vol. II (London: Eyre and Spottiswoode, 1930).

Bythell, Duncan, *The Handloom Weavers* (London: Cambridge University Press, 1969).

Calhoun, Craig J., 'History, Anthropology and the Study of Communities: some problems in Macfarlane's proposal', *Social History*, III, no. 3 (1978) 363-73.

_______ *The Question of Class Struggle: social foundations of popular radicalism during the Industrial Revolution* (Chicago: University of Chicago Press, 1982).

Cameron, Richard M., *Methodism and Society in Historical Perspective* (Nashville, TN: Abingdon Press, 1961).

Carson, W.G., 'The Conventionalization of Early Factory Crime', *International Journal of the Sociology of Law*, VII (1979) 37-60.

Carwardine, Richard, *Transatlantic Revivalism: Popular Evangelicalism in Britain and America, 1790-1865* (Greenwich, Conn.: Greenwood Press, 1978).

Centenary: Townley Street Sunday School (Macclesfield: n.p., 1901).

Chalklin, C.W., *The Provincial Towns of Georgian England: a study of the building process, 1740-1820* (London: Edward Arnold, 1974).

Chaloner, W.H., 'Charles Roe of Macclesfield (1715-81): an eighteenth-century industrialist', *TLCAS*, LXII (1951) 133-56; LXIII (1952) 52-86.

_______ 'The Cheshire Activities of Matthew Boulton and James Watt, of Soho, near Birmingham, 1776-1817', *TLCAS*, LXI (1949) 121-36.

_______ 'Sir Thomas Lombe and the British Silk Industry', *History Today*, 3 (November 1953) 778-85.

Chamberlayne, J.H., 'From Sect to Church in British Methodism', *British Journal of Sociology*, XV (1964) 139-49.

Chambers, J.D., 'Enclosure and the Labour Supply in the Industrial Revolution', *Economic History Review*, 2nd ser., V (1952-53) 318-43.

_______ *Nottinghamshire in the Eighteenth Century: a study of life & labour under the squirearchy* (London, 1932; 2nd ed. New York: Augustus Kelley, 1966).

Chapman, Stanley D., *The Early Factory Masters: the transition to the factory system in the Midlands textile industry* (Newton Abbot: David and Charles, 1967).

_______ 'Fixed Capital Formation in the British Cotton Manufacturing Industry', in J.P.P. Higgins and Sidney Pollard (eds), *Aspects of Capital Investment in Great Britain, 1750-1850: a preliminary survey* (London: Methuen, 1971) 57-107.

_______ (ed.), *The History of Working-class Housing: a symposium* (Newton Abbot: David and Charles, 1971).

Cheshire Women's Institutes, *Cheshire Village Memories* 2 vols (Tilston Court, near Malpas: Cheshire Federation of Women's Institutes, [1952, 1961]).

Church, Leslie F., *More about the Early Methodist People* (London: Epworth Press, 1949).

Church, Roy A., *Economic and Social Change in a Midland Town: Victorian Nottingham, 1815-1900* (London: Frank Cass, 1966).

Clapham, J.H., 'The Spitalfields Acts: 1773-1824', *Economic Journal*, XXVI (1916)

459-71.

Clark, Peter (ed.), *Country Towns in Pre-Industrial England* (Leicester: Leicester University Press, 1981).

Clarke, H.A., 'Residence of the Anglican Clergy in Cheshire: 1775-1825', *Lancashire and Cheshire Historian,* vol. II, no. 9 (September 1966) 509-12; vol. II, no. 10 (October-December 1966) 531-2.

Clarke, W.H., 'On the Charters, Documents and Insignia relating to the Ancient Manor and Borough of Macclesfield', *TLCAS*, XXII (1904) 154-64.

Cockburn, J.S. (ed.), *Crime in England, 1550-1800* (Princeton: Princeton University Press, 1977).

Coleman, Donald C., *Courtaulds: an economic and social history*, vol I (Oxford: Clarendon Press, 1969).

_______ *The Economy of England, 1450-1750* (London: Oxford University Press, 1977).

Collier, Frances, 'The Family Economy of the Working Classes in the Cotton Industry, 1784-1833', *Remains, Historical and Literary . . . Published by the Chetham Society*, 3rd ser. vol. XII (Manchester: Chetham Society, 1965).

_______ 'Workers in a Lancashire Factory at the Beginning of the Nineteenth Century'. *Manchester School*, VII (1936) 50-4 and 126-31.

Cooke, John Henry, *Bibliotheca Cestrensis, or, A Bibliographical Account of Books, etc. relating to Cheshire* (Warrington: Mackie and Co., 1904).

Corfield, P.J., *The Impact of English Towns, 1700-1800* (London: Oxford University Press, 1982).

Coward, T.A., *Cheshire, Traditions and History* (London: Metheun, 1932).

Cressy, D., 'Literacy in Pre-industrial England', *Societas*, IV (1974) 229-40.

Crompton, John, *Packway to Motorway* (London: Wayland, 1974).

Crossley, Frederick Herbert, *Cheshire* (London: Robert Hale Ltd., 1949).

Crozier, Mary, *An Old Silk Family* (Aberdeen: Aberdeen University Press, 1947).

Cuming, G.J. and D. Baker, *Popular Beliefs and Practice,* Ecclesiastical History Society: Studies in Church History, vol. VIII (London: Cambridge University Press, 1972).

Cunningham, Hugh, *Leisure in the Industrial Revolution, c.1780-c.1880* (London: Croom Helm, 1980).

Currie, Robert, Alan D. Gilbert, and Lee Horsley, *Churches and Churchgoers: patterns of Church growth in the British Isles since 1700* (Oxford: Clarendon Press, 1977).

Currie, Robert and R.M. Hartwell, 'The Making of the English Working Class?', *Economic History Review,* 2nd ser., XVIII (1965) 633-43.

Darvall, F.O., *Popular Disturbances and Public Order in Regency England* (London: Oxford University Press, 1934; repr. 1969).

Davies, C. Stella, 'The Agricultural History of Cheshire 1750-1850', *Remains, Historical and Literary . . . Published by the Chetham Society,* 3rd ser. vol. X. (Manchester: Chetham Society, 1960).

_______ (ed.), *A History of Macclesfield* (Manchester: Manchester University Press, [1961]).

Davies, Rupert, *Methodism* (Harmondsworth: Pelican Books, 1963).

_______ and Gordon Rupp (eds), *A History of the Methodist Church in Great Britain* 2 vols (London: Epworth Press, 1965; 1978).

Dawley, Alan, *Class and Community: the industrial revolution in Lynn* (Cambridge, Mass.: Harvard University Press, 1976).

Deane, Phyllis and W.A. Cole, *British Economic Growth 1688-1959* (London, Cambridge University Press, 1967).

[Dent, Emma.], *In Memory of John Brocklehurst, M.P.* (n.p., [1897]).

Dinwiddy, John, 'Luddism and Politics in the Northern Counties', *Social History*, IV (1979) 33-64.

Dobson, C.R., *Masters and Journeymen: a prehistory of industrial relations, 1717-1800* (London: Croom Helm, 1980).

Dyson, J.B., *The History of Wesleyan Methodism in the Congleton Circuit* (London: John Mason, 1856).

Earles, John, *Streets and Houses of Old Macclesfield* (Macclesfield: Robert Brown, 1915).

Earwaker, J.P., *East Cheshire: past and present* 2 vols (London: author, 1880).

Evans, Eric J., 'Some Reasons for the Growth of English Anti-Clericalism *c.*1750-*c.*1830', *Past and Present*, no. 66 (1975) 84-109.

Evans, W.B., *et al.*, *Geology of the Country around Macclesfield, Congleton, Crewe and Middlewich* 2nd ed. (London: HMSO, 1968).

Faler, Paul G., *Mechanics and Manufacturers in the Early Industrial Revolution: Lynn Massachusetts, 1780-1860* (Albany, N.Y.: State University of New York Press, 1981).

[Farrar, J.E.], *A Note on the History of Congregationalism in Macclesfield* (n.p., 1948).

Field, C.D., 'The Social Structure of English Methodism, Eighteenth to Twentieth Centuries', *British Journal of Sociology*, XXVIII (1977) 199-225.

Finney, Isaac A., *Macklesfelde in ye olden time . . .* (Macclesfield: J. Daniel, printer, 1873). (Reprint from *Macclesfield Advertiser*.)

_______ *Notes on the Antiquities of Macclesfield*, 4th ed. (Macclesfield: Brown and Son, printers, 1871).

Foster, John, *Class Struggle and the Industrial Revolution: early industrial capitalism in three English towns* (London: Weidenfeld and Nicolson, 1974).

Freeman, T.W. *et al.*, *Lancashire, Cheshire and the Isle of Man* (London: Thomas Nelson and Sons, [1966]).

French, A.J., *The Life of John Birchenall* (London: Wesleyan Conference, [1881?]).

Fryer, Alfred, *Wilmslow Graves and Grave Thoughts from Wilmslow* (Stockport: author, 1886).

Gadian, D.S., 'Class Consciousness in Oldham and Other North-West Industrial Towns, 1830-1850', *Historical Journal*, XXI (1978) 161-72.

Garden, Maurice, *Lyon et les lyonnais au XVIIIe siècle* (Paris: Flammarion, 1975).

Gauldie, Enid, *Cruel Habitations: a history of working-class housing, 1780-1918* (London: George Allen and Unwin, 1974).

George, M. Dorothy, 'The Combination Laws', *Economic History Review*, VI (1936) 172-8.

_______ 'The Combination Laws Reconsidered', *Economic Journal Supplement* (May 1927) 204-28.

George, M. Dorothy, *London Life in the Eighteenth Century* (Harmondsworth: Penguin Books, 1966).

Gibson, T.E., 'Some Old Country Sports — from the Crosby Records', *THSLC,* XXXIII (1881) 1-22.

Gilbert, Alan D., *Religion and Society in Industrial England: Church, Chapel and social change, 1740-1914* (London, Longman, 1976).

Giles, P.M., 'The Felt-Hatting Industry *c.*1500-1850, with Special Reference to Lancashire and Cheshire', *TLCAS* (1959) 104-32.

Gray, Robert Q., 'Politics, Ideology and Class Struggle under Early Industrial Capitalism: a critique of John Foster', *Marxism Today* (December 1977) 367-71.

Greaves, Robert William, *The Corporation of Leicester, 1689-1836* (London: Oxford University Press, 1939).

Grindon, Leopold H., *Manchester Banks and Bankers* (Manchester: Palmer and Howe, 1878).

Halévy, Elie, *History of the English People in the Nineteenth Century,* vol. I: *England in 1815* (Paris, 1912; New York: Peter Smith, 1949).

Hamilton, Bernice, 'The Medical Professions in the Eighteenth Century', *Economic*

History Review, 2nd ser., vol. IV (1951) 141-69.

Hammond, J.L. and Barbara Hammond, *The Skilled Labourer, 1760-1832* (London: Longmans, Green and Co., 1920).

_______ *The Town Labourer, 1760-1832: the new civilisation* (1917; New York: Kelley, 1967).

_______ *The Village Labourer, 1760-1832* (London: Longmans, Green and Co., 1927).

H[ard], A[rnold] H., 'Silk Throwing in England', *Fibres and Fabrics Monthly*, I (June 1940) 152-5.

Harris, B.E. (ed.), *A History of the County of Chester,* vol. III (London: Oxford University Press, 1980).

Harrison, Brian, *Drink and the Victorians: the temperance question in England, 1815-1872* (London: Faber and Faber, 1971).

Harrison, W., 'Development of the Turnpike System in Lancashire and Cheshire', *TLCAS*, IV (1886) 80-92.

Hartwell, R.M., 'The Rising Standard of Living in England, 1800-1850', *EHR,* 2nd ser. XIII (1961) 397-416.

_______ and E.J. Hobsbawm, 'The Standard of Living during the Industrial Revolution', *EHR*, 2nd ser. XVI (1963) 117-46.

Hay, Douglas *et al.* (eds), *Albion's Fatal Tree: crime and society in eighteenth century England* (London: Allen Lane, 1975).

Head, Robert, *Congleton Past and Present* (Congleton: author, 1887).

Helm, Alex., 'The Cheshire Soul-caking Play', *Journal of the English Folk Dance and Song Society*, VI (1950) 45-50.

Hertz, Gerald B., 'The English Silk Industry in the Eighteenth Century', *English Historical Review,* XXIV (1909) 710-27.

Hibbert, Thomas Dorning, 'Letters relating to Lancashire and Cheshire; — Temp. James I., Charles I., and Charles II', *THSLC*, IV (1851-52) 189-98.

Hill, Michael, *A Sociology of Religion* (London: Heinemann, 1973).

Hobsbawm, Eric J., 'The British Standard of Living, 1790-1850', *Economic History Review,* 2nd ser. X (1957) 46-61.

_______ *Labouring Men: studies in the history of labour* (London: Weidenfeld and Nicolson, 1964).

Hodson, Howard, *Cheshire, 1660-1780: Restoration to Industrial Revolution* (Chester: Cheshire Community Council, 1978).

Hole, Christina, *Traditions and Customs of Cheshire*, (London: Williams and Norgate, 1937).

Howitt, Mary, *Mary Howitt: an autobiography*, edited by Margaret Howitt, vol. II, (London: William Isbister, 1889).

Hume, Rev. Canon, 'Rural Life and Manners, — in the Neighbourhood of Bidstone and Upton, — A Hundred Years Ago', *THSLC*, XXVII [3rd ser., vol. III] (1875) 131-68.

Hunt, Alfred Leeds, *David Simpson and the Evangelical Revival* (London: Charles J. Thynne and Jarvis Ltd, 1927).

Ingham, Alfred, *Cheshire: its traditions and history* (Edinburgh: Pillan and Wilson, printers, 1920).

Inglis, K.S., *Churches and the Working Classes in Victorian England* (London: Routledge and Kegan Paul, 1963).

_______ 'Patterns of Worship in 1851', *Journal of Ecclesiastical History*, XI (1960) 74-86.

Johnson, James, *Memoir of the Rev. David Simpson, M.A.* (Macclesfield: G.J. Goodwin, printer, 1878).

Jones, Gareth Stedman, 'England's First Proletariat: class struggle and the Industrial Revolution', *New Left Review,* no. 90 (1975) 35-70.

Joyce, Patrick, *Work, Society and Politics: the culture of the factory in later Victorian England* (Brighton: Harvester Press, 1980).

[Kelley, Henry], *History of Freemasonry in Macclesfield, from the Year 1717* (Macclesfield: G.J. Goodwin, printer, n.d.).

Kent, John, *The Age of Disunity* (London: Epworth Press, 1966).

Kiernan, V.G., 'Evangelicalism and the French Revolution', *Past and Present*, no. 1 (1952) 44-56.

Knapp, David, 'The Ancient Town of Macclesfield and its Methodism', *Methodist Recorder* (September 1904) 9-10.

Laqueur, Thomas Walter, *Religion and Respectability: Sunday schools and working class culture, 1780-1850* (New Haven: Yale University Press, 1976).

Laslett, Peter, *Family Life and Illicit Love in Earlier Generations* (London: Cambridge University Press, 1977).

_______ and Richard Wall (eds), *Household and Family in Past Time* (London: Cambridge University Press, 1972).

[Leary, Frederick], *The Earl of Cheshire's Regiment of Yeomanry Cavalry: its formation and services, 1797-1897* (Edinburgh: privately printed, 1898).

Levine, David, *Family Formation in an Age of Nascent Capitalism* (London: Academic Press, 1977).

Linebaugh, Peter, 'Labouring People in Eighteenth-Century England', *International Labor and Working Class History*, no. 23 (Spring 1983) 1-8.

Macclesfield Sunday School — Centennial Celebrations (Macclesfield: Heath Bros., printers, 1896).

McLeod, Hugh, 'Class, Community and Religion: the religious geography of nineteenth-century England', *Sociological Yearbook of Religion in Britain*, VI (1973) 29-72.

Malcolmson, Robert W., *Popular Recreations in English Society, 1700-1850* (Cambridge: Cambridge University Press, 1973).

_______ *Life and Labour in England, 1700-1780* (London: Hutchinson, 1981).

Mathews, H.F., *Methodism and the Education of the People, 1791-1851* (London: Epworth Press, 1949).

Mathias, Peter, 'The Social Structure in the Eighteenth Century: a calculation by Joseph Massie', *Economic History Review*, 2nd ser., X (1957-58) 30-45.

Mayor, S.H., *Cheshire Congregationalism: a brief history* ([Chester]: n.p., [1956]).

Mellor, Robert F., *A Short History of the Macclesfield Sunday School* (Macclesfield: Brown and Brown, 1947).

Mellows, C.L., 'Geographical Basis of the West Pennine Silk Industry', *Journal of the Textile Institute*, XXV (1934) 376-88.

Merriman, John M. (ed.), *Consciousness and Class Experience in Nineteenth-Century Europe* (New York: Holmes and Meier, 1979).

Miller, Matthew Henry (ed.), *Olde Leeke* (Leek: *Times* Office, 1891; reprinted from the Leek *Times*).

Mitchell, S.I., 'Food Shortages and Public Order in Cheshire, 1757-1812', *TLCAS*, vol. LXXXI (1982) 44-66.

Mobberly Women's Institute, *A History of Mobberly Village* (1952; reprint. Altrincham: John Sherratt and Son, 1973).

Money, John, *Experience and Identity: Birmingham and the West Midlands, 1760-1800* (Manchester: Manchester University Press, 1977).

Moore, D.C., 'Concession or Cure: the sociological premises of the first Reform Act', *Historical Journal*, IX (1966) 9-59.

_______ *The Politics of Deference* (Hassocks: Harvester Press, 1976).

Moore, Robert S., 'The Political Effects of Village Methodism', *Sociological Yearbook of Religion*, VI (1973) 156-82.

Morrill, J.S., *Cheshire, 1630-1660: County Government and Society during the English*

Revolution (London: Oxford University Press, 1974).
Murphy, Brian, *A History of the British Economy* (London: Longman, 1973).
Musson, A.E., *British Trade Unions, 1800-1877* (London: Macmillan, 1972).
_______ 'Class Struggle and the Labour Aristocracy, 1830-1860', *Social History*, no. 3 (May 1976) 335-66.
_______ and R.G. Kirby, *The Voice of the People: John Doherty, 1798-1854: trade unionist, radical and factory reformer* (Manchester: Manchester University Press, 1975).
Namier, Lewis and John Brooke, *The History of Parliament, 1754-1790* (London: Oxford University Press, for the History of Parliament Trust, 1964).
Neale, R.S., *Class in English History, 1680-1850* (Oxford: Basil Blackwell, 1981).
Norman, E.R., *Church and Society in England, 1770-1970: a historical study* (Oxford: Clarendon Press, 1964).
Norris, Jill, 'Women's and Men's Unemployment in Macclesfield between the Wars', *Bulletin* [*of the*] *North West Labour History Society*, 9 (1983-4) 5-13.
Obelkevich, James, *Religion and Rural Society: South Lindsey, 1825-1875* (Oxford: Clarendon Press, 1976).
Oddy, Derek and Derek Miller (eds), *The Making of the Modern British Diet* (London: Croom Helm, 1976).
Orme, Ernest, *A Brief Centenary History of the Hurdsfield Sunday School* (Macclesfield: Claye, Brown, and Claye, 1908).
Ormerod, George, *The History of the County Palatine and City of Chester*, vol. III, new and rev. edition by Thomas Helsby (London: Routledge, 1882).
Oxley, G.W., 'The Permanent Poor in South-west Lancashire under the Old Poor Law', in J.R. Harris (ed.), *Liverpool and Merseyside: essays in the economic and social history of the port and its hinterland* (London: Frank Cass, 1969).
_______ *Poor Relief in England and Wales, 1601-1834* (Newton Abbot: David and Charles, 1974).
Pevsner, Nikolaus and Hubbard, Edward, *The Buildings of England: Cheshire* (Harmondsworth: Penguin Books, 1971).
Phillimore, W.P.W., Thomas M. Blagg, and Leopold Choice, (eds), *Cheshire Parish Registers: Marriages*, vols. II, III, and IV (London: Phillimore and Co., 1910, 1911, 1912).
Pocock, T.I., *The Geology of the Country around Macclesfield, Congleton, Crewe and Middlewich*, Memoirs of the Geological Survey: England and Wales (London: HMSO, 1906).
Pollard, Sidney, *The Genesis of Modern Management: a study of the Industrial Revolution in Great Britain* (London: Edward Arnold, 1965).
Powicke, Frederick James, *A History of the Cheshire County Union of Congregational Churches* (Manchester: Thomas Griffiths and Co., 1907).
Pressnell, L.S., *Country Banking in the Industrial Revolution* (Oxford: Oxford University Press, 1956).
Prest, John, *The Industrial Revolution in Coventry* (London: Oxford University Press, 1960).
Price, F.C., 'The Italian who brought Silk to Stockport', *Cheshire Life* (October 1967) 112-13.
Radzinowicz, L. and R. Hood, 'Judicial Discretion and Sentencing Standards: Victorian attempts to solve a perennial problem', *University of Pennsylvania Law Review*, CXXVII (1979) 1288-1349.
Rawlley, Ratan C., *Economics of the Silk Industry: a study in industrial organisation* (London: P.S. King and Son, 1919).
Reach, Angus Bethune, *Manchester and the Textile Districts in 1849*, edited by C. Aspin (Helmshore: Helmshore Local History Society, 1972; reprint of articles from the

London *Morning Chronicle*, 1849-50).
Redford, A., *Labour Migration in England, 1800-1926* (Manchester: Manchester University Press, 1926).
Renaud, Frank., 'Contributions towards a History of the Ancient Parish of Prestbury in Cheshire', *Remains, Historical and Literary . . . Published by the Chetham Society*, 1st ser., vol. XCVII (Manchester: Chetham Society, 1876).
Richards, Raymond, *Old Cheshire Churches* (London: Batsford, 1947).
Roberts, David, *Victorian Origins of the British Welfare State* (New Haven, Conn.: Yale University Press, 1960).
Robson, Derek, 'Some Aspects of Education in Cheshire in the Eighteenth Century', *Remains, Historical and Literary . . . Published by the Chetham Society*, 3rd ser., vol. XIII (Manchester: Chetham Society, 1966).
Robson, Robert, *The Attorney in Eighteenth-century England* (Cambridge: Cambridge University Press, 1959).
Rogers, C.D., 'The Bowden Marriage Licenses', *Lancashire and Cheshire Historian,* vol. II, no. 10 (October-December 1966) 533-6; vol. III, no. 1 (September 1967) 603-6.
Rose, E.A., 'Methodism in Cheshire to 1800', *TLCAS*, LXXVIII (1975) 22-37.
Rowlands, Marie B., *Masters and Men in the West Midland Metalware Trades before the Industrial Revolution* (Manchester: Manchester University Press, 1975).
Rudé, George, *The Crowd in History: a study of popular disturbances in France and England, 1730-1848* (New York: John Wiley and Sons, 1964).
Rule, John, *The Experience of Labour in Eighteenth-Century English Industry* (New York: St Martin's Press, 1981).
Rushton, Adam, *My Life, as Farmer's Boy, Factory Lad, Teacher and Preacher, 1821-1909* (Manchester: S. Clarke, 1909).
Schofield, R.S., 'Dimensions of Illiteracy, 1750-1850', *Explorations in Economic History*, X (1973) 442-5.
[Scott, Walter], *The Journal of Sir Walter Scott, 1825-32, Vol. I* (London: Thomas Nelson, n.d.).
Searby, Peter, 'Chartists and Freemen in Coventry, 1838-1860', *Social History*, no. 6 (October 1977) 761-84.
Sedgwick, Romney, *History of Parliament, 1715-1754* (London: Oxford University Press, for the History of Parliament Trust, 1970).
Semmel, Bernard, *The Methodist Revolution* (New York: Basic Books, 1973).
Short, H. Lismer, 'Macclesfield's First Unitarian Minister', *Transactions of the Unitarian History Society*, X (1953) 142-7.
Simon, Daphne, 'Master and Servant', in John Saville (ed.), *Democracy and the Labour Movement: essays in honour of Dona Torr* (London: Lawrence and Wishart, 1954).
Slater, George, *Chronicles of Life and Religion in Cheshire and Elsewhere* (London: Andrew Crombie, 1891).
Smiles, Samuel, *Lives of the Engineers*, vol. I (London: John Murray, 1861).
Smith, Benjamin, *Methodism in Macclesfield* (London: Wesleyan Conference Office, 1875).
Smith, D.M., 'The Silk Industry of the East Midlands', *East Midlands Geographer,* no. 17 (1962) 20-31.
Smith, Dennis, *Conflict and Compromise: Class Formation in English Society, 1830-1914: a comparative study of Birmingham and Sheffield* (London: Routledge and Kegan Paul, 1982).
Smith, F.B., *The People's Health, 1830-1910* (London: Croom Helm, 1979).
Smith, Roger, 'Early Victorian Household Structure: a case study of Nottinghamshire', *International Review of Social History*, XV (1970) 69-84.

Smith, Walter, *King Edward Street Chapel (Unitarian), Macclesfield* (Macclesfield: King Edward St Chapel Committee, 1947; reprinted from the *Macclesfield Courier*),

Speck, W.A., *Stability & Strife: England, 1714-1760* (London: Edward Arnold, 1977).

The Spitalfields Acts: seven pamphlets, 1818-1828 (New York: Arno Press, 1972).

Stevenson, John, *Popular Disturbances in England, 1700-1870* (London: Longman, 1979).

——— and R. Quinault (eds), *Popular Protest and Public Order: six studies in British History, 1790-1920* (London: George Allen and Unwin, 1974).

Stigant, P., 'Wesleyan Methodism and Working-Class Radicalism in the North, 1792-1821', *Northern History*, VI (1971) 98-116.

Stone, Lawrence, ed., *Schooling and Society: studies in the History of Education* (Baltimore: Johns Hopkins University Press, 1976).

Storch, Robert D., 'The Plague of Blue Locusts: police reform and popular resistance in Northern England, 1840-57' *International Review of Social History,* XX (1975) 61-90.

——— (ed.), *Popular Culture and Custom in Nineteenth-Century England* (London: Croom Helm, 1982).

Strumingher, Laura S., *Women and the Making of the Working Class: Lyon, 1830-1870* (St Alban's, Vermont: Eden Press, 1979).

Sylvester, Dorothy, *A History of Cheshire* (Henley-on-Thames: Darwen Finlayson, 1971).

[Symmons, W.G.?], *A Short History of the Macclesfield Borough Police* (Macclesfield: privately printed, [1947]).

Thirsk, Joan, 'Industries in the Countryside', in F.J. Fisher (ed.), *Essays in the Economic and Social History of Tudor and Stuart England* (London: Cambridge University Press, 1961).

Thomas, Hilah F. and Keller, Rosemary Skinner (eds), *Women in New Worlds* (Nashville, Tennessee: Abingdon Press, 1981).

Thompson, E.P., 'Eighteenth-century English Society: class struggle without class?', *Social History*, III (1978) 133-65.

——— *The Making of the English Working Class* (London: Victor Gollancz, 1963 and new edition, Harmondsworth: Penguin Books, 1968).

——— 'On History, Sociology and Historical Relevance', *British Journal of Sociology,* XXVII (1976) 378-402.

——— 'Patrician Society, Plebeian Culture', *Journal of Social History*, VII (1973-74) 382-405.

——— 'Time, Work-Discipline and Industrial Capitalism', *Past and Present*, no. 38 (1967) 56-97.

Tobias, J.J., *Crime and Industrial Society in the Nineteenth Century* (London: Batsford, 1967).

Townsend, William J., *et al.*, *A New History of Methodism,* vol. I (London: Hodder and Stoughton, 1909).

Treble, J.H., *Urban Poverty in Britain, 1830-1914* (London: Batsford, 1979).

[Urwicke, William (ed.)], *Historical Sketches of Nonconformity in the County Palatine of Chester by Various Ministers and Laymen in the County* (London: Kent and Co.; Manchester: Septimus Fletcher, 1864).

Vigier, François., *Change and Apathy: Liverpool and Manchester during the Industrial Revolution* (Cambridge, Mass.: M.I.T. Press, 1970).

A Walk through the Public Institutions of Macclesfield (Macclesfield: Claye, Brown, and Claye, 1888).

Walker, R.B., 'Religious Changes in Cheshire, 1750-1850', *Journal of Ecclesiastical History*, XVII (1966) 77-94.

Ward, W.R. (ed.), *The Early Correspondence of Jabez Bunting, 1820-1829*, Camden fourth series, vol. XI (London: Offices of the Royal Historical Society, 1972).

Ward, W.R., *Religion and Society in England, 1790-1850* (London: Batsford, 1972).

Warner, Frank, *The Silk Industry of the United Kingdom: its origin and development* (London: Drane's, 1921).

Watts, Michael R., *The Dissenters: from the Reformation to the French Revolution* (Oxford: Clarendon Press, 1978).

Wearmouth, R.F., *Methodism and the Common People of England* (London: Epworth Press, 1945).

________ *Methodism and the Working-Class Movements of England, 1800-1850* (London: Epworth Press, 1937).

Webb, Sidney and Beatrice Webb, *The History of Trade Unionism* (1894; rev. ed. London: Longmans, 1920, reissued 1926 and 1950).

Westerfield, Ray B., *Middlemen in English Business* (New Haven, Conn.: Yale University Press, 1915).

Whitley, W.T., *Baptists of North-west England, 1649-1913* (London: Kingsgate Press, 1913).

Wickham, E.R., *Church and People in an Industrial City* (London: Lutterworth Press, 1957).

Willan, T.S., *An Eighteenth-Century Shopkeeper: Abraham Dent of Kirkby Stephen* (Manchester: Manchester University Press, 1970).

Williams, J.E., 'The British Standard of Living, 1750-1850', *EHR*, 2nd ser. XIX (1966) 581-89.

Williamson, F., 'George Sorrocold of Derby: a pioneer of water supply', *Journal of the Derbyshire Archaeological and Natural History Society*, no. 57 (1936).

Wilmot, Darwin, *A Short History of the Grammar School, Macclesfield, 1503-1910* (Macclesfield: Claye, Brown, and Claye, 1910).

Wilmslow Historical Society, Industrial Archaeology Group, *Cotton Town: Bollington and the Swindells Family in the nineteenth century* (Wilmslow: Wilmslow Historical Society, 1973).

Wilson, R.G., *Gentlemen Merchants: the Merchant Community in Leeds, 1700-1830* (Manchester: Manchester University Press, 1971).

Winter, James, 'Widowed Mothers and Mutual Aid in Early Victorian Britain', *Journal of Social History*, XVII (1983) 113-23.

Wootton, John, *Macclesfield Past* [prize essay, 1866]. Printed in parts in the Macclesfield *Courier and Herald* in 1880 and collected in a scrapbook of clippings in the Local History Collection, Macclesfield Public Library.

Wrigley, E.A., *Nineteenth-century society: essays in the use of quantitative methods for the study of social data* (London: Cambridge University Press, 1972).

________ and R.S. Schofield, *The Population History of England, 1541-1871: a reconstruction* (Cambridge, Mass.: Harvard University Press, 1981).

Index